THE
MEANING
OF

Ichiro

THE
MEANING
OF

THE NEW WAVE FROM JAPAN AND THE TRANSFORMATION OF OUR NATIONAL PASTIME

ROBERT WHITING

WARNER BOOKS

NEW YORK   BOSTON

Warner Books

Time Warner Book Group
1271 Avenue of the Americas, New York, NY 10020
Visit our Web site at www.twbookmark.com.

Printed in the United States of America

First Printing: April 2004
10 9 8 7 6 5 4 3 2 1

Library of Congress Cataloging-in-Publication Data
Whiting, Robert.
   The meaning of Ichiro : the new wave from Japan and the
transformation of our national pastime / Robert Whiting.
       p.   cm.
   Includes index.
   ISBN 0-446-53192-8
   1. Suzuki, Ichirao, 1973– .   2. Baseball players—Japan—
Biography.   I. Title.
GV865.S895W55   2004
   796.357'092—dc22   2003027134

In memory of two old friends,
Greg and Dwight, who left too soon.

ACKNOWLEDGMENTS

THERE ARE A NUMBER OF PEOPLE I'D LIKE TO THANK FOR HELPING me with this book. In the research department, Kozo Abe of the *Fuji-Sankei* communications group kept a steady supply of information and checked facts coming my way; Miwako Atarashi of the Baseball Hall of Fame and Museum in Tokyo (*Yakyū Taīku Hakubutsukan*) verified data and responded promptly and kindly to numerous requests I made for material, which usually required her digging into nineteenth-century files; and my neighbor and old friend, the highly regarded baseball author Masayuki Tamaki and translator of *You Gotta Have Wa*, as well as his wife, Kyoko, and members of his family, all provided numerous kindnesses.

Thanks to two of the world's foremost authorities on the Japanese game who were generous enough with their time to check the manuscript for factual errors (and they found more than I'd care to admit). One is ace Yomiuri columnist Jim Allen, the other is Marty Kuehnert, foremost bilingual media commentator on *nihon puro-yakyū* for three decades. Others who read the manuscript in whole or in part and provided helpful advice were Peter Miller, Elmer Luke, Jeff Kingston and Velisarios Kattoulas.

Among those I'd also like to thank in no particular order are Leon Lee, Shuji Tsunoyama of the *Sankei Supotsu*, Wayne Gracyyk, venerable columnist and author of the *Japan Pro Baseball Fans Handbook and Media Guide*, which we've all been referring to for more than a quarter of a century, noted Tokyo author Mark Schreiber, Michael Westbay, System Administrator/Editor of the popular website japaneseball.com, Jim Small, head of the Tokyo office of MLB, Nobuhisa Ito of the NPB Commissioner's Office, Hiroko Tashiro, Toru Matsubara of the NPBPA, Zooher Abdool-Carim, Hannah Beech, Karl Greenfeld, Toko Sekiguchi and Shintaro Kano of *Time-Asia*, Shigeyoshi

"Steve" Ino, Trey Hillman, Bobby Valentine, Tadahiro Ushigome, Rick Roa, Masa Oshima, Ken Belson and Howard French of the *New York Times*, Benjamin Fulford of *Forbes*, Sebastian Moffet of the *Asian Wall Street Journal*, Yuichi Hongo of *Yeah*, Isao Takeda of *Playboy, Japan*, Glen S. Fukushima, chairman of Cadence Design Systems, and his wife, Sakie, Skip Orr, president of Boeing Japan, and his wife, Miko Orr, Kenjiro Sasae of the Foreign Ministry and his wife, Nobuko, Hide Tanaka of the *Asahi Shimbun* and his wife, Yoshie, Professor Machiko Osawa, Akiko and Anastasia Yamamoto-Kattoulas, Leron Lee, Vicquie Lee, Gareth "*Torakichi*" Swain, Professor Seiyu Hosono, Koichi and Machiko Kawamura, Joichi Ito, president and CEO of Neoteny, the English Agency of Japan, Martin Fackler of the *Asian Wall Street Journal*, Yuko Aotani of *NHK*, Eric Prideaux, Editor Jack Gallagher of the *Japan Times*, Rekichi Sumiya, Richard Mei of the U.S. State Department, Wally and Jane Yonamine. And special thanks to Satoru Hayano for many services rendered, as well as to Fusakzu, Etsuko, Yutaka, Yoko, Hisashi and Kae Hayano for the Hawaii Ichiro seminar. To Noriko and Eiji Fukushima. To Masako Sakata. And to Eide and Michiko Haru, for arranging a memorable dinner with Michiko's father (son of Waseda University's Iso Abe, who led Japan's first historic baseball tour of the United States in 1905).

As always, I extend a big *arigato* to Midori Matsui, translator of *The Chrysanthemum and the Bat*, her husband, Kiyondo Matsui of *Bungei Shunju*, and to Satoshi Gunji of Kadokawa.

In Seattle, I'd like to thank old friends Doug and Noriko Palmer, Masayoshi Niwa of *Yeah* magazine and journalist James Bailey, who all provided insights into the Ichiro craze as well as life in Seattle in general. Also special thanks to Bob Bavasi of Bavasi Sports Partners for his generosity.

In San Francisco, a gratitudinal bow of the head to old friends and S.F. Giants fans Rosser and Yin-wah Brockman, Frances Bushell and baseball connoisseur and Pac Bell Park fixture Steve Eisenberg. Also Blake Rhodes of the Giants' front office and Katsunori Kojima. In Los Angeles, thanks to player agent Don Nomura of KDN, Jim Colborn, Jim Tracy, John Olguin and Scott Akasaki of the Los Angeles Dodgers. Derek Shearer of Occidental College. Tom House. In San

Diego, player agent Tony Attanasio of Ada Finanacial and Robert E. Turner. In Chicago, Dusty Baker. In Tampa, John Kraal.

In New York, *domo* to Yusuke Kamata of *Fuji-Sankei*, Gaku Tashiro of *Sankei Supotsu*, Jean Afterman, Joe Torre, and Isao Hirōka of the New York Yankees. Rick Down. Don Zimmer. Kota Ishijima. Jeremy Schapp of ESPN, Gene Orza of the MLBPA, Marvin and Terry Miller. Mark Ryckoff of *TIME*. Melanie Kirkpatrick of the *Wall Street Journal*. Dan Gordon. Richard Siracusa. Nick Pileggi. Clyde Haberman of the *New York Times*. And the merry band of souls at the Japan Society in New York. In Boston, thanks to Bill Givens and Ed Kleven. In Washington, D.C., it's Joe and Leith Bernard, Robin Berrington of the State Department, William R. Farrell and Patricia Kearns and Eri Howard of the Japan-America Society.

Also a tip of the baseball cap to the gang of artistes and reprobates who constitute my neighbors in Kamakura, Kagari, David, Mark, Keiko, Karen, Peter, Yuko, and a nod of appreciation to all my relatives and friends on the Monterey Peninsula, starting with my mother and father, Margo, Ned, Buck and the rest of the tribe. And let us not forget the Kondo, Kobayashi, Hayano and Noble clans.

I am particularly grateful to David Shapiro, poet, writer and Tokyo's foremost horse-racing expert, for editing the first finished drafts of this book and, in the process, saving me from myself on more than one occasion.

Next, at Warner Books, I would like to thank my estimable editor, Rick Wolff, the man primarily responsible for the existence of *You Gotta Have Wa*, for his encouragement, support and editorial sense. I can't think of any other editor I'd rather work for. Also much gratitude to Dan Ambrosio and Bob Castillo, without whom this book would never have happened.

Finally, thanks to my longtime agent Amanda Urban at ICM, who always seems to know the right thing to do.

And to my wife, Machiko, for helping me to read Meiji-era Japanese, among other things.

AUTHOR'S NOTE

This book was inspired by the success and wild popularity of Ichiro Suzuki, Hideki Matsui and other stars from Japan. It was written for North Americans, contemporary fans of Major League Baseball, with little or no knowledge of the Japanese game. Readers familiar with my previous works, like *You Gotta Have Wa,* may notice certain minor redundancies. These are unavoidable given the requirements and the context of *The Meaning of Ichiro.*

CONTENTS

PROLOGUE

PROFESSIONAL SPORTS IN NORTH AMERICA HAS GONE GLOBAL. THE National Football League regularly plays several preseason exhibition games abroad, and it has a subsidiary loop in Europe. The NBA features players from Croatia to China, and telecasts of its games can be seen in every time zone in the world. The National Hockey League draws on talent from Scandinavia, Russia and several different Eastern European countries. Yet, of all the professional sports in North America, it may be Major League Baseball that has become the most internationalized.

As of Opening Day of the 2004 MLB season, players born outside the United States and Canada constituted more than a quarter of all big league rosters (and the percentage in the minor leagues was nearly half). Twenty-one of the participants in the 2003 All Star Game were foreign born, while the contest itself was beamed to 200 different countries. Only two of the nine Florida Marlins starters in the final game of the 2003 World Series were American citizens.

This represents quite a change from the previous generation, when foreign players were more of a novelty. Excessive expansion had threatened to dilute the quality of play, but the influx of players from Latin America and the Caribbean has, in the words of sportswriter Thomas Boswell, "served to reinvigorate the sport." And in recent years, Asia has played an increasingly larger role in that reinvigoration.

The Republic of Korea, whose passion for the high school game dates back to 1905, has already produced a handful of notables from its amateur ranks: Consider beefy stud pitcher Chan Ho Park (6'2" 205), who pitched well for the Los Angeles Dodgers before moving to the Texas Rangers, where injuries sidelined him; and Byung-Hyun Kim, the relief ace with the submarine delivery who helped the Arizona Diamondbacks win a world title in 2001. Kim is particularly remembered for two ignominious deeds: giving up back-to-back walk-off home runs to the Yankees in the 2003 World Series, and extending the middle-digit salute to Fenway Park fans during pregame introductions at the opening of the American League Championship Series in Boston that year, after he was booed for a string of bad pitching performances. Other Major League notables include Seoul-born Braves reliever Jung Bong and 6'5" 240-pound first baseman Hee Seeop Choi.

Waiting back home on the Korean peninsula was a right fielder for the Hyundai Unicorns, Shim Jeong-soo, noted for his power and his gung-ho attitude. Korean baseball's home run record holder, meanwhile, Lee Seung-yeop, who hit 56 out of the park in 2003, an all-time Asian high, was headed for Japan.

Taiwan, winner of 17 Little League world titles, has produced a number of young prospects who have been snapped up by hungry Major League scouts: Lo Ching Lung of the Rockies, outfielder Chin-Feng Chen (the first Taiwanese position player to appear in a pro game in the U.S.), Hu Chin Lung of the Dodgers, Wu Chao Kuan of the Mariners, and Chi-hui Tsao of the Rockies. Taiwan established its own professional loop in 1990, the Chinese Professional League. Readers who want to know more about the history of baseball in Korea and Taiwan (and other Asian nations like China, where former Major Leaguers Jim LeFebvre and Bruce Hurst were invited to coach the national team in the 2003 Asian Games) should read the prize-winning *Taking in a Game*, by Joseph Reaves.

The most influential Asian country by far, however, has been Japan, which has the longest baseball history of all. Amateur play extends back to the early 1870s, while the nation's professional game is seven decades old and rich in tradition. Nippon Professional Baseball had produced a 400-game winner (Masaichi Kaneda), a 1000-base stealer (Yutaka Fukumoto) and a slugger supreme in the form of one Sadaharu Oh, who hit 868 lifetime home runs, more than Hank Aaron or Babe Ruth.

In the decade since Hideo Nomo first tested the waters at Vero Beach in 1995, almost two dozen Japanese have donned the uniform of a Major League team, many of them becoming household names, like the aforementioned Nomo and the iconic Ichiro Suzuki. Collectively they have instructed Americans that there is another way to play the game.

The Japanese may not play baseball with the looseness and joy of the Americans, but they love the game just as much and they play it as if they mean it. They have a respect for the sport that is sometimes lacking in the U.S., and, as such, they have much to offer.

Because of linguistic difficulties and other factors, not that much is really known about those individuals who have made their marks on the American consciousness. Who are they? Where do they come from? What makes them tick? How do they regard their own experiences and their impact on our game, and what lessons can we learn from them? This book is meant to answer those questions.

THE EDUCATION OF ICHIRO

A person does not live alone. Our lives are not our own. They are a gift from heaven. Just like our physical bodies. We are created and nurtured by our parents, by all mankind, by the wind and the rain, by the food we eat and countless other things that have supported our hearts, soul, spirit. So, in a sense, they are not really our bodies. We live because we are allowed to live. I taught this to my son Ichiro again and again.

NOBUYUKI SUZUKI

HE HAD PLAYED BASEBALL ALL HIS LIFE. HE HAD APPROACHED the sport with a passion and conviction that few of his contemporaries could match. For that, he had his father, a former high school pitcher, to thank. When he was three years old, his father had given him his first baseball glove and initiated daily games of catch. Made of shiny red leather, it was the most expensive type available at sporting good counters in and around Toyoyama, a sparsely populated suburb of industrial, smog-bound Nagoya, where the Suzuki family lived. The boy's mother had strenuously objected that at half a month's wages, it was far too costly a toy for a small child, but the father had been resolute.

"It's not a toy," he had said. "It's a tool that will teach him the value of things."

Nobuyuki Suzuki was a practicing Buddhist who believed that all inanimate things—rocks, trees, fish, baseball gloves—were animated with spirit, that they were created by a higher force and deserved to be treated with respect *and* gratitude. He demanded that his son Ichiro follow their daily games of catch in the back yard with a ritualistic cleaning and oiling of the glove (a habit that the son continued to follow religiously for the next three decades).

At age seven, the boy, Ichiro, had joined a local youth baseball team, which played on weekends; shortly after that, he asked his father to teach him the proper way to play the game.

The father in turn asked his son if he could commit himself to practice every day, to stick without deviation to the endeavor, all the way to the end. Could he promise? The answer was yes.

"Good, then," said the father. "We have a deal. Make sure you keep your end of it."

Thus did practice—and what would prove to be Nobuyuki's lifelong mission—begin in earnest. At 3:30 every afternoon, the father would excuse himself from the small family-owned electrical parts factory he managed and join his son at a neighborhood Little League ballpark, an island of manicured grass and raked earth set amongst suburban rice fields and newly built residential houses, bringing with him bats, gloves and a suitcase filled with hard rubber balls. The daily routine included some jogging and a light game of catch to start, then the boy would throw 50 pitches, hit 200 balls tossed to him by his father, and finally finish up with infield and outfield defensive fungo drills of 50 balls each. The father, a slightly built man who as an amateur ballplayer had been distinguished more by his desire than real ability, taught his naturally right-handed son to swing from the left side, which he explained would give him an extra two or three steps' advantage on the sprint to first base. He also taught him to swing so that he would always be in a position to run.

On the way home, around seven o'clock, they would stop at a shop for ice cream, then after dinner and homework, father and son would set out once more, this time to a nearby batting center, located in the shadow of the city's international airport and named, fittingly enough, "Airport Batting Center." The boy would take 250 to 300 swings against a pitching machine. He would assume his stance, imitating the star batters he saw on television like Yasushi

Tao, the smooth-swinging line-drive-hitting outfielder of the Chu-nichi Dragons—the thwack of bat against ball competing with the roar of the passenger jets taking off and landing down the road. The father would stand behind the net, monitoring his son's form, scold-ing him if he swung at a ball that was outside of an imagined strike zone. The batting center closed at 11 P.M. and quite often the Suzuki team was still there when it did. Then, before bed, the father would massage the soles of his son's feet, in the belief that the foot with all its nerve endings was the key to a sound body.

"If the feet are healthy, you are healthy," he liked to say.

This routine went on every day for several years, regardless of the heat or cold, rain or snow. During this time, Nobuyuki Suzuki be-came known in the neighborhood simply as *san-ji-han otoko* (the 3:30 man) for his compulsive habit of leaving work early to play base-ball with his son.

Ichiro, whose name meant "most cheerful boy," was not always so cheerful about practicing, especially during the harsh winter days of central Japan, when his fingers grew so numb from the frigid air that he could not button his shirt.

Once, denied permission to leave practice early to play with his friends, he sat down in the middle of the field in protest and refused to budge. The father angrily began to throw balls at his son, but the boy's reflexes were so fast that he would move his body an inch to the left or right and the ball would whiz harmlessly by, or else a hand would shoot up, like the automatic flag on a Nagoya taxi me-ter, and snare a bullet headed for the bridge of his nose.

"That kid of mine," Nobuyuki would later write. "He was really stubborn, willful. Sometimes I got so mad at him. But it was also times like that that I knew he was something special. He had a great natural talent."

That Ichiro was preternaturally talented became ever more appar-ent as he grew. In the sixth grade, as a rail-thin child who lacked power and strength, he still had better baseball skills than most high school players. He hit the pitching machines so well at the Airport Batting Center, which he now frequented with his father as often as four times a day, that Nobuyuki asked the superintendent there to increase the speed. At first, when Ichiro was in the third grade, the speed was set at 65 miles an hour, which he handled easily, be it fastball, curve ball or *shōto* (a kind of screwball), the different pitches which the machine could be set to throw. Within three years, he was hitting balls at 75 miles per hour, but then even that became too easy, so the manager at the batting center jerry-rigged a machine for his special client with a spring attachment that upped the speed to 80 miles per hour. That, he said, was the absolute limit. But in time the boy complained it still wasn't fast enough. Eventually, when Ichiro turned 15, the superintendent would physically move the machine itself several feet closer to the batter's box, creating, in effect, a 93-mile-an-hour pitch (the equivalent of an upper limit fastball in Japan's professional leagues at the time). His most frequent customer easily mastered even this.

Throughout all the batting center sessions, Ichiro's father continued to stand behind home plate, making sure his son only swung at strikes. This was not an inexpensive proposition. One set, or "game" as it was called, cost the rough equivalent of a dollar for 25 pitches, and as the machine was somewhat erratic, pitches not infrequently missed the mark. Although Nobuyuki could not be described as a wealthy man, he uncomplainingly bore the cost.

Nobuyuki also devised what he called a "life or death" drill, in which he stood just six feet away from his son and delivered pitches that Ichiro was required to swat to the left or right sides of the diamond in order to avoid hitting his father. It was a perilous exercise, because from the fifth grade they had begun using a much harder professional-league-approved ball—hard enough to cause concussions and broken bones if directed with enough force at the human body. The father believed the risk was necessary to teach his son bat control.

In addition, the father, who had been an avid golfer until he decided to devote all his free hours to his son's baseball training, also tried to incorporate the basic elements of a golf swing into Ichiro's batting form, the idea being to shift weight from one foot to the other while completing the swing, to get the entire body fully behind the motion. The result was the eventual development of a style of hitting in which Ichiro swept his front foot in the air pendulum style as he went into his swing. It was a batting form that Ichiro kept all throughout his Japan career, one in which he also made it look as though he was running before he had even finished his swing.

Through it all, the father tried to inculcate in his son his philosophy of life, the four principles of which were *doryoku, konjō, nintai,* and *chōwa* (effort, fighting spirit, patience and harmony). Likened by some to the ethos of the *bushi* or samurai, dating back to the days of the medieval warrior, to Nobuyuki, they were merely the guiding principles that he had learned from his parents. By all accounts, Ichiro had little difficulty in assimilating them. As a child, he was self-composed and betrayed little emotion. Unlike others on his Little League team, he did not jump up and down after a big play. Instead, he acted as if hitting a home run or winning a game in the ninth inning was the most natural thing in the world. He had the word *shūchū* or "concentration" ink-brushed on his glove. It was a state of mind he endlessly sought to maintain.

By the time Ichiro was 12, he had his heart set on a professional career, as an excerpt from a sixth-grade essay he composed made clear:

> My dream when I grow up is to be a first-class professional baseball player. . . . I have the confidence to do the necessary practice to reach that goal. I started practicing from age three. From the age of nine I have practiced baseball 360 out of 365 days a year and I practice hard. I only had five to six hours (in a year) to play with my friends. That's how much I practiced. So I think I can surely become a pro. I will play in junior high and high school. When I graduate I will enter the pros. My dream is to join the Seibu Lions or the Chunichi Dragons. My goal is a contract signing bonus of 100 million yen.

According to published reports, he was, by this time, already practicing his autograph.

Years later, sportswriters reading Nobuyuki's published account of his sessions with Ichiro would find echoes of *Kyojin no Hoshi,* an enormously popular cartoon series that first appeared in the 1960s in *manga* or comic form and was later adapted for television. It told the story of a young boy's long and difficult climb to stardom with the Tokyo Yomiuri Giants, Japan's quintessential professional team. The protagonist learns the game under the tutelage of his father, an impoverished postwar laborer who takes his son to a practice field and subjects him to hours' worth of fierce training that leave him battered and bloodied and crying from pain.

"The only way to become a man and succeed in life," the father says at one point, "is to suffer and persevere." Through years of enduring such hardship, the boy grows into a sinewy young man and becomes a star pitcher for the mighty *Kyojin* (Giants), a left-handed smokethrower who can make a pitched baseball perform impossible gyrations. "*Hoshi*," the boy's name, was also a homonym for "star."

Kyojin no Hoshi was grounded in the harsh work ethic that Japan embraced as the nation clawed its way up from the ashes of war. It also informed the way the country approached the game of baseball in the postwar decades. Several sequels followed until changing generational attitudes began to result in a somewhat less rigorous approach to the art of cultivating young ballplayers.

Although Nobuyuki bristled at such comparisons—"Baseball was fun for both of us," he insisted—Ichiro found them rather close to the mark.

"It might have been fun for him," he said, "but for me it was a lot like *Kyojin no Hoshi*. It bordered on hazing and I suffered a lot. But I also couldn't say no to him. He was doing his utmost to help me."

Meiden

By the time Ichiro entered junior high school in 1975, Nobuyuki had become so convinced his son possessed the ability to make it as a professional, he went to see the coach of the school's baseball team with two requests:

"Do whatever you want with my son," he said, "but please don't change his batting form. He has worked a long time to perfect it."

And then he added the kicker: "No matter how good Ichiro is, don't ever praise him. We have to make him spiritually strong."

With afternoon sessions now out of the question because of the year round practice routine school teams in Japan required, Nobuyuki shifted into a different kind of support mode. He continued to leave his factory at 3:30 every day, but now he went to observe his son's after-school practices. He would stand there behind the backstop, hands in his pockets, and watch silently as Ichiro and his teammates went through their paces. As long as his son was on the practice field, he would not sit down, because his son could not sit down. It was a kind of moral reinforcement. He would drive his son home in the family car after practice and when dinner had been eaten, he would take him to the batting center for their nightly two-hour session, often staying there until the place was closed down. Then it was time for homework and Nobuyuki would always stay awake in case Ichiro had questions that needed to be answered. Neither father nor son ever went to bed before 2 A.M. during this period and never until Nobuyuki had capped the day off with the nightly foot massage.

A big problem was Ichiro's abnormally slender physique, especially since the boy was a starting pitcher as well as the team's cleanup hitter. He was a notoriously fussy eater. His dislike of vegetables was exceeded only by his fondness for Kobe filet steak and sashimi, two of the most expensive items on the menu in Japan. So Nobuyuki proposed a deal that would put a huge dent in his pocket. He offered to allow Ichiro to consume all the Kobe beef and raw tuna he wished as long as he ate a lot and drank abundant quantities of milk at the same time. Ichiro agreed, much to the reported displeasure of his mother, whose say in her second child's upbringing had been steadily diminished.

Ichiro led his junior high school team in pitching, hitting and fielding for three years running, at the conclusion of which he and his father were besieged by high school baseball scouts.

At this point, a major choice was to be made. In junior high school, Ichiro's marks were so impressive that teachers thought he might gain admission to Todai, Japan's top university, if he applied himself in his studies. But that meant he had to choose between attending a rigorous top-ranked academic high school and enduring what was known in Japan as "Examination Hell," as the admission tests for Japan's top colleges were called, or going to a top-ranked baseball school, to prepare for a career in the pros. After what appears to be not a great deal of agonizing, he opted for the latter. Once there, he stopped studying and, by his own admission, "slept in class."

In Japan, high school baseball was almost a religion—akin to Texas high school football, only more so. It had a long, honored tradition that dated back to the Meiji Era (1868–1912). Indeed, by the time the first professional league was established in 1936, high school baseball already had a 50-year history. The National High School Baseball Championship Tournament, established in 1915 and held each summer since 1924 in cavernous 50,000 seat Koshien Stadium, near Osaka, had become a revered national institution. It was the most prestigious sporting event in the land, famous for its ear-splitting brass bands and wild, colorfully costumed cheering groups bussed from home towns all over the country, and even more for its shaven-headed, sweat-soaked participants, dashing madly on and off the field, fighting to the point of collapse for the glory of their alma mater. (A shorter spring invitational tourney that previewed this event was also highly popular.)

It was the dream of every young player who aspired to a professional career to play in the national summer tourney at Koshien, a single-elimination affair involving the 49 regional winners across Japan. This Holy Grail of amateur sports was televised nationwide every day for the two weeks it lasted, attracting huge crowds as well as pro scouts from all the teams in Japan's two professional leagues, the Central and Pacific. Parents of boys with baseball potential chose high schools with the same care that their counterparts in the United States did when selecting colleges for their sons. A youth who starred on a team that made it all the way to the Koshien tournament was virtually guaranteed a pro contract. (Indeed, any athlete who played in Koshien was considered a prime candidate for employment with Japan's largest corporations because high school baseball at that level was considered the supreme character builder.)

The school that eventually selected Ichiro and, wittingly or not, his father was Nagoya's *Aikodai Meiden Kokko*, one of the top baseball schools in the country, and a frequent Koshien participant; Meiden had a proven track record of sending its best athletes to the pros.

Ichiro thus became one of 51 players on the team, all of whom were required to live in the Meiden baseball dormitory year-round, except for the month of January, when they were allowed to go home to visit their parents. He gaped in amazement at the gleaming three-story ferro-concrete building, compared by many to a modern hotel. On the first floor was a huge kitchen and laundry room area, on the second were rows of bunk beds and on the third a huge, cavernous *tatami* room used for weight lifting and shadow swings before bedtime. The ballpark, a short bus ride away, measured 350 feet to center and had equipment that rivaled that of professional teams. A large indoor training facility, for use on rainy days, stood nearby.

At Meiden the game of baseball was approached with the same intense dedication that characterized most other big-time sports high schools in Japan. That meant practice every day, from 3:30 to 8:00, and then, after a break for dinner, special batting practice from 9 P.M. There would be no more late-evening trips to the Airport Batting Center. From March to December, Meiden played a game every single Sunday.

The spiritual voice of high school baseball was personified in a famous college baseball manager and columnist, Suishu Tobita, who compared athletics to *bushido,* the way of the samurai, where one could overcome natural limitations by sheer force of will and where only those who excelled morally could excel on the field. "The purpose of training," he wrote, "is the forging of the soul. If the players do not try so hard as to vomit blood in practice, they cannot hope to win games. One must suffer to be good."

And so suffer Ichiro did.

Only the top 17 players at Meiden were granted the honor of being allowed to practice every day, while the rest, usually underclassmen—and Ichiro was included in this group—were required to spend their time doing menial character-building chores such as raking the field and picking up the balls. It was a time for them to learn humility, to learn how to speak and show respect towards their seniors. They had to earn the right to touch a ball.

Thus, while other boys his age in American high schools were driving cars and going on dates with their girlfriends after practice, Ichiro and his confreres were enduring a routine that was more befitting a military boot camp. Ichiro later called it "the hardest thing I have ever experienced."

When practice was over, for example, they would make the dinner and start the bath. Then while the lucky 17 were taking their evening batting practice, they were consigned to scrubbing the dormitory floors and doing all the dirty laundry, often enduring long waits to use the limited number of washing machines and driers installed in the building. Rather than waste precious time, Ichiro would sneak off to a nearby tennis court to practice shadow swinging a bat by himself. Then at 3 A.M. he would get up to do the wash.

There was no small amount of hazing to be endured. Underclassmen who said the wrong thing or offended seniors in some other way such as letting the rice cooker boil over had to be punished. A common—and extremely painful—form of punishment was being made to sit atop a garbage can in the *seiza* position—legs tucked underneath the hips with all the body weight bearing down on the heels and calves—until the pain became too acute to bear.

Ichiro became a regular in his junior year and his daily chores were replaced by miles of running each day along with a plethora of exhausting baseball drills. Among the esoteric muscle-enhancing maneuvers required of him were hurling automobile tires and attempting to hit Wiffle balls with a heavy industrial shovel—this is where Ichiro is said to have first begun developing his now famous strong wrists and hips.

Through it all, standing there every day without fail, in the first row of spectator seats behind the net, was you know who. For three full years, there was never a time, regardless of how bitterly cold or snowy it was, that Nobuyuki failed to be at his post. The only father there most of the time, he never called out to Ichiro or spoke to the manager (who later confessed he thought the mysterious-looking figure he spotted in the stands each day was somehow plotting to take over his job). As was his habit, Nobuyuki never sat down during the Meiden practices, nor for that matter did he ever eat or

drink anything either. If his son could not do those things, then neither would he.

"Sometimes it got so cold that I thought my heart would stop," he
said later. "But I just wanted to be there in case he needed me. I took
notes for later use. Also it was just fun to watch him."

Nobuyuki always bowed silently before he left—a gesture of respect
to the field. It went without saying that he attended all the home
games, arriving several hours in advance to watch pregame workouts,
and, of course, he was there for *all* the away games as well. Whenever
possible, he made advance scouting trips with Ichiro in tow, to the
fields of opponents Meiden was scheduled to play in upcoming
games, so he could familiarize his son with the lay of the land.

"Doesn't your old man ever work?" was a question Ichiro's teammates would teasingly ask. In time they began to jokingly refer to
Pere Suzuki as "*Chichiro*," a play on the name "Ichiro" and "*chi-chi*,"
which means "father" in Japanese. It was not exactly a compliment.

At Meiden, Ichiro perfected his unusual batting form—now pointing the bat toward the pitcher's mound before going into his leg-in-the-
air swing. And what an effective way to hit it was. Over a three-year
high school career, Ichiro hit for a galactic .502 average. Despite his
flyweight physique, he also had 19 home runs with 211 RBIs and
131 stolen bases. Ichiro struck out only ten times in 536 official high
school at bats and not one was a swinging strikeout. According to
Meiden records, he connected solidly on 97 percent of all the pitches
he swung at. Ichiro also pitched on occasion, displaying an exceptional fastball and deft control of a curve, until an injury sustained in
a bicycle accident adversely affected his throwing form. Ichiro took
Meiden to the venerable Koshien Tournament twice, losing on the
next to last day in his junior year and qualifying for the spring invitational, but being eliminated in the regionals, the year following.

His sharp batting eye and lightning reflexes combined with a
spookily placid temperament earned him the nickname *uchūjin* or
"spaceman" from his teammates. Another nickname was *no-tenki*
("No Weather"), a tribute to his disciplined cool. In fact, a Shiga University research team once included high school star Ichiro in a series of tests of Alpha 2 brain wave activity designed to determine an

athlete's ability to relax under pressure. He was tested ten times over a ten-month period between June 1991 and March 1992, including the day before the opening of the notoriously tension-filled National High School Baseball Tournament. Ichiro's scores registered a super-serene rating of 91 percent, far ahead of the other subjects, who averaged around 60 percent.

In 1990, when his team was eliminated at Koshien, he was the only boy on the entire team (indeed perhaps the only boy on all 48 losing teams) who did not shed a tear. But then, as one cynical sports writer pointed out, "He had had a batting average of .625 in the games. All the pro scouts were watching him. So what did he have to cry about?"

Ichiro had hoped to go high in the November 1991 professional draft, but was taken in the fourth and final round—the 36th pick overall—by the Orix BlueWave of the Pacific League, based in the bustling, historic port of Kobe, just west of Osaka. Kobe is a twinkling gem of a city nestled between green mountains and blue ocean (and a temporary break in a relentless coastline of concrete seawalls and shoreline hydropods, of the type that helped make Japan's "construction state" famous). Number 36 was a somewhat ignominious rank given his high school stats, but scouts were a little dubious about his preshrunk physique—120 pounds on a 5'9" frame. He was so slight that he appeared years younger than he actually was, or, in the words of one bemused American who had seen him interviewed on TV, "He looked like a fifth grader."

All Orix was willing to pay for a signing bonus was $43,000.

The BlueWave

Orix's pint-sized manager Shozo Doi believed in what was known as the *totei seido* (apprenticeship system), long evident in many areas of Japanese society from small factories to large corporations and government offices. To Doi, *totei seido* meant baseball rookies should endure a certain amount of pain and suffering and should not be allowed to experience too much success too early. Doi liked to cite the case of his former teammate on the Yomiuri Giants, Sadaharu Oh, the man who had hit 868 career home runs, a world record. Oh struggled hard in the minor leagues during his first two or three years in the pros. That kind of tempering had built character, Doi would say, which, in turn, helped Oh develop into a great batting star.

Thus, after Ichiro, in his first season as a professional, had led the Japanese minor leagues in batting with a .366 average in 58 games and compiled a .253 average in 40 games with the parent team, Doi returned him to the farm club early the following year.

"Ichiro had come too fast too far," Doi explained. "He was progressing without any problems. A player has to know hardship if he's gong to reach his full potential."

But Doi, himself a former all-star second baseman and accomplished spray hitter for the "V-9" era Giants, so called because they won nine straight Japan Series championships, had also been critical of Ichiro's unorthodox batting form. "You'll never make it hitting that way," he'd said and instructed him to plant his feet and shorten his grip.

Confused with this new wrinkle, Ichiro, ever the perfectionist, kept his mind focused, putting in longer hours on the training field than anyone else in the organization. This was saying something because Japanese teams already practiced more than anyone else in the world.

Consider: Japanese and Americans play similar seasons from April to October (162 games for MLB, 140 for NPB as of 2001), but the way they go about preparing for them is very different. Americans start their training camp in the warm southern climes of Florida and Arizona around the first of March. The players are on the field three to four hours a day and then it is off to the nearest swimming pool or golf course—often with the wife and kids in tow.

Japanese start their training in the freezing cold of the Japan winter with something called "voluntary" training, which is another way of saying "show up or start looking for a vocational counselor." Camp begins on February 1 and consists of about eight or nine hours a day on the field followed by evening indoor workouts and lectures on baseball, and just possibly, Zen meditation sessions. For most teams, it is unheard of to have a wife in camp. Japanese coaches, unlike their American counterparts, demand an extraordinary amount of running and not infrequently order punishing physical exercises like the so-called "1,000 fungo drill," not intended solely for conditioning but also to build inner strength. Americans who experienced this system often compared it to military training. ("It was like serving in the Japanese Imperial Army," is the way former Montreal Expo and Tokyo Giant Warren Cromartie once described it.) All the extra work is one reason why teams in Japan take every fifth day in camp off—to recover, while MLB teams in spring camp take none.

During the season the training regimen continues. Whereas Americans believe that one has to save one's energy for the games, especially during the hot weather, the Japanese believe that the hotter the weather gets, the harder one has to train to compensate.

When the season ends in early October, Americans pack their bags and go home to spend the winter as they like—those who spent their season on the bench might head for the winter leagues, those who didn't might head for the living room sofa. Japanese, by contrast, would go off to autumn training, a reprise of spring baseball boot camp, which lasts until the final day of November. In many cases even the top stars on the team would participate.

For years, the Tokyo Giants have held an autumn camp where typically the workday began at 7:00 in the morning and ended at 9:00 at night. Drinking and mah-jongg were forbidden. So was watching adult videos. One year, each player was required to write an essay entitled "A Self-Examination Concerning Flaws in My Performance During the Past Season."

As a BlueWave, Ichiro always stayed late after practice. Long after practice and long after his teammates had ensconced themselves in Kobe's neon-lit watering holes and fleshpots, he was hard at work on his form in the batting cages by himself. In the winter, with permission from Orix, he played for the Hilo entry in the Hawaiian League.

Out of deference, Ichiro had politely tried his manager's way of hitting for a while. After all, a willingness to conform was a sign of good manners. But he found that the new stance threw his rhythm out of whack. Called back to the big team in midyear, he could only manage a .188 batting average in 43 games, although in one memorable contest he did hit a single and a home run off the PL's leading hurler, Hideo Nomo. He subsequently declared, rather dramatically, that he would rather stay on the farm team than continue trying to alter his swing.

"I've been hitting this way since high school," he said. "That's my batting. I'd rather stay on the farm than attempt a switch now."

"These young guys really say what they want," remarked a somewhat bemused Doi, granting Ichiro's wish to return to the minors.

Ultimately, Ichiro's stubbornness, rare for a player in Japan, paid off. In 1994, Doi was forced to resign because of the team's mediocre record and a new manager, an irreverent spirit named Akira Ogi, took over. Formerly a second baseman with the old Nishitetsu Lions, based in Fukuoka, he and his teammates had been as famous for their postgame debauchery as for any exploits on the field. Ogi, a mere .229 career hitter between the foul lines, was a free-spending night life aficionado who could negotiate the dense thickets of bars in Tokyo, Osaka and Kobe as well as any man alive. He liked to dress in the fashion of a Japanese movie gangster—in white suits, white enamel shoes, gold chains and dark sunglasses— and liked to bring nightclub hostesses with him to the ballpark.

His transition from player to manager seems not to have affected his approach either to the game or to life. Under Ogi, there was no player curfew and few other rules. It was fine with him if an Orix player stumbled back to the *ryokan* drunk out of his mind, as long as said player was up the next morning running around the practice field and sweating the alcohol out of his system.

"Drink hard, but practice hard," Ogi was often heard to say. "That's my motto."

By all accounts, it was a philosophy he personally adhered to well past his middle years. Until he retired as BlueWave manager in 2001, he would lubricate himself until the wee hours, arise in the morning for a run of several miles and follow that with a sauna and a bath, during which he would douse his private parts with alternating buckets of hot and cold water. He boasted that this ritual kept him young well into his 60s, able to vie with his players for the affections of young ladies in cities all over Japan.

His on-field strategy was not remarkably different from the dogged step-by-step, base-by-base approach followed by the Giants and most other Japanese teams, who worshipped at the altar of the sacrifice bunt. (After seeing Nippon Professional Baseball's button-down style of play during a lengthy stay in Tokyo, author David Halberstam was moved to remark, "They play as if they were wearing blue business suits.")

However, Ogi *was* unburdened by a belief in *totei seido* and the widely-held notion in Japan that orthodox form was all-important. He did not think there was anything at all wrong with Ichiro's swing and confessed that he could not figure out why Doi had not used him more. Thus, one of Ogi's first acts as manager was to stick Ichiro in the starting lineup, mostly in the leadoff spot, and let him hit any way he wanted. Ichiro responded with a breakthrough season that baseball fans in Japan still talk about. Playing in Kobe's idyllic new park, Green Stadium Kobe, notable for its fan-shaped playing field and multicolored seats, he became the first Japanese player to accumulate over 200 hits in a season, finishing with 210 in 130 games for a batting average of .385. The latter was a new Pacific League record, just shy of the Japan record of .389 held by American Randy Bass, set in 1986. Batting leadoff, Ichiro also whacked 13 home runs, drove in 54 runs and, demonstrating exceptional foot speed, stole 29 bases. He was chosen the Pacific League MVP and awarded a Gold Glove for his fine defensive efforts in center field, where he had unveiled the best throwing arm in the Japanese game.

It was in 1994 that he also officially became known by the handle "Ichiro," rather than Suzuki—which was the second most common surname in Japan. It was a PR stunt dreamed up by Ogi and an Orix coach in an effort to change the image of a team that had grown weak and complacent, as well as to separate their new outfielder from the anonymous clutter of all the other Suzukis in Nippon Professional Baseball. It was an idea Ichiro initially thought frivolous. He found it embarrassing to be introduced that way over the P.A. system. By the end of the season, however, with Ichiro a household word and commercial endorsement offers flooding in, he did not want to be called anything else.

The following year, picking up where he left off, he propelled the BlueWave to their first pennant in 12 years and copped his second MVP in a row. He topped the league in hitting again, with a .342 average, and led in RBIs with 80. What's more, he belted 25 home runs, while upping his number of stolen bases to 49.

By this time, he was so famous it was difficult for him to walk the streets of Kobe, now, tragically, reduced to rubble in many neighborhoods by the great earthquake of 1995, which had collapsed the city's overhead highway and turned many of the downtown office buildings into grotesque shells of twisted metal, leaving some 300,000 people—one-fifth of the metropolitan population—homeless. Ichiro had quietly donated considerable amounts of money out of his own pocket to help in the relief effort.

Basking in the reflected brilliance of Ichiro's luminosity was *pater* Nobuyuki, who attended every Orix home game he could, making the two-hour drive west from Nagoya. He had just authored a book, *Musuko Ichiro* (My Son Ichiro), in which he recounted his relationship with his son, and, in the process, turned the Airport Batting Center into a tourist attraction. As a result of that tome's substantial sales, he had become a minor celebrity himself, fielding dozens of media requests every day. He could be seen sitting in the infield stands at Green Stadium Kobe signing autographs for fans and being interviewed by sports reporters. However, it was a turn of events that embarrassed Ichiro. He complained to his father, who subsequently moved to the outfield bleachers, where he might be less easily spotted.

The press had dubbed Ichiro the "Human Batting Machine" and he continued to do justice to the name, putting together the most impressive skein of hitting seen in Japan since the heyday of Sadaharu Oh. In 1996, he batted .356, won his third straight MVP and led his team to a victory in the Japan Series win over the Yomiuri Giants. In 1997, moving to third in the batting order, he hit .345. A year later it was .358, then .343 and .387 after that. That made seven batting titles in a row, baby, an unprecedented feat in the NPB, as was his aggregate batting average over that period of .353. He had become such an adroit, dexterous hitter that he was downright eerie at times. In 1997, for example, he went two entire months—

216 plate appearances in all—without striking out. In the 1999 season, he managed to get hits on 70 percent of the strikes he swung at—an esoteric if nonetheless astonishing baseball statistic. His bat control was so good that in one game in the year 2000, he hit a pitch that bounced in front of home plate for a single to the outfield (the video highlight of this sensational hit is often played these days on American television). Ichiro believed himself on the verge of hitting .400, something that had never been done in Japan. By then the press had come up with another word for him: *kaibutsu* (monster). It was praise of the highest order.

Hip Hop

As he was being catapulted into superstardom, Ichiro was also morphing into a symbol of the assertive new youth in image-conscious Japan. He would appear at the park dressed in baggy jeans, T-shirt and backwards baseball cap, rap music blaring from his Walkman—the strains of "Fuck you mother fucker" and other popular lyrics of the time audible, if not intelligible to non-English-speaking listeners, as he strolled by.

In pregame practice he would entertain the fans with a flashy routine normally associated with showoff Americans, shagging fly balls with behind-the-back catches. While warming up between innings, he would demonstrate his arm strength by throwing all the way across center field to the left fielder, from his right field position. During a delay in one game he sauntered onto the pitcher's mound and began hurling pitches—at 85 miles per hour—delighting the restive crowd. While waiting out a long argument involving the umpires in another contest, he passed the time by playing catch with the bleacherites.

Newsweek International featured him on the cover of an issue in mid-1996. "He's hot. He's hip. He's the new face of Japan," blared the magazine, ". . . a new breed of brassy ballplayer intent on breaking the mold in which everybody marched to the same beat."

Well, not entirely.

In reality, Ichiro was not quite the iconoclast some journalists made him out to be. Like all of his young teammates, he helped clear the field of equipment at the end of practice. Although he could now afford a luxury apartment, he continued to live in the BlueWave's spartan dormitory throughout the season so he could be near the team's batting cages.

What's more, at the end of each season, he packed his bags and headed off to the team's fall camp—a five-week rerun of spring training. Ichiro never attempted to use his status as the game's brightest young star, one who was in constant demand for lucrative commercial endorsements, to gain special dispensation.

When Orix offered less-than-heart-palpitating salary raises, he did not take his case to the press, as a player in America might, but instead uncomplainingly signed his contract. After his MVP year in 1996, many baseball watchers had expected the BlueWave to double Ichiro's 1995 pact of 160 million yen, which would have made him the third-highest-paid player in the game. But the club made a surprisingly low offer of 260 million yen, which Ichiro meekly accepted. He himself had had to negotiate the deal as NPB rules at the time banned agents for Japanese.

"I have actually only been playing professional baseball for three years," he explained to the *Asahi Shimbun,* a leading daily newspaper. "I wonder how it would appear if I had asked for the same kind of money that the top guys are making."

The Yakult Swallows' curmudgeonly manager Katsuya Nomura, a man notoriously critical of young players, had nothing but praise for this brightest of new stars in the NPB constellation.

"He's wonderful," gushed Nomura. "He hits well. He runs well. He plays good defense. He's polite in his private life and is kind to his parents. I've never seen anyone like him. It's strange that such a person is born into this world."

At the end of the millennium, Ichiro won a nationwide poll conducted to determine Japan's favorite sports star, while yet another survey determined him to be the best baseball player in NPB history. As he closed in on his ninth year, which would qualify him for free agency, he began to get attention from abroad, where he had developed a small cadre of distant admirers.

One of them was Bobby Valentine, who had spent the 1995 season in Japan managing the Chiba Lotte Marines of the Pacific League. At the time, Valentine had called him "one of the five best players in the world."

Ichiro himself had begun mulling a career move to America as far back as 1996, after a standout performance against a group of visiting Major League All-Stars featuring Cal Ripken, Barry Bonds, Brady Anderson and Pedro Martinez, in a postseason series of exhibition games. ("That little shit can really hit the ball," Bonds was overheard saying.) Los Angeles Dodgers manager Tommy Lasorda, who later saw the videos of Ichiro demolishing those visiting MLB pitchers, urged owner Peter O'Malley to sign him up. As one veteran observer of the game on both sides of the Pacific Ocean put it, "For Ichiro, Japan was an aquarium. But he really deserved an ocean. He belonged in the major leagues."

"I was in a funk," Ichiro himself said after the 1996 series finale. "I saw those MLB players and I thought to myself, 'That's what I want to do.'"

But actually doing it was not that simple. Despite disturbing signs of change, the most disturbing of which to Japanese purists was the abrupt defection of Pacific League ace pitcher Hideo Nomo for the States in 1995, through a technicality whereby a voluntarily retired player could sign with any team he chose abroad, baseball in Japan had not quite yet turned into a game of raging individualists. Deep down, Ichiro was still anchored by the traditional Japanese concept of *on* and *giri* (obligation and duty). That meant that as long as his manager required his services, Ichiro was going to stay put and not seek a subterranean way out of the NPB and into the major leagues. He could have used the loophole Nomo used, which came to be known as the "Nomo Clause," but he refused to betray his manager, the man who had helped make his fantastic career possible.

When Ogi told him, "As long as I'm manager of this team, I'm going to need your services," Ichiro snapped to attention and replied, by all means, he would continue to provide them.

Under Japanese rules, he would, however, become a free agent after nine years of service, and he determined to make himself ready when the opportunity presented itself. He spent two weeks as a guest participant in the Seattle Mariners' spring training camp in early 1999. On his return to Kobe, he began seeking advice from American players in Japan, like teammate George Arias, about the differences between the two games, as well as what he would have to do to succeed in the United States. He also embarked on a sophisticated weight-training program to develop the explosive capacity of his muscles and took to using a regulation major league baseball in practice sessions (the Japanese professional baseball is slightly smaller than the one used in the major leagues). In addition, he managed to develop a new way of running, switching from a chest-puffed-up form to a crouching style which, sports writers remarked, resembled that of a lion chasing its prey (it was actually patterned after Carl Lewis).

Finally, in 2000, his chance came. According to one version of this story, Ogi, after six years as a manager, and the BlueWave steadily sliding into the second division, had begun to feel guilty about standing in the way of his star's inevitable date with destiny. In the age-old Japanese clash between *giri* (duty) and *ninjō* (human feeling), *ninjō* was now winning out. Thus, one evening that fall of 2000, he invited Ichiro and his new bride Yumiko to dinner at a Chinese restaurant in Kobe for a heart to heart talk.

"Tell me again, Ichiro," he said, laying down his chopsticks when the main course was finished. "Do you really want to go to the major leagues?"

"Yes," Ichiro replied. "I really want to test my ability."

"He'll do anything you tell him to. He's that loyal," Ichiro's wife chimed in. "But please let him choose his dream."

At this, Ogi sighed and said, "I want him to stay, but that's selfishness on my part. He's already done a lot for us. If Ichiro really wants to go to the States, I'm just getting in the way."

Then he turned to Ichiro and said, "I can't very well stop you from going now, can I?"

With that, Ogi gave the couple his blessing and released Ichiro from any further obligations.

It was a touching, heartwarming story.

And it was even partly true.

But there was another version as well. At that point, Ichiro had only one year to go before he did become eligible for free agency. If the team let him go early under a new system called "posting," devised jointly by the baseball commissioners of the U.S. and Japan (see Chapter 6 for details), Orix stood to earn a substantial lump sum from the MLB team that signed him. His Orix salary was already at five million dollars a year, an expensive proposition for a team that, even with its all-world luminary, was not exactly a cash cow. He had just hit .387. What if Ichiro batted .400 the next season and legitimately demanded a doubling of his pay? It was a burden Orix would not be overly eager to assume. Would it not be the better part of valor to let him go now and make it look as if they were doing him the favor?

In the end, the answer to that question turned out to be "yes." Orix received $13 million from Seattle and left Ichiro to negotiate his own deal with the major leagues.

An important part of Ichiro's master plan to emigrate to the States had been finding a wife, a goal he accomplished in late 1999, the wedding taking place in the U.S. in a small private ceremony at Los Angeles's Riviera Country Club to avoid the media crush.

The lucky young lady was one Miss Yumiko Fukushima, a television reporter for the Tokyo Broadcasting System (TBS), one of the major commercial networks in Japan, and the news of their engagement received wide media coverage of the type the American press might devote to a royal wedding. Press reports unfailingly pointed out that Yumiko was conveniently fluent in English and familiar with the United States, which would no doubt be a big help to her husband in making the adjustment to a new culture. Writers glowingly noted that she was also well-versed in baseball, having been previously engaged, albeit temporarily, to a ballplayer in the Central League, before switching her affections to the Pacific League. Coming in for the most favorable comment, perhaps, was the fact that she was seven years Ichiro's senior, a bit long in the tooth for a Japanese anchorette, but ideal for a young man like Ichiro lacking in worldly experience and requiring the stabilizing influence of a mature woman. As one reporter less than tactfully pointed out, "Ichiro can see the seams on a

150 kilometer per hour fastball, but he can't see the wrinkle lines around Yumiko's eyes."

Ichiro had not been lacking in female companionship prior to meeting his bride. Far from it. He had been involved with a number of high-profile young women, bimbonic and otherwise, including a former singing and dancing star in the famous all-female Takarazuka troupe, and a beautiful, impulsive young actress named Leona Suzuki, later famous for a *kamikaze* marriage to a Honolulu sushi shop employee she had just met, one which lasted all of one week. Said teammate Shigetoshi Hasegawa, "One of the reasons Ichiro stayed in the team dormitory was that it was easier to carry on his romantic liaisons from there than it would be operating out of a private apartment, under the constant eye of the press. The team would always arrange a hotel for him and smuggle him out somehow, like under a blanket in the back seat of a van."

However, the more old-fashioned of Ichiro's followers believed a supportive wife to be a necessity if their hero was to realize his dream of big-league stardom and Yumiko, in the manner of so many other Japanese women before her, did not disappoint them. She surrendered her career to become a dutiful wife, moving back home to study cooking and brush up her English language skills. As if to confirm her adherence to old ways and reassure an anxious public, she could be spotted by Japanese photographers walking three steps behind her husband in postwedding excursions. It was a customary and respectful distance long observed by traditionally minded wives in Japan. However, not everything about Yumiko was conservative. It was she, according to reports, who persuaded him to grow a beard—"You'll look like Brad Pitt," she had reportedly said—and encouraged him to wear rock star sunglasses when he was in public.

The union survived a postnuptial scoop by the popular Japanese weekly photojournalism magazine *Friday* which reported on Ichiro's lengthy affair with a 30-year-old married woman and the secret $100,000 *tegirekin* (solatium for severing relations), arranged by lawyers, he had been obliged to pay as a result. The indiscretion was made public when the husband (of whom Ichiro was reportedly unaware) discovered the deal and leaked it to the press.

Fortunately for Ichiro, he was able to afford it. And then some. In the fall of 2000, he signed a three-year deal worth $12 million with the Seattle Mariners, negotiated by his new American agent Tony Attanasio.

He was finally on his way.

THE MEANING OF ICHIRO

We still can't get over the fact that he is a real hero to Americans.
We still can't see that.

SATOSHI GUNJI, BOOK EDITOR, KADOKAWA PUBLISHING,
NOVEMBER 2002

Ichiro is the first cool Japanese I've ever met.

UNIDENTIFIED AMERICAN SPORTSWRITER

THERE HAD ALWAYS BEEN A SPECIAL CONCEIT IN THE LAND WHERE baseball was born that a small man could not play in the major leagues. A small Japanese man, that is. That particular species was viewed with the same disdain which Americans used to have for products bearing the label "Made in Japan"—once a synonym for poor quality.

As the first position player ever from Japan to seek his spot in the major leagues, Ichiro was considered too slight and too fragile. An advertised 5′9″ 156-pounder, his seven batting titles in Japan were regarded as insignificant by the vast majority of MLB insiders, Bobby Valentine and company notwithstanding, because they believed the Japanese played a second-rate, Ping-Pong type of game. Sure, there might have been a few pitchers capable of performing at the top levels of the American game, but they were the exception. Playing every day was something else.

Suzuki's detractors snootily declared that the bigger and stronger

MLB pitchers would cut the 27-year-old wisp down to size with high inside fastballs. ESPN's Rob Dibble, in a preseason interview with the Seattle Mariners' then manager Lou Piniella, had stated flatly that he would strip naked and run through Times Square if the little squirt won a batting crown.

Actually, size turned out to be less of a problem than people had anticipated. From mid-2000 to the spring of 2001, while no one was really watching, Ichiro had gained nearly 20 pounds on top of his listed weight of 156 pounds through intensive weight training. In fact, when he reported to the Mariners camp in sun-drenched Arizona, the uniform they had readied for him was too tight, thanks to new muscle mass in his arms, shoulders and legs. This raised suspicions in some quarters, although never proven, that he had been taking steroids, suspicions fueled by the fact that he had refused to join other NPB stars and play on Japan's baseball team in the Australian Olympics. Reporters speculated that he was afraid to take the required drug tests. Whatever the reason, Ichiro was stronger than he had ever been. He also insisted that the Mariners' 5'9" height listing was off by nearly two inches.

Ichiro did, in fact, endure a period of adjustment. Initially, he found it difficult to get used to the pitching motion of American hurlers, which was much quicker than the "one-two-and-three" herk-and-jerk style of many Japanese pitchers, incorporating as they usually did a brief pause at the height of their delivery to throw off a batter's timing. With Americans, he discovered, there was simply no "and." They just wound up and came right at you. Because of this, Ichiro found it necessary to eliminate the pendulum-style leg lift he had used all his years in Japan and employ a new, more compact stance that, ironically, would have pleased his former manager Shozo Doi.

His new manager, Piniella, also had his doubts. After watching his expensive rookie bat in the first several games of the exhibition season, during which he hit balls nowhere but to the opposite field, Piniella took him aside and asked, in some frustration, "Don't you know how to pull the ball?"

"Sure," came the reply. "Anytime. That's easy." It was just that for the time being, he was focusing on a more important task: building a zone for himself in his head. He was working on chopping the ball to left field and, in the process, creating a mental "wall" in the outer part of the strike zone, for use as a permanent point of reference. Once he had done that, he would shift his focus to left center and when he had that mental zone down pat, he would hit to center, then right.

Piniella was not impressed. "Why don't you show me right now that you can pull the ball to right," he said.

So in the very next exhibition game, Ichiro banged out three sharp line drives to right field and put a permanent end to all discussion about where he could and could not hit the ball.

Piniella later confessed his astonishment that a batter could have that much bat control.

Ichiro wound up batting an impressive .321 for the exhibition season, and once the season started, it did not take long for the man (now sporting a new spiky hairdo and Day-Glo sunglasses) to serve notice that he was indeed special—that it was the pitchers who would have to learn to adjust to him and not the other way around.

On opening day against Oakland, in front of Nobuyuki Suzuki (who had been robbed on his way in from the airport) and 43,000 other fans at Safeco Field, Seattle's beautiful, sparkling new gem of a park, he collected his first two official MLB hits, including a perfect drag bunt single in the ninth inning that left the Oakland infield searching for their athletic supporters. That surprise tactic led the Mariners to a dramatic come-from-behind victory and earned the famously reserved Japanese star a big, wet, sloppy kiss from the famously extroverted Piniella, an impulsive display of appreciation which the embarrassed Ichiro bore with some discomfort. As he told a Japanese TV crew, "It's something that makes most Japanese men want to throw up."

Back-to-back hitting streaks of 15 and 23 games followed, highlighted by three four-hit performances and a 10th-inning, game-winning home run in Texas. By the first week of June he was on the cover of *Sports Illustrated* (in the same week that the movie *Pearl Harbor* opened nationwide, ironically enough), leading the American League in hits with an overall batting average of .366. He also had a mark of over .500 with the bases loaded, totally obliterating the misconception that Japanese batters could not handle major league pitching.

Opposing pitchers discovered that he could hit everything they threw at him: curves, sliders, changeups, split-fingers and pure unadulterated heat, in-high or low-and-away. It didn't matter. He was an equal opportunity batsman. So exceptional was his hand-eye coordination that it was calculated he swung and missed only 6 percent of the time. These were figures that had not been seen since Wade Boggs was in his prime.

Although the Japanese flash could smack line drives to either gap and pull the occasional pitch into the stands, his specialty was slashing pitches in the dirt to the left side of the infield and then beating the throw to first base—his time down the line was a Mantlesque 3.6 seconds, the swiftest in the major leagues. In fact, he was so quick out of the box that it looked to most observers as though he was running even before he had hit the ball. Opposing teams radically revised their infield defenses to cope, moving in only to leave larger holes through which Ichiro punched one-hoppers to the outfield.

This was, it should be pointed out, not exactly the Ichiro that Japanese fans were used to seeing. In the major leagues, Ichiro had half again as many infield hits as he had ever had in Japan, where he was rather more noted for whipping line drives over the infielders and for occasional bursts of power. The change was largely due to Piniella, who, when not showering his new star with affection, was ordering him to eschew the fly ball and chop pitches into the dirt, the better to take advantage of his blinding speed and force errant throws.

Seattle, a team that had heretofore relied primarily on home run power from its former slugging stars Ken Griffey Jr. and Alex Rodriguez, was now transformed into a gang of scrappers, scoring runs on infield hits, stolen bases and sacrifice flies, thanks to the spark plug from the Orient. In fact, the Mariners frequently scored a first-inning run before their cleanup hitters even had a chance to bat. Their offense was so diabolically effective that by mid-June, they found themselves leading the American League West by more than 22 games and were on pace to match the all-time single-season win record.

The new guy on the team also turned out to have one of the best throwing arms on the planet. In one frigid night game in Oakland, he launched a 200-foot missile that nailed Oakland baserunner Terence Long attempting to go from first to third on a single to right field. Long, who had expected to make the trip easily, was so astonished to be thrown out that he turned, faced right field and tipped his cap.

"I'm not the fastest guy in the world," he said later. "But that has to be the best throw I've ever seen." ESPN agreed. "The Throw," as it came to be known in Seattle baseball lore, quickly won a spot on the sports channel's highlight clips.

By the midseason break, the verdict was in. A survey of baseball managers, conducted by *Baseball America,* voted Ichiro the best base-runner in the American League, its second-best hitter and its third-best defensive outfielder. Catching great Ivan Rodriguez declared flatly, "Ichiro is the best player in the game."

In the voting for the All-Star Game, held fortuitously enough in Seattle, Ichiro garnered 3,373,000 votes—an all-time record, as was the 800,000-vote margin he boasted over his nearest rival. Although he had benefited from newly instituted Internet polling as well as convenience store voting in Japan, where zealous fans were notoriously un-shy about voting multiple times, he had also dominated the hard ballots filled out at stadiums across North America.

Piniella, sitting atop the baseball world, couldn't believe his good fortune. "This guy Suzuki, he hits, bunts and steals," he said. "He scores before you know it. He sets the tone for the team. He's phenomenal. . . . I'll bet if you ask the managers today what they really want, it's a leadoff man like him. And of course Ichiro is the best in the game." Said Mariners veteran first baseman John Olerud to a Japanese reporter, "He's without question the driving force on this team. He's the one who makes it go."

The effect that Ichiro's presence had on the city of Seattle and the entire Northwest was electric. Attendance at Mariners games surged, on its way to a new single-season record. Ichiro posters, T-shirts and jerseys flew off the shelves. Autographed Ichiro baseballs went for $500. An Ichiro bobblehead doll, a Mariners promotional giveaway in July, caused a 30 percent jump in ticket sales. One man drove all the way from Boise, Idaho, just to get one of them, purportedly for his son.

In addition, airline and hotel reservations rose 20 percent, the latter thanks primarily to visitors from Japan who were paying up to $2,000 for baseball package tours. This caused the subsequent debut of sushi stands at Safeco, selling "Ichirolls" (tuna rolls for $9), for example. Headbands emblazoned with the *kanji* slogan for "Water Warrior" (a Mariners nickname) also went on sale, and a large Nissan sign in *Katakana* was erected inside the park. The Pacific Northwest had never seemed more Japanese.

Analysts predicted that the Ichiro factor—when one included ticket sales, souvenirs and advertising—would move over $100 million into Seattle's economy over a five-year span.

NHK, Japan's quasi-national television network, which had opened up a permanent booth in the Safeco upper deck, was telecasting live all Seattle games—182 of them including exhibition and playoff games—back to Japan, where Ichiro was suddenly the talk of the land. Almost overnight, solely because of him, Japan had gone from a country that sporadically watched American baseball to one that watched Seattle Mariners games with something approaching religious fervor, even though the 16-hour time difference meant that the games were televised in the morning.

Tokyo taxi drivers plied the streets with their radios tuned to the Mariners' play-by-play in Japanese, while the numerous sports dailies—14 in all with circulations of up to several hundred thousand each—carried detailed reports on every move Ichiro made. His success in the big leagues was the story of the year in Japan, the story of the decade, perhaps. He got more attention than the Emperor and the Prime Minister combined. Everybody wanted a piece of him, from the mainstream newspapers, with circulations running well into the millions, to the myriad network TV shows, as well as the weekly and monthly magazines. The *Yukan Fuji,* an evening tabloid, featured the exploits of Ichiro on its back page every single day and saw its sales jump dramatically. The Yomiuri Giants, a national institution whose games had been televised nationwide nearly every evening since April 1954, saw their ratings drop.

With homegrown baseball suddenly relegated to second-tier status, "How did Ichiro do today?" became a new way of saying hello in Japan.

The Mariners had given credentials to 166 reporters dispatched from Japan, many of whom were to take up permanent residence in the Puget Sound area and follow Ichiro around 24-7 the entire season. This caused not a few headaches for the Mariners media relations department, bombarded as they were daily with requests for information.

The Japanese reporters on the scene were on orders from their editors to file something new and interesting about Ichiro every day, along with photos. This was not easy, because the object of their attentions followed the same unvarying, if lengthy, pre- and postgame routines with such religiosity that a minor event such as the delivery by Ichiro of a *bentō* of pickled *onigiri* packed by Mrs. Suzuki for Bret Boone (or even a gratuitous nose-picking) qualified as news. After one workout, a Japanese writer approached Seattle coach John McClaren and asked, "Yesterday, Ichiro swung 214 times in batting practice. Today he swung only 196 times. What is the problem?"

Desperate for something different, reporters staked out the house on Mercer Island where Ichiro and his wife lived. They sifted through the Suzuki family garbage and badgered the neighbors for information. When a pictorial scandal magazine offered $1 million for a photograph of Ichiro in the nude and photographers took to hiding out in the bushes near his back yard, Ichiro was forced to move to a highrise condominium to protect his privacy, as well as shower in private at the ballpark. (He declined an offer from an insouciant fellow Mariner to take a snapshot in the altogether and split the money.)

Observing all this, ESPN reporter and noted wit Jim Caple was moved to remark, "This is what it would have been like if Princess Di had played baseball."

As the season wore on, Ichiro proved impossible to intimidate. Opposing pitchers who tried to knock him back with high, inside pitches found his bat so quick he could snake their offerings down the line. Knock him down and he'd get right back up and stand that much closer to the plate. Send him to first with a pitch in the ribs and he'd promptly steal second, maybe even third for good measure. He was, in the words of fellow outfielder Mike Cameron, "one feisty little sucker."

The longer schedule (162 games in 180 days in the MLB in 2001 as opposed to 140 games in 199 for the NPB) and a much heavier travel load than he had ever experienced in geographically compact Japan also proved to be less of a problem than many had predicted. Indeed, the only pitch that proved effective against Ichiro was an unexpected curve thrown by a long-legged 20-year-old Japanese exchange student—a young lady whom Ichiro had reportedly met at a hostess club for expatriate Japanese in San Francisco.

After a game in Oakland one night, as the story went, Ichiro had invited her to his hotel room at the Westin for a romantic encounter. He was unaware, when the young lady arrived, that the cell phone in her handbag was turned on and connected to a number that would record their subsequent activities.

A transcript of the recording subsequently appeared in the pages of *Friday* and caused a huge scandal. Among other things, it had Ichiro saying, "I'd like to tie you up with the bathrobe sash. The thought of it really turns me on." Some readers compared its contents to the infamous Charles and Camilla tapes.

The embarrassment of it all plunged Ichiro into an 0–21 slump, his batting average plummeting from the .347 mark he had taken into the All-Star classic all the way down to .325 and prompted a flurry of wisecracks in the Japanese media. Typical was that of a *Shukan Post* journalist who wrote, "Ichiro might have great bat control, but this is one time he forgot to exercise it."

Reportedly, Ichiro's wife did not speak to him for a long time after that, while Ichiro and relief ace Kazuhiro Sasaki, who had joined Seattle a year earlier from the Yokohama BayStars, launched a brief boycott of the Japanese press for hounding them in such a manner.

Operation Tapegate proved to be only a temporary setback, however. In time, Ichiro regained his old stroke and by the end of the season he was leading the American League in a multitude of categories. He won the batting title, hitting .350, and led the league in

hits with 242 (59 of the infield variety). The latter was an American
League rookie record, as well as a Seattle Mariners team record and
was the highest total anyone had seen in 71 years. He also led the
AL in runs scored (127) and stolen bases (56), as Seattle finished
with 116 victories, which broke the American League record for total wins heretofore held by the New York Yankees, with 114 in 1998.
Ichiro had helped the Mariners achieve victory in the AL Divisional
Playoffs (collecting 12 hits) before losing out to New York in the AL
Championship Series in five games. He was chosen the American
League's Most Valuable Player as well as its Rookie of the Year (only
the second man in history to earn both honors in one season) and
won a Gold Glove. All in all he broke 13 MLB, AL or franchise
records and his former critics now were saying that he had the ability to become the first man in over 60 years to hit .400.

Rob Dibble, true to his word, ran through Manhattan wearing
nothing but a G-string.

American Hero

Americans liked Ichiro because, for one thing, he was a throwback
to another time. He had reintroduced them to a style of offense that
many MLB fans, accustomed to andro-induced sluggers and tape-
measure home runs, had forgotten—an attack based on the single,
the hit and run, and intrepid baserunning that had once defined the
game. Said the *Washington Post*'s Thomas Boswell, the MLB poet lau-
reate, "To see Ichiro hit is to be taken back almost a century to the hit
'em where they ain't technique." Some commentators compared him
to Ty Cobb, Rogers Hornsby and other old-time greats. It was telling
that before long, his teammates began copying his technique of slashing the ball to the opposite field.

But there was far more to his appeal than that. Fans had never seen
anything quite like the contortionist ritual Ichiro put himself through
before each and every at bat: an unvarying set of squats, stretches,
shoulder rolls, quad stretches and practice swings designed to keep
him relaxed, to empty his mind, and, at the same time, to prevent him-

self from looking at the opposing pitcher before he was ready to mentally confront him.

Then, standing in the batter's box like some modern-day Musashi Miyamoto (a famous 16th century swordsman), he would hold his bat one-armed, swinging it over his head in a clockwise arc, pointing it directly at the pitcher. Bending his elbow to touch his right shoulder and tug on his uniform sleeve, he would lock his arms and cock his hands, then, drawing a breath, he would wait for the first pitch in utter concentration.

It was a form of attack that, with its unvarying routine of getting set, breathing, exhaling and emptying the mind, then directing all concentration into two movements after being perfectly still, enabled Japanese practitioners of the martial arts, from *zen* archers to *kendō* combatants, to see their philosophy at work. It was also a way of hitting that Little League ballplayers all across America began copying.

On top of that there was Ichiro's perfectionist attitude and a work ethic which put his teammates to shame. His pregame workouts were models of consistency and persistence—a demanding regime of running, calisthenics and weight lifting, followed by the detailed viewing of videotapes of the day's opposition, that surpassed what everyone else on the Mariners did. It prompted Mariners second baseman Bret Boone to say, "I get tired just looking at him."

Ichiro, in fact, opined that if his teammates spent more hours on the practice field they'd be even better off. He had expressed disappointment that in the Mariners' spring camp, Piniella had eschewed practice games and gone straight into the exhibition matches, and that the team did not really start to play hard until opening day. There were no defensive relay drills for the infield and outfield, or other fundamental drills. It was greatly different from the Japanese camp where such things were practiced in great detail. If, on the one hand, he had found Japanese camps a little too rigid and had admired the way the American system allowed its athletes to relax, he, on the other, was concerned about MLB's neglect of fundamentals.

"Theirs was the type of practice that made you wonder whether they could really play the game or not," he said. "Many times during the season we made errors and I thought, 'If we had just worked on that in camp.'"

In time, many of his teammates did begin imitating aspects of his practice routine, following the sophisticated set of stretching exercises he performed before games, as well as the special tee batting drills he did. In fact, in 2003, a new manager, Bob Melvin, would incorporate some of Ichiro's ideas on defensive practice in his camp and pregame regimens, and so would Tony LaRussa of the St. Louis Cardinals, after having a lengthy off-season discussion with Ichiro about the differences between Japanese and American spring training.

Ichiro's dedication also showed in the respect he accorded his equipment. As his father had taught him, he religiously cleaned and oiled his glove after every game. He shined his shoes on a daily basis. He kept all his bats in a humidor and his game bat beside him in the dugout, propped against a pair of wooden tongue compressors taped together by the trainer. (His substitute bats were cradled on a rack above his head.) Once he reportedly felt so bad about throwing down one of his bats after an unproductive plate appearance that he brought it back to his hotel room and polished it. None of these habits were followed by American players, a state of affairs that Ichiro had a hard time grasping.

"I couldn't understand how my teammates could sit down on a glove I'd just cleaned and placed on the bench," he once complained. "I couldn't understand why they didn't take care of their equipment more. How can you play well and improve if your equipment is not in good condition? Cleaning the glove cleans the heart. It's all part of a 24-hour process, in which everything—eating, sleeping properly, doing correct pregame workouts—is all intertwined."

Chikara wa keizoku ("continuity is strength") was his personal motto.

In some ways, Ichiro seemed a cypher. With him, there were never any untoward displays of emotion, which was something else that separated him from many of his American colleagues. As had been his habit in Japan, there were no excessive celebrations of victory; no wallowing in the pain of defeat. No pumping of his fist in exultation after a home run. Not once during his time in Seattle did he ever lose his temper or his cool, even when victimized by a bad call or a fastball in the ribs. (That was a lesson from his father, who repeatedly cautioned him that such boorish behavior would only affect his mental state and lead to a lapse of concentration on the next play.) At the same time, he never ever seemed to get rattled under pressure no matter what the situation—as his fat batting average with the bases loaded would indicate.

"I get nervous and upset like everyone else," he said, "but I just don't want others to know it or see my fighting spirit on the surface."

He needn't have worried.

As an admiring Japanese baseball philosopher put it sometime later, adding his own spin on the cool Ichiro persona, "Ichiro knows the *mu* or nothingness of *zen*."

Ichiro tapped into America's nostalgia for baseball the way it used to be in still other ways. After pregame workouts, he would amble over to the fans in the stands down the right-field line and sign autographs—yet another thing that fewer and fewer major leaguers could be bothered with. Following a season that most players could only dream about, no one heard him complaining about his relatively low annual salary of $4 million. Indeed, prior to coming to America, he had told his agent Attanasio that he did not care how much money he made in MLB as long as he could play there. He would also turn down $35 million in endorsement offers by 2002, because he thought the products would either detract from his image or the effort required would impede his concentration on baseball in some fashion. He continually displayed a profound reluctance to discuss his accomplishments. Summing up his record-breaking first MLB season in a special 90-minute documentary for NHK, he said:

> I really don't like the word success or a lot of talk about records. Records are a way of saying a person is better than another. People use them. It's a way of comparing players. I don't mean to say that they have no value or are insignificant, but the most important thing is doing your best, preparing, giving your all. If you get a record without preparation, it's not satisfying. If you really prepare, try hard, do your best and you succeed in surpassing yourself, that is really satis-

fying. If you do that and someone else surpasses you, then *shogonai*, it can't be helped. So instead of thinking about who is number one and who is number two, you should think about whether you have given your best.

It was the kind of intelligent, well-thought-out statement that Ichiro was capable of, if the spirit moved him, but one that American fans seldom got to hear, partly because of the language barrier, but also because of, well, Ichiro's chronic and unfortunate distaste for interviews. After a game he would sit in front of his locker, massaging his feet with his back to the gaggle of reporters standing behind him. He would direct his answers to their questions through an interpreter or intermediary who then relayed them to the gentlemen and ladies of the press. American writers, who had never encountered anything like it, wondered, "Is that the way it's done in Japan?" "Is that Zen?"

Well, yes and no. It certainly wasn't the way things were done in NPB because access there was more controlled and reporters were never allowed inside the clubhouse. Even in permitted interview settings, however, there was a premium was placed on taciturnity. There was a saying in Japan that: "The man who says nothing, says everything." And that indeed was *zen*.

But, even in a country where evasive answers were par for the course, Ichiro had been known as a notoriously difficult interviewee. A writer who made the mistake of asking him what his objectives were in baseball was apt to be dismissed with an abrupt "I'm working toward my own inner goals. As for what those goals are, I can't tell you." Another common response was "I find that question too vague to answer."

Said well-known sportswriter Masayuki Tamaki, a longtime Ichiro watcher, "He's a control freak. He thinks that if he stays quiet then nobody will know what he thinks and he won't be criticized. He's a great player, but he's also arrogant. Deep in their hearts, most people in the media in Japan don't like him because he is so uncooperative. Most of them were hoping he would fail in the U.S."

Ichiro's general aloofness had not endeared him to all of his former Japanese teammates either. Said one Orix player, "He didn't join us in our morning walk. He was always the last one on the bus. He didn't care if he kept his teammates waiting. He was a standoffish guy." Nor had his attitude captured the hearts of Japanese residents of greater Seattle, who criticized him for not socializing more with them. Said a Seattle-based Japanese businesswoman in her 40s, "It's too bad that someone like him had to be the one to represent Japan to the American people."

Be that as it may, Ichiro still managed to connect with his American teammates—Bret Boone, for one, who had become addicted to the *bentō* (boxed lunch) Ichiro's wife made for him—as well as his fellow MLB players. He would go out of his way to try to speak Spanish to the Latin players and English to the others. Cynics said that he tried harder to integrate in the United States than he did back home.

Not, it might be remarked, without a substantial measure of success.

Seattle

Asked once what he thought the significance of his accomplishments in the U.S. was, Ichiro replied simply, "I think I have narrowed the gap between America and Japan." And indeed, he had. For openers, he had introduced his country to a segment of the American population that had never given Japan much thought. Twenty years earlier, most Seattleites had not even known what sushi was. Now they were eating it at the ballpark and shouting *"gambaré,"* along with other demotic Japanese phrases of encouragement. It was no small achievement.

Seattle had, in fact, undergone a remarkable transformation over that time—morphing from an insular, redneck, blue-collar industrial town of mostly aircraft line workers, loggers and fishermen, to a white-collar, high-tech, sophisticated corporate city of "Microserfs," home to three of the world's 10 richest men, even *after* the NASDAQ meltdown of 2000.

With that transformation had come a desire to white out all that had been small-town and small-minded about Seattle's past—which was not inconsiderable. The events portrayed in the bestselling novel *Snow Falling on Cedars,* a story of a murder set in Puget Sound in the 1950s amidst lingering memories of World War II and internment camps, were not altogether fictional—involving as they did racial prejudice, forbidden love and a falsely accused Japanese-American fisherman, a lifelong resident of the area.

Against that background, a kind of historical watershed occurred in 1991 when then Mariners owner Jeff Smulyan was on the brink of moving his team, a perennial loser with depressed attendance, to Florida. In an effort to keep the club where it was, a group of Seattle politicians and business leaders led by Slate Gorton prevailed upon Nintendo president Hiroshi Yamauchi, whose firm's American branch was based in Redmond, to buy a majority share in the franchise. Yamauchi, an eccentric Kyoto aristocrat whose passion for *go* far exceeded his minimal interest in *bēsubōru* and who had never been to Seattle to see the Mariners play, agreed to do it as a "gift" to the community.

However, the idea of a foreigner, or rather a *Japanese* foreigner, buying an MLB team was not warmly received in the country at large, thanks to the growing economic friction with Japan. At that particular time, Japan was at the height of its economic power. Its firms were buying up U.S. landmarks like Rockefeller Center, Pebble Beach and Columbia Pictures. The U.S. trade deficit with that country was so huge, courtesy of burgeoning Japanese automobile and electronics exports, that many Americans had begun complaining of a "Japanese invasion" and the threat it posed to the future of the faltering U.S. economy. It was a time when the rhetoric flew hot and heavy.

In January 1992, for example, in response to U.S. Japan-bashers, the Speaker of the Lower House of Parliament in Japan had termed the Americans "lazy and illiterate," while Shintaro Ishihara, a popular novelist turned politician, claimed that Japanese could always make a better product than the Americans. That latter remark prompted U.S. Senator Ernest Hollings to retort undiplomatically that Ishihara was forgetting who made the atomic bomb. In a visit to a weapons factory in South Carolina, Hollings suggested employees "draw a mushroom cloud and put underneath it: Made in America by lazy and illiterate workers and tested in Japan." In a highly charged incident some months earlier, a group of U.S. lawmakers had been photographed smashing a Japanese car with a sledgehammer.

Against this background, Philadelphia Phillies owner Bill Giles declared his opposition to the sale of the Mariners to Nintendo. "It's a patriotic issue for me," he sniffed, while Major League Baseball commissioner Fay Vincent announced it was not in the best interests of U.S. major league baseball to have foreign ownership by any other than a Canadian organization. A poll conducted at the time revealed that 70 percent of Americans queried were opposed to having Japanese own a major league franchise.

However, Seattleites, for their part, were beginning to view their region as part of the Pacific Rim. Not only did Asians constitute by far the largest minority in the Puget Sound area, the territory was dependent on the exports of Microsoft and other companies to Japan and the rest of the Asian economies. Many jobs also depended on the very Japanese imports that were taken to task in the country at large. There were enough folks who appreciated Nintendo's record as an upstanding member of the corporate community in the Pacific Northwest to successfully push the idea of Japanese ownership through, although it did not survive completely intact.

Although the major leagues had eventually agreed to Yamauchi's acquiring 60 percent of the Seattle franchise, they did so only on the humiliating condition that he restrict his voting interest to less than 50 percent. It was a restriction described by Donald Hellman, director of the Institute for International Policy at the University of Washington, as "out and out racism."

Nonetheless, Yamauchi, described by one business writer as "a likeable crab," agreed to pay $75 million of the estimated $125 million total price of the team, and consented to leave the day-to-day management of the Mariners to Nintendo America's chief, Howard Lincoln. Lincoln hired Pat Gillick as general manager, a man who had a reputation for creating competitive teams on less than exorbitant payrolls, and the Griffey/Rodriguez era was launched. Then in the winter of 1999, Gillick signed Kazuhiro Sasaki, relief ace of the Yokohama BayStars, who became an instant success with the Mariners, winning the 2000 Rookie of the Year award with a record of 37 saves and an ERA of 3.16. That year, the Seattle Mariners made a profit (of $10 million), the first in the history of the franchise. And, of course, they made even more money in 2001 when Yamauchi suggested the team acquire Ichiro Suzuki. By the end of that year, Japanese was virtually a second language at Safeco Field, with ideographs featured in advertisements all over the park. Suzuki was unable to walk in downtown Seattle without being mobbed.

Ironically, those owners who initially opposed Yamauchi's acquisition wound up benefiting from it heftily thanks to MLB TV broadcasting contracts with Japan that proved to be worth tens of millions of dollars.

Author Shawn Wong, an Asian-American professor of English at the University of Washington who had himself experienced discrimination, was particularly happy about the way things ultimately turned out. He was so moved by the sight of 45,000 people in Safeco Field chanting Ichiro's name when he came up to bat (and yelling *"sanshin"* when Sasaki struck out an opposing batter) that he declared the people of Seattle had become global citizens without leaving home.

In an article he wrote for the *Seattle Times,* he praised the respect and loyalty, "distinctly Japanese traits," exhibited by Ichiro and Sasaki. The latter had quietly signed a contract extension without the bargaining in the media that was standard for American stars. When it was over Sasaki made the simple public statement, "I love the city of Seattle and my teammates." Wong also movingly described a little white boy holding up at sign at Safeco which read, "I want to be Ichiro when I grow up."

"Today," wrote Wong, "the corporation known as Major League Baseball is looking like a global missionary, marketing its products in Japan and around the world. . . . I'm beginning to think that an entire city can understand how race changes their culture and society and can embrace and even encourage that change."

The View from Japan: Members of the World

For Japan, the significance of Ichiro's accomplishment was a slightly different matter. His success was one of those great postwar moments for the Japanese that inspired a sense of triumph—like the exploits of Rikidozan, a former sumo wrestler who popularized pro wrestling in Japan by defeating outsized American wrestlers in carefully orchestrated matches. Rikidozan's first match, in 1954, was seen by a record 24 million people, nearly one-third of the nation's population at the time, who crowded in front of promotional TV sets set up in public squares around the country and watched in delirious joy as their hero pounded an American, Ben Sharpe, into submission.

His matches gave an enormous boost to the nascent television industry in Japan, as well as an incalculable lift to the spirit of the nation, still trying to recover from defeat in war. Said Matsutaro Shoriki, the president of the Yomiuri media conglomerate that had telecast the Rikidozan matches, "Rikidozan, by his pro wrestling in which he sent the big white men flying, has restored pride to the Japanese and given them new courage."

Another triumph was the conquering of the U.S. auto market in the 1980s. This inspired an enormous wave of self-congratulation, endless platitudes from political leaders in Tokyo and hundreds of books and TV documentaries about the end of the U.S. century and the rise of the Japanese one. *The Japan That Can Say No,* a saber-rattling polemic by the aforementioned Shintaro Ishihara, one which essentially extended a middle finger to the U.S.A., sold a million copies.

The Ichiromania that swept Japan was certainly no less intense, as evidenced by the full-frontal blast of coverage in the ubiquitous sports dailies, featuring large photos and detailed pitch-by-pitch charts of each Ichiro at bat. In NHK's twice-daily broadcasts of Mariners games (shown once live, once on tape on the network's thirteen-year-old satellite channel), viewers were treated to endless shots of their idol doing knee bends in the outfield, joking with his teammates on the bench, stretching in the on-deck circle. These were interspersed with taped replays of his pregame warm-ups, autograph signing sessions and, of course, earlier at bats, ad infinitum. After watching all this for half a season, one Tokyo-based TV reviewer suggested sarcastically that NHK change the name of its daily gamecast from "Major League Baseball" to "The Ichiro Show."

The telecast of the 2001 All-Star Game by the Tokyo Broadcasting System (TBS), a major commercial TV network, represented a new high in such narcissistic reporting. It marked the first time in history that two Japanese players had appeared in a Major League Baseball All-Star Game and a bevy of Japanese TV personalities appeared on the program to offer color commentary on the newest hero. When Ichiro was taken out of the game in the early innings, a luncheon show featuring guests singing Ichiro's praises came on to occupy all but a small corner of the screen, where the all-star telecast continued. It stayed that way until the other Japanese participant, Ichiro's team-mate Kazuhiro Sasaki, was called into the game to pitch the ninth inning. Then, suddenly, the live full screen baseball telecast resumed. The priorities could not have been clearer.

A similar, although lesser, media display had occurred when Hideo Nomo first entered the major leagues, pitching every fifth day. But Ichiro was the first to appear front and center every single day—a slender Japanese among pumped-up musclemen, sparking his big American teammates to victory—and the public could simply not get enough of this delectable sight. It was an unprecedented opportunity to massage the national ego and the press took full advantage of it.

There was no small degree of irony here, because, outside of the BlueWave home city, hardly anyone had watched Ichiro play in Japan. He had been the country's premier player, with a string of batting titles under his *obi,* and owned the highest paychecks in either league, not to mention his own clothing line, numerous endorsements and his face adorned billboards all over Japan. Yet he nearly always played to half-empty stands, in games that were almost never telecast nationally. This sorry state of affairs was largely due to the existence of the Tokyo Yomuri Giants, Japan's oldest and winningest and most beloved franchise. The Giants are owned by a puissant media conglomerate that includes the largest daily newspaper in the world, the *Yomiuri Shimbun,* with an average daily circulation of about 13 million including morning and evening editions, and the largest commercial television network in the land, Nippon Television. They were the only baseball organization so blessed.

The *Kyojin* (Giants) were the living definition of the term "wretched excess." Thanks to their habitually winning ways (31 pennants in their first 70 years) and the fact that they had always attracted the best players in the land, they drew capacity crowds to nearly every game they played, attracting over three million fans a year. Tokyo Giants primetime telecasts had enjoyed consistently high ratings, which peaked in 1982 to a nationwide Nielsen rating of 27.5 percent for the season. Surveys regularly showed that one out of every two persons who followed baseball was a Giants fan, which meant that no matter where the *Kyojin* ventured, at least half the stands were rooting for them.

They were in the forefront of the nation's consciousness for so long that, cynics argued, the country had essentially been brainwashed into following them. Even when the team finished in last place in 1975, or in the second division as they did in 1991 and 1997, far out of contention, they still outdrew *all* the pennant contenders. Indeed, many viewers complained of suffering withdrawal symptoms if a Giants game was rained out and there was no nightly fix available—no matter where the team was in the standings.

Yomiuri was the reason the Central League had an average attendance of about 13 million a year while the Pacific League drew only around 10 million. In Ichiro's breakout year, the Orix BlueWave attracted 1,700,000 fans—not bad, if still far behind the Giants—but then attendance slipped in succeeding campaigns as the novelty wore off. Tabloids that featured Ichiro on their back cover in 1994 and 1995 found that his drawing power did not last as the public turned back to more familiar Giant heroes. The number of times Orix played on nationwide TV during Ichiro's entire Japan career could be counted on one hand. Elvis could have come back to life and played in the BlueWave outfield and the result would have no doubt remained the same, such was the enduring allure of the magical *Kyojin* name.

Although Ichiro could certainly attract a crowd on an afternoon stroll through the Ginza, and complained constantly about intrusions into his private life by the media, it was, if the truth be told, the *lack* of attention from *bēsubōru* fans that prompted him, at least in part, to make the move to the States. He viewed himself as a far better player than his contemporary, the Giants' popular center fielder Hideki Matsui, now with the Yankees (see Chapter 10). Matsui was a home-run slugger, but, as a general all-around player, he was, in Ichiro's quoted opinion, *"ichi-ryū ja nai"* (not first class): an athlete who had yet to take his game to the level that was demanded of a superstar. Despite this, however, Matsui continued to command the headlines almost daily over Ichiro—even after the Orix BlueWave had defeated the mighty *Kyojin* in the 1996 Japan Series.

"I could hit .400," Ichiro muttered, "and still they would not come to see me."

Thus it was not until he left his homeland to play in the U.S. that Japanese fandom finally gave him the attention he deserved. Only then did he go from being a star player to a nationwide phenomenon and one who, ironically, caused a significant drop in the Giants TV ratings. These actually fell to single digits at times in the 2001 season, the first time that had ever happened to the team during *Goruden Awa* ("Golden Hour") as the Japanese referred to prime time. Moreover, while their games still played to capacity crowds, discount tickets were now easy to come by, a circumstance most people had once thought impossible.

Ask Japanese why they suddenly became so fixated on Ichiro and they would give you a variety of reasons. He helped people take their minds off the bone-wearying recession that had infected Japan since the early 1990s. He proved the high level of baseball in Japan— prompting even the Japanese baseball commissioner to say, improbably, as he watched his NPB lose its best talent to the major leagues, "It's an honor for me as commissioner to see Ichiro playing well in the U.S." And he also validated the national ego, as evidenced by the turgid encomium of Prime Minister Junichiro Koizumi, who announced to all citizens, "Ichiro makes me proud to be a Japanese."

Indeed, the response of an NHK announcer, when asked if she worried that the local professional game was being reduced to a farm sys-

tem for MLB, was telling. "No," she replied, "Japanese are excited because this shows Japanese superiority over America."

However, there was something even deeper going on here. For
decades, Japan had impressed itself on the world's consciousness,
primarily through its products, its currency, its visible cross-border
acquisitions (like the Mariners), and its well-disciplined tourists flush
with cash. Japan was seen as a place where highly trained and largely
faceless "organization men" marched efficiently in lockstep—a place
that produced few stars or exceptional talents worthy of mention.

But now, finally, here was Ichiro, a real live human being in Oakley
Juliet sunglasses, besieged for autographs everywhere he went.
American kids loved him. Their parents admired him. His fellow
players respected him. TV sports announcers all across America
were giddily singing his praises. Famed writer Frank Deford hailed
him in a piquant documentary for Bryant Gumbel's *Real Sports.* Jeremy Schaap did the same for *Sports Center,* while S.L. Price penned
a loving profile in *Sports Illustrated.*

The Ichiro-in-America phenomenon was a fantasy that many Japanese had long wanted to experience, if only vicariously. It had special
resonance in Japan because it gave the people something they had
never quite had before: a full-fledged Japanese hero who was idolized
by Americans themselves. It was the Asian version of *Damn Yankees.*
It was something the Japanese had not been able to do in the political arena or the entertainment world, or anywhere else.

These baseball triumphs also seemed somehow more substantive
than the economic triumphs of years past. Ichiro's rookie hit record
mattered; it would retain its significance over time. True, during the
peak of the Bubble, the Nikkei hit an all-time high of nearly 40,000
and was hailed as an economic Seventh Wonder—until the ensuing
collapse revealed the smoke and mirrors that had disguised the underlying weakness. In Ichiro's case, however, no one was going to come
along in ten years and claim that his p/e ratio was out of whack.

At the same time, many Japanese back home found it difficult to
fully grasp the idea that Ichiro was truly, madly and deeply accepted
into the fold by the American public, given the unpleasant history the
two peoples shared. The sense of insecurity was palpable enough that

some Japanese sought confirmation from their American acquaintances that Ichiro was indeed as popular as they had been led to believe and not simply the beneficiary of overzealous and slanted reporting, as was often the case in Japan.

They found it odd that although he had made a sustained assault on the long-standing single-season hit record of 257 held by George Sisler and had monopolized the batting leader board all year, he received almost uniformly positive treatment by American fans and media—his success failing to activate any nativist, xenophobic strain in the American character. To Ichiro fans, this was puzzling because it was in marked contrast, for example, to what American sluggers in NPB had experienced when chasing titles or attempting to break Japanese records.

In point of fact, the pride and satisfaction in Ichiro's achievements coexisted with a strange, indelible desire in Japan to hold the world at arm's length—as reflected in 2001 by the remark of one Ministry of Justice official who explained, to a UN representative, the minuscule number of refugees Japan took in annually by saying, "Japanese don't like foreigners." This attitude, which waxes and wanes, has been dubbed a "*gaijin* allergy" and its sneezes continue to resonate through many areas of Japanese society.

Some historians trace this allergy to the centuries of isolationism dating back to the Tokugawa Shogunate, whose rule of Japan from 1600 to 1868 was marked by the fear that interference by foreigners and foreign ideas would threaten its hegemony. The shogunate had initiated a policy of national seclusion that banned foreign travel. With a few minor exceptions, anyone caught trying to leave or return to Japan was liable to face execution.

After Commodore Matthew Perry and his Black Ships arrived at the white sands of Shimoda in 1853, demanding that the shogunate abandon its isolationist pose and open its ports, that era was supposed to have ended.

But it hadn't. Not quite.

With the fall of the shogunate and the ascension of the reform-minded Emperor Meiji to the throne 15 years later, Japan began a campaign to absorb foreign learning and technology in order to catch up and overtake the more industrially advanced West. The phrase which, for the most part, characterized this effort, *wakon-yoshi* (Japanese spirit, Western skill), meant, essentially, Give us your technology but don't intrude in our society or disrupt our national spirit of *wa* or harmony.

The resulting bi-polar relationship with foreign culture was marked by an intense interest for the Japanese in how they sized up against the West. The country's self-esteem soared to new heights when Japan defeated Russia in the war of 1905 and expanded its military power throughout Asia, eventually pulling out of the League of Nations. It sank to new depths in the aftermath of World War II when it was utterly dependent on the outside world to keep from starving. Then it rose once more in the postwar era, during which Japan threatened to flood the world with exports.

Boasting of technological superiority, Japanese companies manufactured and exported high-quality products, but the country had not been successful in producing human beings who could truly interact with others in foreign lands. In the eyes of many consumers of Sonys and Hondas, the Japanese themselves remained two dimensional—a sort of caricature taken from *Madame Butterfly* and the numerous published accounts of Japanese corporate Groupthink.

Midori Masujima, a prize-winning sports journalist, touched on this when she wrote in 2002, "We've never really been a member of the world community, not in the Edo period, not in the Meiji era and not today. Though we may have been a guest, or a provisional member, or a member-in-training, we have never been a full-fledged, card-carrying member." She addressed what she called Japan's "complex"—a language complex stemming from a chronic inability to master the English language, and a sports complex stemming from its inability to prevail in international sports events, save for the odd marathon or judo triumph. Thus was there a craving for approval from overseas, for a vindication of Japan itself, that attached itself to the athletes who made their way across the Pacific.

The measure of the success of Ichiro, Nomo and the others is, in Masujima's words, that "these Japanese athletes had taken the Japanese sports inferiority complex—the sense that Japanese are not physically or experientially ready for world competition—and proved it wrong."

As she put it, they were taking their place on the world stage and giving young and old "a new vision of the world," and went on to say:

> I believe that the statistics and the records and the splendid skills dis-
> played by Japanese athletes are not just about athletic talent. I believe
> that these athletes in this brand new century represent a new way of
> thinking, a new philosophy that has arisen within Japanese society,
> and that this new philosophy will have a tremendous influence.
> . . . Stock prices are falling and Japan's long recession continues. Vi-
> olence and crime appear to be on the rise as a result. Yet, today's ath-
> letes—active overseas in greater numbers and in more sports than
> ever before—have made us remember the confidence and the pride
> we have lost. "Maybe we can make it through these hard times after
> all." "Maybe the world will finally accept us . . . for what we truly are,
> regardless of whether we are good or bad at foreign languages." I
> think Japan's athletes can inspire such hopes in the Japanese people.
> . . . Not only are they standing shoulder to shoulder with their over-
> seas peers, in some cases they are leading the way.

SOME HISTORY AND
SOME PHILOSOPHY

I watch baseball which was introduced by the Americans and it
is not boring.

EARLY MEIJI-ERA HAIKU
Shiki Masaoka

The day passes with nine people doing nine different things at
baseball.
  The three bases are full; I'm very excited as to what is going
to happen
  The soaring ball goes high into the clouds,
  Then comes down into someone's hands.

EARLY MEIJI-ERA WAKA
Shiki Masaoka

Some History

Jim Colborn was a onetime Milwaukee Brewers pitching star who
was brought to Japan in 1990 to coach for the Orix BlueWave.
Hired to teach MLB methods to the pitching staff there, he found
himself learning from his hosts instead. Lesson One began on the
opening day of spring camp. With the permission of Orix manager
Shozo Doi, Colborn had ended his first session at one o'clock in the
afternoon. However, he discovered later that his assistant coaches,
fearing ridicule from other organizations over this early dismissal,
held an afternoon practice in Colborn's absence—with the players'
enthusiastic support. They repeated this the next day, and the follow-

ing one and the one after that, until Colborn realized what was going on and agreed to incorporate the afternoon workout into his own formal agenda.

"What I was trying to do was to get them to conserve some energy," said the soft-spoken California native. "I knew from talking to other Americans who had played or coached in Japan that those long workdays the Japanese put in tended to wear the players down over the course of the season. And at first, I couldn't understand why they kept knocking themselves out. But then I eventually came to realize that there were other more important objectives on their mind. Their practices, I found out, were designed to teach patience and perseverance—'*doryoku*' (effort)—as much as the skills of baseball, to instill character as well as to prepare for the game. That was why they were so long."

In time, Colborn also came to comprehend another truth about the Japanese system—the extreme importance of process. Whereas in America you were always looking for new ways to do things, that wasn't necessarily true in Japan. They had a set SOP, a predetermined way of approaching the game, and they protected it like Fort Knox. The difference might be summed up by saying, "In the U.S. we say 'Just win baby.' In Japan, it was 'Just do it the right way.'"

"All Japanese institutions were like that," said Colburn, an intelligent, educated man who learned to speak Japanese during his four-year stint with Orix and refined it in his subsequent capacity as a Pacific Rim scout for the Seattle Mariners (where he recruited a young man named Ichiro Suzuki). "Our baseball reflects Western culture: aggressiveness, innovation, surprise. But their baseball reflected Japanese values. Proper form. Rote learning. Harmony. Constant effort. It frustrated Americans on our team who were just trying to win the game. They'd ask, 'Why do we have to hop and skip for 30 minutes beforehand?' Of course, the answer was because that was the way it was done."

Other students of Japan have made similar observations. In 1992, for example, a team of researchers did a study on cultural differences between Japan and America as reflected in sport and came to this conclusion: Japanese practiced "democratic conformity," in which players demonstrated control over their own wills by moving toward consensus within the group, while Americans showed something called "reluctant conformity."

It was the difference, they reported, between a "harmony-oriented strategy and one which stressed fulfillment of individual potential and responsibilities." Their findings were published in the *National Strength and Conditioning Association Journal*, in an article written by Bill Shang, president of NSCA's Japanese affiliate.

Shang wrote: "In Japan, the team is thought of as a 'household'—a close-knit community with hierarchical organization and sub-leaders for its various groups, such as freshmen and sophomores. A successful leader in Japan motivates his people to win for the coach or the captain rather than for personal glory or achievement.

"In Japan, the coach is the master; the athlete, a disciple," he added. "The teacher-disciple (coach-athlete) bond is a very important one and fits into the whole group orientation of the Japanese. . . . Moreover, whereas American athletes practice long and hard, but concentrate simply on developing skills, in Japan, there's a Zen approach to practice as more a development of inner self than muscle and a player is bound to work out until he reaches mental limitations, which in most cases (are) far beyond physical limits."

Although not everyone agrees that sports reflect culture (indeed, some profess to find terms like "national character" and "patterns of culture" downright offensive), the differences between baseball as it is played here and baseball as it is played there are certainly impossible to miss—and, as we have seen, they date all the way back to the 19th century.

Baseball was first taught to the Japanese by visiting American professors shortly after Emperor Meiji assumed the throne in 1868, thereby ending centuries of feudal, isolationist rule, and initiating the nation's all-out effort to modernize, which became known as the Meiji Reformation. During the emperor's reign, which lasted until 1912, Japan devised a new constitution based on that of Bismarck's Germany. The Japanese built an army trained by French officers and fashioned a navy modeled on that of Great Britain, importing educators, scientists and engineers from Europe and North America to help them develop their schools, railroads, hospitals and police, as well as their postal and bureaucratic systems. This period was initially defined by an intense interest in all things Western and a proportional disdain for things homegrown—a time when many Japanese men, for example, exchanged kimonos for three-piece western-style suits and bowlers.

Baseball, at the time known as *bēsubōru* or *tama asobi* (playing with a ball), initially met with more approval in some quarters than the traditional fighting techniques like *kenjutsu* or *jujitsu*, believed by certain progressives at the dawn of the Meiji Era to be anachronistic and dangerous remnants of Japan's feudal past.

Later, however, as discontent arose over the unequal treaties Japan had been forced to sign with the West, a backlash against Western values occurred. In 1890, for example, an Imperial Rescript on Education reemphasized the centuries-honored traditions of Shinto and Confucianism, while an elite educational institution called the First Higher School of Tokyo, or *Ichiko*, founded in 1886, emerged as a bastion of Japanese culture, standing firm in the face of outside influences that seemed to be overwhelming Japan.

Although Ichiko embraced some key Western technologies, its students also studied the martial arts and practiced zen in the pursuit of purity and mental and moral discipline. Ichiko students lived in campus dormitories, symbolically isolated from the rest of society by a fence deemed sacred by the student body. Ichiko was, in fact, the premier prep school in the land and a major stepping-stone for students who wanted to attend Japan's most prestigious institution of higher learning, *Teikoku Daigaku* (Imperial University), the elite hopper from which the future leaders of Japan would emerge.

Ichiko's baseball team was established in 1886. In contrast with the baseball played at *Meiji Gakuin*, its archrival and a Christian missionary school noted for its laid-back, American-style approach, Ichiko developed something called *seishin yakyū* (spiritual or spirit baseball), which essentially turned the game into a new sort of Japanese martial art.

According to historians, the Ichiko baseball regimen drew on the concepts of *bugei* (military arts), with a strong emphasis on constant training (which would grow into harsh summer and winter baseball camps) and the development of fighting spirit or inner strength. A team motto urged participants to practice so hard that they urinated blood, while another team rule forbade complaining of injury or pain. The underlying ideology also embraced group loyalty, love of school and nationalism. (With peanuts and Cracker Jacks coming in considerably further down the list.)

The Ichiko baseball phenomenon did not occur in isolation. For one thing, it closely paralleled the development of a new school of judo, established in the mid-1880s, under the guidance of Gakushuin University professor Jigoro Kano, which was attracting a lot of attention at the time. Kano's creation was an amalgam of modern scientific techniques and the old pre-Meiji art of *jujitsu*, with a focus on blood-and-guts training. The Kano school's month-long winter camp was held in February, the coldest part of the year; participants arose at 4 A.M. for a run of several miles before beginning an intense two-hour morning workout, followed by another two-hour workout in the evening.

Kano, unlike some of his contemporaries, had great respect for the old masters, whose teachings he believed need not be set aside in the quest for enlightenment from the more industrially advanced West. A respected scholar who served as headmaster of Ichiko for a time in the mid 1890s, he held that ancient concepts could be harmonized with modern thought and he took pains to incorporate the idea of *seishin* into his new martial arts. He wanted to preserve the sweat, agony and ordeal that characterized the training of men in olden times—stressing development of strength, skill, stamina, courage, "martial timing" and an immovable mind. In particular, he thought that with the proper combination of technique and mental willpower, a man could be made unstoppable. At the same time, *kenjutsu* enjoyed a similar revival in the form of *kendo*, thanks to its popularity with the police force.

A driving force behind the development of the Ichiko baseball team was its playing manager, Kanae Chuman. In 1894, he gave the imported sport a bona fide Japanese name that would stick: *yakyū* (field ball). It was also the title of a book Chuman would write in

1897, said to be the first ever book solely on baseball in Japan. In it, he described proper training methods and other aspects of the games, emphasizing that "Ichiko players should ignore the American way and devise a system that suits Japanese." He advocated that his team practice two or three months before playing its first game.

Another key figure was Chuman's teammate Jutsuo Aoi, a pitcher/infielder whose "1,000 swing" batting drills evoked associations with the famed 16th century swordsman Musashi Miyamoto. In his classic work, *The Book of Five Rings*, Miyamoto preached the Way of the Martial Art, which he exhorted devotees to "put into practice morning and evening, day in and day out."

"Surpass today what you were yesterday," Miyamoto wrote. "See to it that you temper yourself with one thousand days of practice, and refine yourself with ten thousand days of training."

The Ichiko baseball team's success in defeating a team of American traders and missionaries belonging to the private Yokohama Country and Athletic club in a series of historic games in 1896 received prominent newspaper coverage—a first for baseball in Japan—and caused the game's popularity to soar. Suddenly, "spirit ball" was elevated to the status of national sport.

Ichiko games were rich in symbolism because they demonstrated to the nation the potential fruits of hard work and conveyed the message that if the Japanese could defeat the Americans at a game the foreign barbarians had invented, then surely they could surpass them in trade and industry as well. The fact that U.S. sailors were added to the Yokohama team at one stage and still the Ichiko players prevailed made the experience especially sweet.

Star pitcher Tseunetaro Moriyama, a lefthander who later pitched a shutout against the Yokohama Americans, became Japan's first baseball legend, hypostatsizing the grand virtues of *konjō* (fighting spirit) and *doryoku* (effort). Moriyama threw so hard every day at the Ichiko grounds, using a brick wall on the field for target practice, that he eventually wore a hole in it—a permanent tribute to fighting spirit that is now commemorated by a plaque. He was also famous for his habit of setting up a lit candle as a target and trying to extinguish the flame with his pitches. He threw so many curve balls in practice that his arm became bent; to straighten it out, he would dangle from the limbs of the cherry trees that bordered the field, pretending to ignore the pain. Moriyama expanded Chuman's philosophy about preparation when he said, "Two or three *years* are needed before a team can play its first game."

Ichiko was also memorialized in a 1905 poem entitled "*Yakyū Buka,*" an abridged version of which follows:

> The crack of the bat echoes to the sky
> On cold March mornings when we chase balls on the ice
> Year in and year out, through wind and rain
> Enduring all hardship, we practice our game
> Ah for the glory of our Baseball club!
> Ah, for the glitter it has cast! Pray that our martial valor never
>   turns submissive
> And that our honor will always shine far across the Pacific.

From the early part of the 20th century, the baseball teams of prestigious private universities Keio and Waseda came to the forefront, incorporating the Ichiko ethos, which came to be known as *bushido bēsubōru* (*bushido* being the term for the way of the samurai warrior).

In 1905, Waseda made a historic tour of North America. It marked the first time intercollegiate squads from the two countries would face each other, but it was significant in other ways, as well. At the time, Japan was in the midst of a war with Russia—one from which it would emerge victorious and demonstrate convincingly that it had become a major power. It was the idea of Waseda dons and Japanese government officials that by sending a team of college athletes all the way across the Pacific just to play a sporting contest, while simultaneously fighting and winning a war with behemoth Russia, the small island nation would declare in no uncertain terms its arrival on the world stage.

The Waseda nine won only nine of 26 games against teams from Stanford and the University of California, among others, but thoroughly impressed critics everywhere with their grasp of the game. The *San Francisco Chronicle* declared that the "little bronze-faced athletes" ("Japs" as the paper also put it) played "gilt-edged baseball," and that although they were defeated more often than they emerged victorious, they were not in the least disgraced. As the *Eugene Register* put it, "They made every spectator realize that the students of Waseda University know how to play baseball."

The trip gave a healthy boost in confidence to the players from Japan. Waseda returned home loaded with the latest in equipment and technique (pitcher's windups, sacrifice bunts, sliding into base), as well as American style cheering. Back home, the team drew 60,000 to some of its subsequent intercollegiate games. The Keio-Waseda games, played in the separate spring and fall seasons which came to characterize intercollegiate and interscholastic competition, were especially popular and attracted increasing newspaper coverage.

A book called *Saikin Yakyū Gijutsu* (Modern Baseball Techniques), which was inspired by and published shortly after the 1905 trip, stressed the application of Japan's "3,000-year-old martial arts . . . combining physical and spiritual strength" to baseball, as well as to other imported sports like football and boat racing. This, the author maintained, would eventually produce a type of baseball superior to that of the U.S.

Credence was lent to that theory in 1924 when Waseda hosted a strong University of Chicago team and defeated them convincingly in a series of contests representing new heights for the Japanese game and once again elevating baseball to a symbol of national pride. The manager of that Waseda team, Suishu Tobita, a squat, intense individual, became famous as a practitioner of his own brand of *bushido* ball. He encouraged his players to practice—as he himself had done during his playing days at Waseda—until they had "collapsed on the ground and froth was coming out of their mouths." His infield ground ball drills were so ferocious that he would often back his victims all the way to the outfield fence. Although college managers at other schools like Keio and Gakushuin had on occasion tried a less regimented, less groupist approach to *yakyū*, *bushido* ball was so successful it spawned many imitators.

By the time the first professional league in Japan had been established, in 1936, amateur baseball already had a solid grip on the public's interest. The annual National High School championship baseball tournament, established in 1916 by the *Asahi Shimbun*, drew capacity crowds for the two weeks it lasted. The newspaper used the tournament to increase circulation with reports on the games, as well as to promote the concept of Ichiko's *bushido* spirit and to tout baseball as a tool of education. The highly opinionated Tobita became a regular columnist for the *Asahi*, extolling the virtues of student baseball as "the only true form of the game." Samples of his musings about the new fighting technique based on old spirit include: "The only real baseball is year-round baseball. . . . Character is more important than technique. . . . Baseball is more than just a sport. It is an expression of the beautiful and noble spirit of Japan." This paralleled, incidentally, similar arguments being made in favor of the game in the United States at the time, which extolled it as an expression of democratic values and good citizenship.

Some More History

Japanese had actually gotten their first taste of professional baseball in 1908 when a team of minor and major leaguers from the U.S. called the Reach All-Americans won all of its 17 games versus amateur competition on a tour of the archipelago. Similar tours followed, reaching an historical peak of sorts in 1934, when Babe Ruth, playing his last game in a Yankee uniform, headlined a team of big-name American players that won all of its 16 games against a team of former college players, semiprofessionals and high schoolers, mostly by lopsided scores. Ruth, who during the series hit .408 and clubbed 14 home runs, led a huge confetti parade through the Ginza before several hundred thousand wildly cheering Japanese fans.

That 1934 tour had been sponsored by the *Yomiuri Shimbun*, which would vie with the *Asahi* for the title of Japan's leading daily newspaper. Despite the unsuccessful assassination attempt on the life of Yomiuri owner Matsutaro Shoriki by an extreme right wing group named the Warlike Gods Society, who were angered that he had allowed foreigners to play baseball at Jingu Stadium, located on the grounds of the sacred Meiji Shrine in Tokyo, it was by far the most successful of the professional tours from America—thanks in part to bright-eyed pitcher Eiji Sawamura, a fastballer said to throw in the high 90s, who struck out Ruth, Lou Gehrig and two other major league stars in succession, in a 1–0 loss.

Shoriki, who carried a 16-inch scar on his skull from the broadsword that the Warlike Gods had buried into it, was thus persuaded to establish his own professional team, the *Dai Nippon Tokyo Yakyū Kurabu* (The Great Japan Tokyo Baseball Club), which later became the Tokyo Giants, to promote his newspaper.

Sawamura was among the first amateur stars the club signed up. Another was a high school pitching sensation named Victor Starfin, the stateless 6′4″ son of Russian aristocrats who had taken refuge in Japan at the time of the Bolshevik Revolution. Then there were a pair of infielders, Keio star third baseman Shigeru Mizuhara and second baseman Osamu Mihara, a Waseda stalwart—who would both achieve lasting fame in their later years as pro baseball managers.

The Dai Nippon squad celebrated their founding by touring the United States in 1935, where, billed as the team that had faced down Ruth and company behind Sawamura, they won 93 of 102 games against various semipro outfits and minor-league teams and drew enthusiastic crowds.

The success of the Tokyo Giants abroad prompted the Hanshin Railways and six other major companies to organize their own professional franchises and, in 1936, the Japanese professional league was born—under a charter that outlined the goals of fair play and improving the national spirit. The league's director general pledged that the new pro game would "purify the baseball world" and lead to a real world series between Japan and the United States.

Morinji Camp

Pundits like Tobita charged that the professional game—which began as autumn and spring seasons starting in the fall of 1936, before moving to a regular one-season format in 1939—was sullied by monetary considerations and the inability of the players to resist the temptations of the flesh. The pros, in fact, however showed abundant fealty to the concept of *seishin yakyū*, as witnessed by the memorable training camp held by the Giants to prepare for the 1936 fall season. The Giants had lost a spring tourney and numerous summer exhibitions in dismal fashion. Tokyo manager Sadayoshi Fujimoto had determined that the galling defeat was the result of his players' spiritual weakness. "These guys smoke and drink too much," he said, "they're always out at night chasing women. No matter how much I complain, they don't listen." To rectify this unendurable situation, he devised a special pre-autumn-season camp to toughen them up.

It was held at a remote practice field near Morinji Shrine in the town of Tatebayashi, Gumma Prefecture, a rickety, teeth-rattling three-hour train ride from Tokyo. It was not an ideal site for honing one's baseball skills. The infield was strewn with rocks and pockmarked with potholes, the outfield was a sea of weeds. However, to Fujimoto, who had played at Waseda in the immediate post-Tobita era, that was irrelevant.

"The purpose of this camp is not to improve our fielding or our hitting," he declared at the outset, "but to hone our fighting spirit. It will be a battle between me and the players and only one side will prevail. The players won't like it, but this is necessary in order to build the Giants."

For nine days in boiling early September heat that reached 94 degrees that year, beginning at seven each morning and lasting all day, Fujimoto put his charges through Torquemadan workouts, making them chase after hundreds of flies and grounders, an exercise which left their bodies covered with raw bruises and abrasions from the irregular bounces batted balls took on the uneven surface. Not a few players, their uniforms torn and ripped, were seen vomiting on the sidelines from the exertion.

A number of young players were singled out for special ordeals including an untested 19-year-old shortstop candidate named Shiraishi. Shiraishi was subjected to the infamous exercise the "Thousand Fungo Drill," in which he was made to dive for ground balls until he collapsed from exhaustion. After an hour of this punishment, Shiraishi, his face covered with welts from the cascade of balls, was on his hands and knees, holding his stomach and gasping for breath. Still the drill continued, a coach peppering his body with sharply hit balls. Afterwards, for good measure, he was put through a lengthy run. At the end of the day, the teenager was so exhausted, he lacked even the strength to hold onto the straps on the train taking him and his confreres back to the team *ryokan* and collapsed on the floor instead.

However, the young infielder returned for more the next day and was afforded a vivid opportunity to demonstrate his newly acquired fighting spirit. While taking batting practice, he was hit in the temple by a routine *shōto bōru* that broke in too far. The ball collided with Shiraishi's skull with such a sickening thud that the BP pitcher later confessed, "I thought I had killed him." But Shiraishi, against all expectations, did not collapse. His face rapidly swelling, he stood there swaying and making threatening gestures toward the mound. Teammates tried to take him back to the bench, but he pushed them away. "I'm still hitting here," he growled through clenched teeth. It was only when his manager ordered him out of the batter's box that he finally staggered back to the dugout. With wet towels applied to his head, he implored his manager to let him return to the batter's box once more, before passing out on the bench.

Daily practice was followed by a baseball workshop each evening to study rules and strategy, as well as blistering speeches by the manager in which he warned his players that they would have to try harder and sacrifice their egos and individual statistics for the team. All in all, it made what the New York Yankees went through in the preseason look like a Disney vacation.

Osamu Mihara, the team's star second baseman (and former Waseda player under Tobita) recalled in a memoir years later, "The Giants, at that time, did not resemble a professional team. Therefore, there was no other choice but to mold them into one. Shiraishi, Horiuchi, Ito and the others never stopped practicing. They

did not have a moment's rest. They were near tears because the
training was so hard. . . ." Even national hero Sawamura, who had
been confidently relaxing off to the side in the shade much of the
time, was ordered to participate. When he saw how hard his teammates were working, according to Mihara, he confessed he was
deeply moved. "I've never seen people training like this before," he
was quoted as saying, and vowed to redouble his own efforts in pitching practice.

Fujimoto's training, which was appropriately dubbed "vomit practice" and continued for four more days after the team returned to
Tokyo, proved fruitful. The Giants went on to compile a 27-18-9
record and seize the fledgling Japan league crown. It was the first of
many national championships for the team, and fans as well as players would look back at that memorable Morinji camp as the one that
started it all. As one Giants historian would later write, "It was from
the mud and sweat of the training at Morinji that the soul of the Giants was born."

Able to attract the game's brightest stars, like bespectacled line-
drive-hitting first baseman Tetsuji Kawakami, who went on to become
known as the "God of Batting," the Giants succeeded in capturing the
imagination of the public from the beginning, drawing tens of thousands of people to some of their early games. Emphasizing *konjō* and
the idea of team harmony, they became the focus of the pro game for
decades to come.

A succession of managers expanded and built on the Morinji
camp. After the single-season system was instituted in 1939, tough
preseason camps became more common, eventually, as did the "autumn training league," making baseball the year-round profession
that Suishu Tobita had envisaged. Players recalled sessions in which
they were forced to perform their daily drills with heavy *kanji* dic-
tionaries strapped to their backs. Shigeru Mizuhara, the former Giants third baseman and manager of the team throughout the '50s,
instituted taxing spring camp exercises like the "100 fly ball drill,"
where an outfielder was made to chase fly balls barely out of his
reach—to his left, to his right—until he collapsed; it was designed
to teach the players that baseball was "not an easy game." Tetsuji

Kawakami, who took over in 1960, ushered in his famous system of *"kanri yakyū"* (controlled or managed baseball), taking collective discipline (he forbade his players to read comic books in public for fear it would hurt the image of the team) and commitment to practice to a new level, mirroring the corporate management practices that were leading the resurgent Japanese economy to worldwide success.

Many teams copied the Giants in various forms. (Fujimoto went on to manage the Hanshin Tigers, Mizuhara, the Chunichi Dragons and the Toei Flyers.) Although some organizations like the Nishitetsu Lions of the '50s and '60s were known for their relative lack of rules—the Lions were managed by Osamu Mihara, an opponent of *seishin yakyū* (who nevertheless wore out his starting pitchers with horrific overuse)—a basic pattern of boot-camp-style programs emerged, much as Ichiko style baseball formed the basis for most big-time high school programs and Tobita's system was a model for many top university teams. Demanding postgame and off-day practices during the seasons became routine.

In the pros, standard operating procedure for the two pennant winners came to be spending a week before the Japan Series sequestered in hotels away from their families, devoting every waking hour to practice and study of the opposition.

Cracked the iconoclastic sportswriter Masayuki Tamaki, "Japan should replace the Japan Series with a 'practice tournament' to see who can practice the most."

And not a few have pointed out the toll that such zealousness takes. Said Leon Lee, father of major leaguer Derek Lee and a man who played, coached and managed in Japan for years, "Japanese players are in terrific shape in April, but they wear themselves out and run out of gas by midseason."

But, despite such criticisms, the answer to running out of gas by and large remained—what else?—more practice. Under manager Shigeo Nagashima, for example, the Yomiuri Giants held a seven-hour-a-day postseason autumn "Hell Camp" on Izu peninsula in 1997—a time when most major leaguers were relaxing on the golf course. Lasting the entire month of November, it required every pitcher to run 10 kilometers a day and every batter to take 1,000 swings; more than one player collapsed on the field before he finished. Nagashima, dissatisfied with the team's fifth place finish that season, had declared at the outset that he fully expected such dire consequences to occur and had presciently ordered an ambulance to be at the ready.

"Bashing the players this way cultivates spirit," said Nagashima, a man not averse to slapping younger players. "It will help them grow as human beings."

There were a lot of players who scoffed at the term fighting spirit, including a member of that Izu camp, a star pitcher named Suguru Egawa who had run his 10K a day there. Said Egawa, "I hate the word *konjō*." But there were also a lot of players who went along, among them a slugger named Hideki Matsui. Ichiro Suzuki was heard to comment that such rigors are "an extremely valuable thing."

When one added to this certain practical considerations like the need to perfect one's form or *kata* (another legacy of the martial arts), it was not difficult to understand why this practice of endless training remained alive and well in Japan. Most starting pitchers, for example, throw hard on the sidelines nearly every day, in contrast to Americans who rest three or four days between starts. In camp, they'd do even more.

Said Jim Colborn of his Japan experience, "I tried to tell my pitchers it wasn't necessary to throw 1,000 pitches in three days in camp, about ten times what the Americans did, or throw 100 pitches the day before a start. I tried to tell them that they would wind up hurting their arms. But they wouldn't listen. They had too many different pitches to master, they said, like the fastball, the curve, the *shōto*, the slider and the forkball, which was one reason why they had such heavy throwing regimens in the first place. Americans could get by on speed and the changeup, they would admit, but Japanese, who could not throw as hard, needed the variety to succeed. But on top of that, I also found that there was a physical and psychological need for them to do it. Mastering proper form was how they grounded themselves as players."

The *Wa* Factor

The term *wa* (group harmony), some Japanese will tell you, is one of the most fundamental concepts of Japan's moral system. It arose, some say, out of Japan's agricultural past when cooperation between farmers was imperative in order to maintain the irrigation systems necessary to grow rice and other crops. Since Japan was a mountainous island country with few natural resources and little available land for farming and living, people had to work together to survive. In the seventh century, when Prince Shotoku Taishi issued Japan's first constitution, he decreed in Article 1 that *wa* was to occupy a premier place in the value system, stressing the word several times in that document.

The spirit of *wa* was pursued over the centuries with fluctuating degrees of enthusiasm, and success, from the halcyon peace of the Heian Era to the bloody internal wars of the 16th century. It was tempered through a millennium of Buddhism, Confucianism and feudalism (where behavior was dictated right down to the food a person could eat and the clothing he could wear).

Although feudal rule was abolished with the advent of the Meiji Era, the emphasis on the unity of the group remained central to the Japanese way of thinking, influenced, it was said, by feudal family and apprenticeship systems which had made the sense of belonging to a group important. After the Second World War and the establishment of a new democratic constitution, the concept and pursuit of individual rights was not always paramount as the nation went about the task of rebuilding the war-shattered economy with renewed *konjō*. Every aspect of the corporate culture was infused with *wa*—from consenus-based decision-making to promotions and even to elevator etiquette. The emphasis on loyalty, cooperation and trust was cited in many circles as a main reason for Japan's eventual success on the world economic stage.

Thus, company employees and government workers respected their seniors and worked long hours uncomplainingly, including a substantial amount of *"sābisu sangyō"*(unpaid overtime). Industry saw merit in continuation and seniority, not individual flash. The old cliché "The nail that sticks up gets hammered down" was elevated to the status of a national slogan. With all this came Japan's image as "the world capital of consensus-oriented groupthink," as one writer put it.

Enhancing this view was the absence of lengthy worker strikes, a low crime rate, well-mannered passengers on impossibly packed commuter trains—and fans in sports stadiums who were models of restraint and courtesy, careful not to shout out of turn in consideration for the fans sitting next to them. It all reflected what Japan sage Donald Richie described as the general "Japanese ability to put up with things, to conciliate."

The socially accepted escape valves were well known, like those famous after hours drinking sessions with colleagues for the salarymen, (which was why commuter train stations not infrequently smelled of vomit late at night—overworked baseball players were not the only ones puking their guts out for the greater glory of the team). But as author Sebastian Moffet put it, "More than most other societies, appropriate behavior in Japan depended on place and occasion and the Japanese could switch their inhibitions on or off accordingly." For sports fans, it was only when they joined the highly organized ōendan or cheerleading groups that they could really let loose.

The Japanese postwar school system helped prepare students to take their place in such a society. In contrast to the American system, where students were encouraged to cultivate that which made them different from others, Japanese students were taught to focus on finding common denominators. Instead of being urged to think for themselves and express their opinions as part of the democratic process, Japanese were taught to guard their opinions and submerge their interests into those of the group. Individuals, like those annoying Americans, who pressed their thoughts on others, even their elders, were considered likely to disrupt harmony and therefore looked at askance.

Sports reporter Kozo Abe, who covered baseball in the United States for three years in between stints of reporting on his country's own game, came to this conclusion about the essential differences between the two cultures. "Japanese players talk much less than Americans," he said. "Americans expect people to voice their own opinions and express themselves freely. MLB players are always spouting off to the press. But in Japan, it's the opposite. You have to rein in your feelings to maintain harmony. At the same time, it's also a way to keep from having to form an opinion or putting yourself on the spot."

Wa was reflected in *yakyū* in other ways, like uniform playing styles, a mostly conciliatory players' union and the paucity of player agents and heated salary disputes, even though players' salaries were typically one-fifth to one-sixth of those of their North American counterparts. There has never been a baseball strike in Japan.

One might also mention the long history of pitchers who throw without proper rest, sacrificing longevity in their careers for their teams. Most notable was Tadashi Sugiura, who pitched all four games of the 1959 Japan Series and was forced out of baseball with a bad arm at age 30. Or Katsuhisa "Iron Man" Inao, a contemporary of Sugiura's, who won 42 games in one season and also suffered a shortened career. Although such abuses diminished in succeeding decades, starting pitchers in Japan still tended to throw more than their U.S. counterparts, due to pressure from their managers, causing comparatively early retirements.

Then there was the high number of sacrifice bunts (two to three times as many as in the major leagues). As longtime coach Shozo Eto put it, "The Japanese love to sacrifice for the team. It's considered an honor." In 2003 when Tokyo Giants infielder Masahiro Kawai set an all-time record for career sacrifice bunts with 514, it was greeted with as much fanfare as if he had surpassed the home run record. There were fireworks on the Tokyo Dome electronic scoreboard and a flowery ceremony involving Kawai's wife and children, accompanied by tears of joy all around.

But if the history of Japanese baseball has tended to mirror such traditional values as *wa*, *shūdanshugi* (groupism) and deference to authority, it has not been without its own homegrown contrarians. Masaichi Kaneda, the great 400-game winner of the '50s and '60s, dictated to his coaches when he would pitch, demanding no less than three days of rest. In the '70s it was the iconoclastic multi–Triple Crown winner Hiromitsu Ochiai, who disdained practice and refused to listen to any team instruction that pertained to his batting routine. In the '80s there was Kazuhiro Kiyohara, who proclaimed that the only reason to become a professional baseball player was to be able to attract beautiful young women and drive fast sports cars. A 6'4" 220-pound love hunk, who became increasingly thick of girth and prone to injury as his career progressed, slugger Kiyohara was notorious for his addiction to high-end hostess clubs in the posh Ginza district and was a regular target of Japan's infamous scandal magazines (more than once for reputed association with organized crime figures).

However, it might also be noted that Kaneda went on to become one of the most demanding, dictatorial, discipline-conscious managers in the game. "My Way" Ochiai made a postretirement living by writing commentaries criticizing the improper batting form of active players, instituting his own autumn Hell Camps when he became a manager in 2003, while Kiyohara sought to amend his ways by "purification" at Zen temples and publicly expressed horror at any suggestion of a player strike for higher pay. He was once heard to say, "A strike wouldn't be fair to the fans or the owners."

Postwar generations of youth have indeed asserted themselves in different ways—as younger generations tend to do. During the '50s, there were the massive, and often violent, leftist student protests against the government's Security Treaty with the United States. During the '60s, protesters in long hair, jeans and hippie beads marched against the war in Vietnam and smoked marijuana. During the booming '80s era of rising stock markets and real estate values, it was the so-called "shinjin-rui," or "new breed," who wore Armani fashions and gold necklaces, drank imported beer, sniffed cocaine (if their parents were wealthy enough to provide them with the appropriate allowance) and mocked the worker bee ethic.

However, it was also clear that as even the more rebellious members of each generation grew older and confronted the realities of daily living, they became more conservative, eventually acquiescing to the values of the docile organization workers at whom they had scoffed not long before. Blind corporate loyalty at the cost of unpaid overtime and diminished family life continued to manifest itself, even in the face of (or perhaps exacerbated by) the corporate restructuring which took place in the post-Bubble era. *Karōshi* (death from over-work) remained a major social issue, while stress from overwork or the inability to satisfy superiors was among the major causes of some 30,000 suicides that were committed in Japan each year.

In fact, one of the more notable such episodes involved the man who originally scouted Ichiro Suzuki out of high school and urged the Orix BlueWave to sign him against the advice of others who thought that Suzuki was way too thin, even for the NPB.

His name was Kazutoshi Miwata and he had been troubled by his inability to sign another high school star, pitching sensation Nagisa Arakaki, who was the BlueWave's top pick in the 1999 draft. Miwata had been "ordered" by the Wave front office to sign Arakaki, but when the player rebuffed all of his advances and declared instead that he wanted to play for the Fukuoka Daiei Hawks, managed by legendary home run slugger Sadaharu Oh, the scout was forced to admit failure.

Miwata, who had worked long hours on his task, under intense pressure from the team, began to show classic symptoms of extreme stress—loss of appetite, sleep disorders, memory loss. Finally one day, he cracked. On a trip to Naha, Okinawa, to beg for Arakaki's parents' signature on a contract, he went up to the 11th floor of an office building in Naha and jumped to his death. A court later ruled that pressure from work had caused his actions, entitling his family to receive government compensation in the amount of $17,000 a year.

In the '90s, as the deep post-Bubble recession gripped the country, a disenchanted, impatient and narcissistic generation of twenty-somethings emerged. Wearing earrings, bleaching their hair hues of orange and blonde, and displaying, their apologists insisted, a more independent, adventurous streak than any of their predecessors, they were seen to be more in tune with the global youth culture.

Nowhere was this more evident than in the new professional soc-cer loop, the J.League. The J.League had been established in the early 1990s and met with a considerable amount of success, although it still lagged somewhat behind professional baseball in terms of fan popularity.

Soccer, originally introduced to Japan in the 1940s, had, as yet, developed no discernible culture of its own. Thanks to a modern, internationally minded founder and commissioner, the J.League stressed individuality and freedom. Players were allowed to let their hair grow long, to dye it, to have beards and even to grab their crotches in jubilation after scoring a goal.

Baseball's first poster boy for the new generation of restless youth was a reticent moonfaced pitcher named Hideo Nomo, a pitching ace with the Kintetsu Buffaloes, who had long nursed a burning ambition to play in America. Nomo was fed up with the traditional constraints of group loyalty and the wear and tear on his arm that his manager was causing. "I'm not going to ruin my career for one man," he was heard to say.

With the secret help of an agent, Nomo found an obscure loophole in the Japanese rules that enabled him to sign with the Los Angeles Dodgers, despite not yet being eligible for free agency. The first Japanese pro baseball player to defy the system, he was subjected to a brutal attack by Japan's media, which labeled him a "traitor," a man who did not understand the concept of *wa*, as well as condemnation from the powers-that-were in the NPB.

But a former Kintetsu pitching coach named Hiroshi Gondo, after visiting Nomo in the United States, was able to offer an explanation of why a ballplayer of his caliber would actually want to defect.

"Compared to the American way, Japanese baseball is just like being in the army," he said. "Playing in the major leagues might be very tough, but they leave things up to the individual player. Players there know major league team practice is not really enough so they will do their own training afterwards. In Japan, everybody, regardless of whether you are on the first team or the farm team, does the same training. Team management doesn't treat players as professionals. Players are so controlled by team management here that it makes you wonder why more Japanese players haven't left for the big leagues."

"You shouldn't worry about what other people think," Nomo himself drawled, in a rare, talkative moment. "If you think you are right, you should go ahead and do it. The important thing is to have a strong sense of who you are."

This was not exactly the received wisdom of Japanese classrooms and offices. But Nomo eventually managed to overcome his considerable difficulties, to carve out a new life for himself and prevail. How he did it is a story that comes later.

ACCIDENTAL PIONEER

In 1964, I was the first Japanese to play in the major leagues. At the time I was only 20 years old. Because of various circumstances, I had to return to Japan to play baseball. I actually wanted to stay there, but at the time I couldn't express those feelings to many people. I say this to all you young people. You only live once. So don't listen to what the people around you say and follow the path you think is best for you.

MASANORI MURAKAMI, MAY 1995

WHEN THE NEWLY FORMED TOKYO GIANTS TOURED THE United States in 1935, a Pittsburgh Pirates scout tried to sign their ace pitcher, Eiji Sawamura, who was billed on that trip as "The Man Who Struck Out Babe Ruth and Lou Gehrig." But Sawamura flatly refused. He wanted no part of living in the United States, he said; the rice there was no good, the women were too haughty and he couldn't understand the language. Thus did the first recorded attempt by an American major league team to recruit a Japanese baseball player come to an end, and it is safe to say that given the comparatively low level of the game in Japan at the time and the onset of war in the Pacific, similar efforts did not soon follow.

Then in 1961, however, when the Tokyo Giants made the unprecedented move of training at the Los Angeles Dodgers camp in Vero Beach, Florida, Dodgers owner Walter O'Malley became so enamored of Shigeo Nagashima, Yomiuri's clutch-hitting, charismatic third baseman—dubbed "Golden Boy" in Japan for his movie-star good looks—that he tried to buy the cleanup star's contract. Nagashima was interested, but the Giants' aging founder and owner Matsutaro Shoriki turned the offer down flat. He was building a new baseball dynasty and made it clear that unless Nagashima could find a way out of his Yomiuri contract, which bound the superstar to the proud *Kyojin* for life, duty to team—and country—would have to come first.

Now, hundreds of American players, mostly refugees from the U.S. minors, had played in Japan, both before and after the war. In the early '60s Japan became a lucrative market for aging major leaguers like Daryl Spencer, Jim Marshall, Ken Aspromonte, Bob Nieman, Chuck Essegian and Norm Larker, no longer in demand by teams back home. However, traffic the other way was nonexistent, thanks to a combination of NPB contractual restrictions and cultural barriers. It took a freak occurrence for a Japanese to finally be allowed to don the uniform of an MLB squad. The year it happened was 1964 and the player's name was Masanori Murakami. And, as a result of his adventures in America, he found himself in the middle of a battle royal that threatened to destroy baseball relations between Japan and the U.S., not to mention his own career.

It was a conflict that pointed up certain differences between the U.S. and Japan in their respective attitudes toward contracts and *ningen kankei* (human relations).

Murakami was a baby-faced lefthanded pitcher, a trim six-footer, barely out of his teens, who belonged to the Nankai Hawks of the Pacific League. In 1964, the unproven farm team hurler was sent to America, along with two other young players, to spend the season honing his craft in the lower rungs of the San Francisco Giants' minor league system. He was part of a novel player exchange agreement, approved by both the Japanese and American baseball commissioners, that the Nankai and San Francisco organizations had created, the latter purportedly anticipating that one day they might send players from their farm system to train in Japan.

While awaiting that highly unlikely event, they had seen fit to insert a standard option clause in the agreement which allowed San Francisco to purchase the contract of any of the Japanese players who made the parent team for the princely sum of $10,000. The Hawks' general manager at the time, Makoto Tachibana, had agreeably okayed the clause, feeling certain that none of the players he had dispatched would ever advance out of the bowels of the North American farm system, in view of the stiff competition that existed for spots in the almighty major leagues, as well as the obvious fact that none of the three players chosen for grooming abroad had, as yet, demonstrated they had enough ability even to make the Hawks' main roster—which was why they were being sent to America in the first place.

Two of the players sent to America were dispatched to Twins Falls, Idaho, the lowest rung in the San Francisco system, where they would not do very much to distinguish themselves. Young Murakami, for his part, was assigned to the Fresno team in the Class A California League. There, much to everyone's surprise, he suddenly blossomed. With a darting fastball, a sharp breaking curve and uncommon control, he compiled a strong 11–7 record with an honor-roll ERA of 1.78, prompting his crusty manager Bill "Bugs" Werle to croak, "Kid, you're too good for this league."

In September, the parent team beckoned. Signing the requisite MLB contract that a Giants executive thrust in his face, Murakami made his big league debut, pitching an inning of scoreless relief against the Mets at Shea Stadium, before a thunderous crowd of 50,000 fans. He thus became the first son of Nippon to play in a major league game, an accomplishment noted with great pride by the Japanese ambassador to Washington, D.C., to his friends on the cherry blossom circuit there. Murakami went on to pitch ten more scoreless innings before someone finally managed to score a run off him. He was an overnight hit in windswept San Francisco, especially with its large Japanese-American population. Bay Area fans took to Murakami's friendly, gregarious manner and Pepsodent smile, and found especially endearing his habit of doffing his cap and bowing from the waist on the mound when a teammate made an especially good play in the field to help him out of a jam.

Back in old Nippon, Murakami had suddenly vaulted to the top of the news, thanks to wire service reports and film clips flown across the Pacific by JAL in that pre-satellite era. His fellow countrymen were elated. No Japanese had gotten this much favorable attention in the continental United States since Kyu Sakamoto's improbable (and misnamed) hit single "Sukiyaki," a tune, incidentally, Murakami liked to hum on his way from the bullpen to the pitcher's mound. (The Japanese title, *"Ue wo Muite Aruku,"* literally means "Walk with Your Head Held High.")

"Mashi," as his San Francisco teammates had dubbed him, loved pitching against the big, free-swinging Americans. "In Japan, batters only swing at strikes," he told Los Angeles sports writer Jim Murray. "Here, they try to hit everything out and they don't care if you throw a strike or not. It's easier to pitch against them."

Murakami appeared in a total of nine games that season, finishing with an eyebrow-raising ERA of 1.80 in 15 innings pitched. The Giants, delighted with their find, offered him a contract for the 1965 season and Murakami cheerfully signed. "There's nothing I'd like better than to keep playing here," he was quoted as saying. San Francisco owner Horace Stoneham had $10,000 wired to Nankai for Murakami's services, as per their option clause, and assumed they had a done deal. Then Murakami hopped on a jet clipper for Osaka to spend his winter with his family in rustic Yamanashi.

San Francisco was so happy about the experience that they tried to sign the long, lanky, lefthanded pitching sensation Masaichi Kaneda, perhaps the best pitcher in the history of the NPB, a two-time 30-game winner who was coming off a season in which he had compiled a record of 27–12 with an ERA of 2.79 in 310 innings and 231 strikeouts. He had recently been freed from a 14-year contractual obligation to the Kokutetsu Swallows and was initially willing to go, but then changed his mind over concerns about the language barrier, as well as the fact that by leaving, he would have to give up his career quest for 400 wins and 4,000 strikeouts. Instead, he went on to join the Tokyo Giants and retired in 1969 with a lifetime record of 400–298, 4,490 strikeouts and an ERA of 2.34.

Meanwhile, the next chapter of the Murakami saga was beginning to unfold. After meeting several times with Nankai officials, who informed him he might never be allowed to play in Japan again if he returned to San Francisco, and talking with family members who demanded he stay, Murakami suddenly changed his mind about returning to the U.S. and decided to remain in Japan, then signed his *second* contract for the 1965 season. On January 31, the day before spring training started in Japan, he appeared at a press conference and grimfacedly explained his reasoning. He was an only son. His family wanted him at home where his future would be less uncertain. And he was Japanese. He belonged in Japan with the Hawks.

This astonishing turn of events was not welcome in San Francisco. The Giants' incredulous owner Stoneham complained to the U.S. commissioner of baseball, the aging patrician Ford Frick, the man who had become famous three years earlier by refusing to recognize Roger Maris's single-season mark of 61 home runs as having surpassed Babe Ruth's total of 60. (Maris had played in a newly expanded season schedule of 162 games, as opposed to 154 for Ruth.) The Murakami problem also caught the attention of other MLB owners who viewed the conduct of the Hawks and Murakami as a clear violation of *major league* baseball's reserve clause—a time-honored rule that essentially bound a player to the team that had originally signed him via a series of one-year contracts. Murakami had signed a contract with the Giants and he was obligated to honor it. So were the Hawks. If Murakami flouted the rules, then wouldn't other U.S. major league players feel free to leave their teams whenever they wanted? Frick wrote a letter to Japanese baseball commissioner Yushi Uchimura demanding in the strongest terms that he urge the Hawks to send Murakami back to San Francisco.

Uchimura urged, but the Hawks refused. Shigeru Nīyama, who had replaced Makoto Tachibana as the general manager of the Hawks, on loan from Nankai Railways, the Osaka-based transportation monolith that owned the team, indignantly retorted that there had never been any intention on his part of selling Murakami's contract to the Giants for a lousy ten thousand American dollars. They pointed out that they themselves had only recently paid Murakami a ten-million-yen signing bonus, equivalent to nearly $30,000, upon his graduation from high school. What Nankai had done, in effect, explained the Hawks official, was rent Murakami to San Francisco for a year. They interpreted the $10,000 check from San Francisco as a bonus payment for Murakami's services—a payment for which they had signed a receipt in the belief that it was a thank-you gift for all the fine pitching Murakami had done for the Giants in September. And yes, they knew what a reserve clause was. The NPB had one as well, one which they planned to use to keep Murakami for themselves. Frick was unpersuaded. He insisted that the Giants had a valid contract with Murakami and reiterated his demand for the player to return. A stand-off ensued.

The dispute, in essence, arose out of very different attitudes Americans and Japanese had in regard to contracts. The Japanese believed more in the *spirit* of a contract than the letter, that the purpose of a contract was to ensure that both sides benefitted. Since situations changed, the parties to a deal should not be locked in by mere words or the interpretation thereof. For Japanese, a contract did not define a relationship, it signaled the beginning of one. Therefore, a contract's contents could always be changed to suit evolving circumstances. What was most important was mutual understanding and the cultivation of *ningen kankei*, or human relationships.

The Hawks had never anticipated upon signing the agreement with San Francisco that one of their players might be good enough to make it in the majors. Since they had never expected the situation to arise, they paid no attention to the option clause in the contract. They reasoned that the clause was merely a standard part of American contracts, but also assumed that the Bay Area team understood *their* feelings and the *ningen kankei* involved in this trans-Pacific relationship. In all honesty, how could the Giants expect them to give up a promising pitcher so easily? Viewed in that light, wasn't San Francisco in the wrong?

San Francisco, of course, had not understood. A contract was a contract. An option clause was an option clause, and $10,000 for a pitcher who had spent most of the season in Class A baseball was fair compensation. San Francisco officials fully expected the option clause would apply if the tables had been reversed and the Hawks

had decided to keep a player the Giants had sent to Japan for training. The unlikelihood of that idea notwithstanding, neither Stoneham in San Francisco nor New York–based Commissioner Frick,
who was now the point man in the dispute, was about to change his
mind. Murakami belonged to San Francisco and that was that.

The next couple of weeks were not a high spot in the history of
U.S.-Japan baseball relations, as the Hawks turned to other, more
devious ploys to buttress their case. First they claimed the club signature on Murakami's release—which accompanied the $10,000
check—was a forgery. When Frick would not swallow this, they tried
to get their erstwhile pitcher back via a "homesick clause," buried in
the initial agreement, which provided that a Japanese player unable
to adapt to the American way of life be immediately released and allowed to return home. Frick didn't buy that either in light of Murakami's earlier professed eagerness to stay with San Francisco.

Finally, Nankai abandoned all attempts at legal niceties and out
and out refused, unilaterally, as it were, to deliver Murakami. No
more explanations provided.

On Feb 17, 1965, Frick thereupon suspended baseball relations
between the two countries. He also instructed the Pittsburgh Pirates,
scheduled to visit Japan that fall on a goodwill tour, to cancel their
trip until the matter was resolved. Had MLB had an ambassador
posted to Tokyo he would no doubt have been withdrawn as well.

On hearing this, the president of the Nankai Hawks, Osamu
Tsubota, also on loan from the railroad, decided to throw in his two
yen worth. "Let the Pirates stay home," he sniffed. "Japanese baseball
will not suffer. Frick's actions are proof that he is holding Japanese
baseball cheap and it is certainly regrettable."

Things hadn't been this bad since the demonstrations against re-
newing the Security Treaty in 1960, which caused U.S. president
Dwight Eisenhower to cancel his visit to Japan. In fact, things were
so bleak that they had actually galvanized the commissioner of
Japanese baseball, Yushi Uchimura, into doing some work.
Uchimura, a retired college professor of some note, who had also
been a lefthanded fastball pitcher when he attended Todai (the Harvard of Japan), was primarily a figurehead responsible to the own-

ers—or rather, to Matsutaro Shoriki, since the Giants wielded all the power in the NPB—and his duties largely consisted of sitting behind a desk and issuing proclamations. Now, however, he was put on the spot.

His first decisive act was to check into the hospital for an operation, where he stayed for a month mulling his problem. There, he came to the conclusion the Hawks had been careless in their dealings with the American team. He, in fact, had not even seen the San Francisco–Nankai player exchange agreement his office had approved, and when he finally read a copy of it, which was only in English, he found the document difficult to understand, even for a Ph.D. like himself. He guessed then that the Hawks had signed a contract they did not fully understand, naively assuming that no problems would arise, because, after all, what was a little misunderstanding among friends.

Still, he decided it was unreasonable to expect the Hawks to part with their young prospect under such conditions. Moreover, he faced intense pressure from other owners who feared that an agreement in San Francisco's favor might somehow encourage other young players to find ways to flee Japan. They demanded an example be made.

On March 17, he finally came up with a counterproposal—a compromise to Frick whereby Murakami would return to San Francisco for the 1965 season, but come home to stay for good in 1966. He allowed that the Hawks had made a serious error in misinterpreting their agreement with the Giants, but asked that the American side understand that the Nankai club had, indeed, never had any intention of surrendering Murakami permanently to San Francisco.

Frick declined the offer, averring that Murakami's return to Japan in 1966 would still constitute a violation of the reserve clause. He insisted that Murakami come back to the States before any further settlement could be made. Without question, he declared, the first step in breaking this impasse had to be the absolute recognition of the validity of Murakami's contract with the Giants.

Uchimura's response: "I believe Mr. Frick should more deeply appreciate our position."

Uchimura decided to let things simmer for a while. Then he brought Murakami's father, a local postmaster, into the equation. In a letter to Uchimura, the father had explained that he would never have given permission for his son (a minor under Japanese law when the Nankai–San Francisco pact was struck) to go to the U.S. if he had known that Masanori would wind up as the property of an American team.

"He's my only son," pleaded the elder Murakami. "I want him here with me, not stuck in some foreign country."

Uchimura relayed these sentiments to Frick and Stoneham. Surely, as fathers themselves, they could understand, he said.

That apparently did the trick and the U.S. side caved.

On April 28, at Stoneham's initiative, Frick ruled that although Murakami still had to play in San Francisco in 1965, he could return to Japan in 1966, if *he* still wished to do so. In a joint statement, issued by the Giants and Frick, both parties said that they felt obligated to remind their Japanese friends that "in any international agreement, sanctity of contract is the most essential feature." Frick then lifted the suspension.

Uchimura, relieved that he could now to return to doing nothing, replied, "I feel the elder brother has given in to end the family dispute." The Hawks returned the $10,000 to the Giants, and Murakami, who had been working out at a Nankai training facility, packed his bags and flew to California to catch the remaining five months of the season.

There were later unconfirmed reports that the U.S. State Department had intervened at the behest of the Japanese government and asked MLB to back off supposedly because it needed the support of the Japanese government on the Vietnam War. But William Givens, who was on the Japan Desk in State at the time, said he heard nothing to suggest any U.S. involvement, on an official or unofficial basis, in the dispute. Neither, for that matter, had anyone in the Foreign Ministry of Japan. Said spokesman Kenjiro Sasae, "It is unbelievable that the government of Japan would interfere in such a personal matter."

Uchimura denied there was any government intervention and so did Murakami. Said Cappy Harada, a San Francisco official in charge of handling Murakami (and a well-known and highly regarded sports figure who helped organize many a tour of Japan by U.S. major leaguers), "The idea that there was a political motive or political pressure is false."

"It was Mr. Stoneham's decision," said Harada. "He gave in because he did not think it was something worth ruining international goodwill for. Besides, he had gradually come to understand and appreciate the situation with Murakami's father and that in Japan being an only son counted for a lot. In the end, it was a pretty amicable resolution."

However, the then Los Angeles Dodgers executive Buzzie Bavasi, who was highly familiar with the affair, had a more pecuniary explanation as to what had gone on, and why none of the MLB owners objected to the final compromise. "At the time," he said, "the Japanese clubs were paying more money than we were for certain players [i.e., the aforementioned Spencer, Marshall, Larker, et al.]. Japanese clubs were purchasing player contracts from MLB clubs at fairly good prices. It kept some of the clubs afloat." (Selling the contracts of aging MLB name players to the Central and Pacific Leagues was a pattern that continued into the late '60s and early '70s; the A-list of over-the-hill players includes names such as George Altman, Don Blasingame, Willy Kirkland, Dick Stuart, Zoilo Versalles and Don Zimmer, among others.)

In San Francisco, Murakami picked up where he left off, pitching effectively and getting on famously with his teammates, especially Willie McCovey, whom he affectionately called "Horse Face." Catcher Jack Hiatt taught the linguistically challenged bullpen ace that the customary phrase all American pitchers used to salute their manager when he came out to the mound to talk was "Take a Hike!" (Murakami denied reports that he greeted the home plate umpire with the English phrase "cocksucker-san," taught by other teammates. "I had already learned all those bad English words in spring camp," he said.)

Murakami was also given a day by Japanese-American fans in the Bay Area, which took place on August 15 of that year, the 20th anniversary of the end of World War II. As part of a TV program aired in Osaka to celebrate the festivities, Hawks catching great Katsuya Nomura telephoned Murakami, urging him not to forget his "real" fans and teammates back in Japan—as if that were possible.

Murakami enjoyed himself so much that when he came home, he declared he was contemplating a third year in America. San Francisco had offered him a whopping $15,000 to re-sign in 1966 and Murakami indicated that the very least the Hawks could do was to match it. He inquired at the Japanese commissioner's office as to what his status would be should he opt to continue playing in San Francisco for another year—perhaps two. This was a stunning display of cheek and it raised the hackles of the leading sports daily *Hochi Shimbun*, the PR rag owned by the Yomiuri group which had naturally been upset by all the media thunder Murakami had stolen from the Tokyo Giants. The paper ran a story entitled "Selfish Murakami," criticizing him for business techniques he had so obviously learned abroad.

In fact, a bidding war did ensue for a time between Nankai and San Francisco, which in time upped their offer to $30,000 and even volunteered to bring Murakami's parents to the Bay Area for a month. But, in the end, Murakami opted to stay home, signing a pact with the Hawks for "somewhat less than $30,000," as he put it.

"I felt it was my personal obligation to the Nankai manager Kazuo Tsuruoka and others in team management to come back, but my heart wasn't in it."

Other sources said the decisive factor was more pressure from his father. According to Harada, the father was growing increasingly alarmed at the Americanization of his son. He was reportedly horrified at the fact that "Mashi" had a blonde-haired stewardess for a girlfriend—a co-resident of the San Mateo Hotel where his son had been staying.

In December, after Masanori had agreed to stay in Japan, his father negotiated the final contract, with special bonuses to come if Murakami proved himself in *Japanese* baseball.

Unfortunately, that was something Murakami would have a surprisingly difficult time doing. The Hawks had converted him from a reliever to a starting pitcher, as one optimistic team representative put it, so that he could "aim for the all-time wins record in Japan." However, dissuaded by Nankai coaches from throwing the feared, but impolitic brushback pitch—a technique he had learned in the U.S., but which was considered at the time unsportsmanlike in Japan—he lost much of his effectiveness. Playing in Nankai's tiny bandbox of a ballpark, a decaying, molding structure distinguished by its skin infield and chipped paint, which was a depressing comedown from San Francisco's spanking new state-of-the-art home Candlestick Park, and under the constant pressure of outlandish expectations, it took Murakami two seasons to win nine games, his overall ERA a blush-inducing 4.05. He was frequently stung by cries of "Go back to America" when he was knocked out of the box.

Murakami's leading critic, the *Hochi*, reported that he had learned bad habits in America such as chewing gum during games or throwing his glove at the bench and kicking things when his pitching was off, behavior that pure-hearted Japanese athletes would never have been guilty of. The paper also noted that Murakami was "morose" and didn't seem to get along well with the other Hawks. He would eat at a separate table in the team dining hall and was always the last player to leave the ballpark, long after the others had departed.

Murakami did have one good season in 1968, when he won 18 games, lost but four and compiled a 2.38 ERA—a record he achieved ironically not as a high-octane speedballer, but as a breaking-ball technician. But then, he faded back into mediocrity. In 1982, he retired from baseball to become a sports commentator—one who would find new life in later years when Japanese stars began emigrating to the United States. He was heard telling some interviewers curious about his inner feelings during the international flap over his services that he had wanted to remain in the States, while telling others who asked him the same question that his fondest desire had always been to return to Japan. In the conflicted world of Masanori "Mashi" Murakami, it depended on who was asking the question.

For those who had fought so hard over his services, his failure to succeed at home amongst his peers was just further evidence that Japanese baseball was gaining respectability, and that the day was approaching when Japan could take on the Americans in their own game.

Indentured Servitude

In addition to Murakami, there were, in fact, any number of Japanese players with the talent to excel at a higher level, performing well against big league teams making biannual postseason tours to Japan. As the Japanese stars developed in size and strength in the postwar era, in striking parallel to the then booming Japanese GNP, the goodwill games themselves moved from laughable one-sided matches to rather closely fought encounters—although the visitors were clearly there on vacation, often playing with hangovers. Yomiuri owner Shoriki, whose greatest team, behind Nagashima and Oh, would win nine straight Japan championships (1965–1973), was now talking of an eventual "Real World Series" with the U.S. champions—an idea that was not total and complete lunacy anymore (albeit one that would not be realized in the 20th century). In 1955, the New York Yankees would win 15 games and tie one on their fall tour. A decade later, the Los Angeles Dodgers would struggle to a 9-8-1 mark.

American ballplayers who had played in Japan and were familiar with the Japanese game estimate that, at any given time, there were two or three dozen players in Japan, mostly the pitchers, who had what it took to earn a spot on a big league roster. There was Yutaka Enatsu, who packed a cruise missile for a fastball and set the single-season Japan strikeout record with 401 in 1968. Choji Murata had a world-class forkball, according to Americans who faced him throughout the '70s and '80s, while the entire starting pitching rotation of the Yomiuri Giants in the late '80s was deemed by Matt Keough, a former Oakland A's pitcher who played for the Hanshin Tigers during that time, as the "best pitching staff in the world, bar none."

But none of these stars would ever get the chance to follow in Murakami's footsteps. As a result of the trans-Pacific tiff over Murakami, the U.S. and Japan commissioners had signed something called the United States–Japanese [sic] Player Contract Agreement, informally known as the "Working Agreement," in which both sides pledged to respect each other's baseball conventions. Since Japanese owners were very much like MLB owners—titans who ruled with an iron hand and their very own reserve clause—bolting for the U.S. was not considered an option by the game's luminaries.

So strong was the grip of the owners that the term "indentured servitude" was perhaps the only way to describe the situation of the players—as it was with the Americans at the time. But the inability of these athlete-serfs themselves to change the situation contrasted greatly with what their counterparts across the Pacific would do and pointed out some seemingly basic differences between the Japanese and American way of doing things.

The baseball reserve clause was an American invention, officially known as Section 10A of the UPC (Uniform Players Contract) in MLB. Dating back to the 19th century, it essentially bound a player to one team for life by rendering baseball clubs the rights to their players in perpetuity. Its language went like this: "On or before January 15 . . . the club may tender to the Player a contract for the term of that year by mailing the same to the Player. If prior to the March 1 next succeeding said January 15, the Player and the Club have not agreed upon the terms of such contract, then on or before 10 days after said March 1, the Club shall have the right to renew this contract for the period of one year."

The renewal was *automatic*. Thus a player was always separated from freedom by two years: one for the length of the standard contract and one year for the club's option on it. It was argued that the club's option was renewable into perpetuity.

A player dissatisfied with what he was paid could decline to sign his contract and refuse to report to spring training, but that was about all he could do besides complain to the press about the way he was treated. If the player did not come to terms by March 1, the owner of the team could fill in whatever salary he liked, up to the maximum allowable cut of 25 percent. The owner could keep him, sell him, trade him or send him down to the minor leagues. The player could scream until the cows came home but there wasn't anything he could do about it. As John Helyar, author of the classic *Lords of the Realm*, put it, "The reserve clause amounted to modern-day slavery."

In the U.S., it should have been a violation of the Sherman Anti-Trust Act, passed by Congress in 1890 to control American business monopolies. However, a U.S. Supreme Court ruling handed down in 1922 exempted baseball from that antitrust law on the somewhat dubious grounds that the game was not "interstate commerce" and should not be subject to control by the federal government.

A famous lawsuit filed against Major League Baseball by Curt Flood, an All-Star center fielder employed by St. Louis who refused to accept a trade in 1970, unsuccessfully tested the reserve clause. Flood claimed that baseball had violated his basic rights as a citizen, but his argument was ultimately rejected by the Supreme Court in 1972, which said that although the reserve clause was illogical and inconsistent, it was up to the United States Congress—not the judicial branch of government which had set the precedent in the first place—to address the matter and legislate accordingly.

In 1975, however, two other players who followed Flood's lead and challenged the clause wound up changing history. One of them was Andy Messersmith, a 6'1", 200-pound blond-haired surfer from Los Angeles who won 20 games for the Dodgers in 1974 and opted to play the 1975 season without a new contract. Instead of challenging the legality of the reserve clause as Flood had, however, Messersmith decided to question its *interpretation.* He argued that any fair reading of his contract clause by an unbiased court would conclude that a player who played a full season without signing his contract would automatically become free at the end of the year. The other player was Dave McNally, a four-time 20-game winner from Billings, Montana, who was nearing the end of his long career. McNally was extremely bitter because his bid for a two-year contract with his new team, the Montreal Expos, had been summarily rejected. Thus McNally too, using the same line of reasoning as Messersmith, decided to play without a contract.

Messersmith enjoyed another standout season, winning 19 games, and when it was over, he declared himself a free agent. McNally finished with a less inspiring mark of 3–6 and an ERA of 5.24 and declared himself a free agent as well. Both men were advised by Marvin Miller, a polished Brooklyn economist who had come from a long career fighting on behalf of steelworkers to run the MLB Players Association in 1967—eventually molding it into one of the most powerful unions in history, on the basis of several strikes.

Instead of going to court again, the Messersmith and McNally cases were heard by an outside arbiter named Peter Seitz, who had been hired by MLB to arbitrate salary disputes. And much to the shock of the management side, in late November 1975, Seitz ruled in favor of the players, a decision that forever altered the balance of power in the major leagues.

Fearing total chaos with all the restrictions on player movement removed, the owners struck a deal with the union whereby a player joining the big leagues would be required to stay with the team that signed and nurtured him in its farm system for six years. But from then on, free-agent declarations came in droves and salaries suddenly skyrocketed. Multiyear contracts and sophisticated sports agents became a permanent part of the MLB scene. In short, it was the American willingness to *confront*, however belated it may have been, that led to free agency and the earth-shaking changes that baseball subsequently underwent.

In Japan, such a dramatic shift in the status quo was not so easily achieved. The Uniform Players Contract long used in NPB was a descendant of a direct translation of a 1930s U.S. minor league contract. It had the same annoying reserve clause in it and it denied the right of collective bargaining. But Japan was not the United States. Whereas litigation and courtroom confrontation, rightly or wrongly, was a part of the fabric of American life, in Japan, a society whose members traditionally shied away from legal confrontation to resolve disputes, there had never been a movement to challenge the UPC in court.

One need only look at the long tradition of Confucianism and feudalism, where the obeisance of subordinates was as marked as the arrogance of those with high social rank, and where civil disputes and grievances were redressed by a powerful feudal magistrate from whom there was no appeal. Although that situation changed somewhat in the Meiji Era (1868–1912) and its aftermath, as Western institutions were adopted, the lawyers who appeared during that time to represent the common man were generally regarded as being in the same suspect class as reporters and gangsters. The image of the legal profession received a boost in the wake of postwar allied occupation, but the new postwar system, with its tight constraints on the number of attorneys permitted to practice and subsequently on the number of judges, meant that lawsuits and trials could take ages and ensured that litigation remained an endeavor that ordinary Japanese would not enter into lightly. By the end of the 20th century, Japan had only a fraction of the lawyers the U.S. did.

However, there was also a cultural bias against insisting too emphatically on one's individual rights. Parties involved in a litigation were invariably encouraged by judges to accept a *wakai* or harmonious settlement. It was an arrangement that the general populace seemed to prefer.

Pro baseball in Japan reflected and was affected by this condition. Thus, modern Japanese pro players, unlike their American counterparts, tended to see themselves by and large as company employees, rather than performers with special skills to sell to the highest bidder. The sense of individual rights and responsibilities that arose from the U.S. brand of democracy remained foreign.

Japan did indeed have a Professional Baseball Players Association, a famously cooperative *wa*-oriented one. It wasn't until 1985 that, after some lengthy and quiet behind-the-scenes maneuvering, it managed to obtain the legal right to strike—a right it seemed unlikely to exercise. The players themselves made it quite clear from the outset that they would not be following in the footsteps of Miller's union, which by this time had succeeded in raising the minimum salary twentyfold, beefing up the players' pensions and giving them their rightful share of merchandising money by calling several crippling strikes. Instead, the NPBPA's player representative at the time, Kiyoshi Nakahata, the captain and first baseman of the Giants, behaved as if he was representing management. In his memorable declaration before the national TV cameras, he said, "Although we hope to work for higher pay and better working conditions, we could never strike like the U.S. union has. It would not be right."

Four years later, when discussing the possibility of a work stoppage, Hiroshi Ogawa, the player representative for the Fukuoka Daiei Hawks, would be equally resolute.

"Although there may technically be the possibility of a strike," he told *Japan Times* veteran columnist Wayne Gracyzk, "most players would be bothered by their consciences. We realize we are playing for the fans and could not enjoy peace of mind if we stopped playing. We would walk out only as a last resort. In that way, the attitude in Japan is very conservative and quite different from that of the American major leagues."

Indeed, the majority of the players in Japan continued to speak not only of team loyalty and a greater sense of obligation and duty to each other but also a feeling of responsibility to the parent company, the stadium food vendors, the parking-lot attendants, the transportation companies and other individuals and businesses dependent on professional baseball who would suffer economically in the event of a work stoppage (although whether or not they actually felt that way deep inside was unknown). With the exception of the *Akahata* (Red Flag), the Communist Party organ in Japan, and a few other publications, the Japanese media generally supported this position and many unequivocally condemned the actions of the MLBPA, comparing them to those of old labor unions in the U.S. that demanded more money, even if it bankrupted the company that employed them. Some American fans might agree they had a point.

In the middle of all this, however, there was also the complicating fact that ball club ownership, for the most part, was not primarily concerned with making a profit. Generally speaking, it was P.R. for the parent firm that they wanted, which rendered the specter of a player strike not very relevant.

Japan's game was set up differently than its American cousin. In the U.S., professional baseball was run as a business. The teams existed purely for profit, maintained extensive farm and scouting systems to keep up their competitive level and were run by people with years of experience in the pro game. In Japan, by contrast, the teams of the Central and Pacific Leagues existed to advertise the products and services of their corporate owners. Thus, when the Kintetsu Buffaloes met the Nippon Ham Fighters it was a battle for supremacy between a private railway and a pork manufacturer. Although the independently owned venues changed over the years from dark, dank utilitarian parks to high-tech outdoor stadiums and domes, the franchises were operated largely by officials temporarily dispatched from the parent company who knew little about baseball and, in some cases, even disliked the sport. (The Daiei Hawks and the Seibu Lions were two notable exceptions.) They invested sparingly in player development—with only one farm team composed of 35 players per franchise—and, on the balance sheet, at least, they generally reaped as they sowed. Although the parent organizations usually had revenue to spread around, they just preferred to spread it elsewhere.

Few clubs made any real money from baseball itself. The Tokyo Giants, the franchise to end all franchises in Japan, raked in as much as the New York Yankees, from combined ticket, TV and souvenir sales, and more than doubled that of their nearest competitor, the Tigers of Osaka owned by the Hanshin Railway Company. Much of the Giant revenue was said to be funneled back to the parent company, the *Yomiuri Shimbun*, to support costs and losses in the company's vast communications and publishing empire. However, many other teams in NPB, mostly in the Pacific League, played to sparse crowds and operated at an annual loss—a state of affairs the parent companies have simply shrugged off. With the corporation's name in the sports pages every day and, locally at least, on TV every night, it was cheap advertising . . . a loss leader. When Orient Leasing bought the Hankyu Braves from the Hankyu Railway company in 1988 and renamed the team the Orix Braves, then the Orix Blue-Wave, the firm's name recognition value shot up to 90 percent nationwide.

If the players wanted to strike, so be it. The parent company would spend its advertising budget elsewhere. In theory, of course, a strike could be embarrassing, if not economically damaging, but as no one would dare ruffle the game's all-important "*wa*," it wasn't a real threat. And the truth of the matter was that the owners were so power-hungry and egocentric that they would rather shut down baseball altogether than give in to American-style player demands.

"A baseball team in Japan," remarked author and prize-winning reporter Yoichi Funabashi in the *Asahi Shimbun*, summing up the game for his readers, "is similar to a corporate fiefdom where the 'company first' attitude dictates the nature of competition. . . . The Japanese approach to sport incorporates moral guidance, business management and company-based role assignments, making professional baseball a simple job for wages."

It was so simple, in fact, that ties even counted. The 1988 and 1989 Pacific League seasons went down in history because in both years, the team that won the most games did not win the pennant, due to the fact that the championship team had more ties and therefore a higher winning percentage. When, in an interview for the magazine *SPA*, a sportswriter quizzed the PL president whether something was going to be done to change this awkward state of affairs, he was told, "No. Ties suit the Japanese national character. They reward both teams for playing well."

"Playing a 12-inning tie game," said Funabashi, with just a hint of sarcasm, "is considered competition at its finest in Japan, because nobody loses face, or the game." By contrast, when the professional J.League was established, Chairman Saburo Kawabuchi opted for a "golden goal" sudden-death overtime, proclaiming "Ties don't suit Japanese fans."

The NPBPA's pursuit of free agency further demonstrated the odd lopsided nature of the power structure in NPB. (The word "pursuit" is used loosely here.) For years, the union leaders had continually requested that the owners implement a free-agency system paralleling that of the United States, but for years, the owners had stonewalled, offering instead only a token form of free agency to unwanted minor league players. In 1992 the union player representative, infielder Akinobu Okada of the Hanshin Tigers, in what must have been a fit of temporary madness, threatened to call an opening day strike if free agency was not immediately granted. It was telling that no one took him seriously, not even the union's own lawyer, who immediately issued a polite correction saying that Okada had spoken in error. A year later, well after he had regained his senses, a chastened Okada would tell the *International Herald Tribune* that a strike was "unimaginable" in Japan.

Free agency finally did make an appearance in Japan, in 1993. But, typically, it came about not because of anything the union did, but only because of the actions of one man, the tyrannical boss of the Tokyo Giants, Tsuneo Watanabe, who deemed its imposition an evil necessary to protect the Yomiuri dynasty. Watanabe, who had taken over the reins from Matsutaro Shoriki's successor Mitsuo Mutai (known as the "god of newspaper sales" and for his boast that he could even sell blank paper) in 1991, had been concerned by the initially explosive popularity of the newly formed soccer "J.League," with its dynamic, eye-catching, hip-wiggling, hair-dyed youth-oriented culture. In its first season, the J.League threatened to loosen the grip that Japanese pro baseball held on the nation's sports fans. The Central and Pacific Leagues, whose players wore solemn expressions and short unretouched hair, much like the officer workers who went to see them play, had just gone through one of their most colorless seasons in history. Worse, the proud *Kyojin-gun* (Giant Troop) had fielded one of its most boring squads ever, struggling to finish above .500—a fact that was reflected in slumping TV ratings. The Giants games had always had prime time percentage ratings that averaged in the 20s for the whole season. But that year, the ratings had slipped into the teens. It wasn't life-threatening, mind you. The Giants still dominated all sports on the airwaves. But if you were an owner who was accustomed to having everything go your way, it was cause for some concern.

Watanabe's solution was to construct a free-agent system by which he could sign many top stars from others teams and create one super Giants squad that would strengthen the pre-existing monopoly. A cantankerous silver-haired sexagenarian, Watanabe had long made his presence felt in Japanese society. A onetime leader of the leftist student group *zengakuren*, which opposed the Mutual Security Treaty between the U.S. and Japan, he had joined the *Yomiuri Shimbun* and had risen through the ranks, first as a star political reporter, than as editor, whose support had helped Yasuhiro Nakasone attain the prime ministership in 1982. He was appointed president of the *Yomiuri* in the late '80s which brought with it automatic control over the ballclub and honorific title of team *ohna* (owner).

Running a baseball team was something he knew little about—he had been a longtime fan of sumo and was a ranking member of the sumo association—but this did not prevent him from trying anyway. Like Yankees owner George Steinbrenner, to whom he was often compared, he was a blustering alpha male who did everything but urinate on the floor to make his mark. He was used to being obeyed and earned himself many enemies with his totalitarian ways.

When 10 of his fellow owners voiced their objection to his proposal for a new free-agency system, Watanabe threatened to withdraw from the NPB and start his own new baseball association if they did not change their minds. Accustomed as they were to the fringe benefits of the Giants' tremendous drawing power, the other owners reluctantly buckled.

"Watanabe didn't give a damn about the other teams, or players' rights, for that matter," said former Orix general manager Shigeuyoshi Ino, one of the many NPB executives who had unsuccessfully opposed Watanabe's demand for a free-agent system. "He just wanted all the superstars on his team."

The free-agent system that was subsequently introduced was not a hallmark in the history of human rights struggles. Players could only become free agents after ten full years of service on the parent team; time on the farm club did not count. Moreover, under this agreement, while compensation in the form of money and a minor league player would be sent to a team losing a free agent from the team gaining his services, the salaries of free-agent signees would be limited to only 150 percent of their previous season's pay. It was largely designed to appeal to those players who wanted the cachet of wearing a Yomiuri Giants uniform. And there were, of course, lots of those, the Giants being one of the most exclusive private clubs in Japan.

Yet another restrictive aspect of the Japanese free-agent system was the banning of player agents from any kind of negotiating process. Only foreign players who entered Japanese baseball from abroad were allowed that privilege. The Japanese players tepidly accepted such conditions, prompting one disgusted baseball critic to write that theirs was "the behavior of people who belong to a welfare state."

Indeed, it wasn't until the 2001 season that the owners finally decided to allow player agents, but with restrictions so severe they might as well have continued the ban. The agent had to be a bona fide attorney in Japan and said attorney, who must also be a Japanese citizen, was limited to only one baseball client. At the same time, Watanabe, true to form, made it clear that he would not tolerate any of *his* players using an agent, and even publicly scolded his manager, Shigeo Nagashima, for being seen at a dinner party *talking* with one.

"If one of my players brings an agent into contract negotiations," he was quoted as saying, "then we'll cut his salary. If he's expecting five or six hundred million yen, we'll give him two or three hundred instead. If he doesn't like it, we'll release him. There are lots of guys who would want to take his place."

MLB owners could only drool with envy.

The early results of the new free-agent era in Japan were as different from the U.S. as they were predictable. Whereas in America, scores of eligible free agents changed teams annually in pursuit of bigger bucks, in Japan, movement was all but invisible. Of the 60 eligible in the first year, only five filed for free agency. The next year, only four of 59 free-agency qualifiers worked up the courage to switch uniforms, while the figures in years immediately following were no better—two of 58, three of 64 and so on. It took a while to get used to the idea. Kimiyasu Kudo, perhaps the best pitcher in the Pacific League in 1995, left the Seibu Lions to join the Daiei Hawks in order to be reunited with his former general manager who had become the Hawks GM, for *no* raise and a one-year contract. In a magazine interview, Kudo said he thought the free agent system was a "bad influence" on the players and should be abolished. However, this did not stop him from moving on to the Giants a few years later.

Salaries did rise somewhat. Then, in the 1997–1998 off-season, in exchange for a lowering of the free agency time limit to nine years, the union made a stupefying concession: they agreed to a complete *freeze* on salaries for a year. Their compliant attitude puzzled MLB union leaders, who were watching from afar. Said players' association attorney Gene Orza, "It makes you wonder why they ever established a union in the first place."

It was not surprising to learn that after that particular nine-year deal was instituted, the secretary-general of the NPBPA took a position with Yomiuri. He followed in the footsteps of the aforementioned union chief Kiyoshi "A strike wouldn't be right" Nakahata, who became a TV commentator with the Yomiuri group.

At no time in the union's existence was there even an attempt by its leaders to wrest control of the rights to the players' names and their likenesses from the ball clubs, which had held such rights since the game's inception. If a company wanted to use a ballplayer in a TV or print media advertisement, it had to first negotiate with the club he played for; the club then decided yes or no, and if the answer was yes, took a sizable 20 percent commission off the top.

Said one NPB official, who preferred to remain anonymous, "In the U.S., the players effectively took over control of their game, but I think it will be a long time before we ever see anything like that in Japan. It takes a lot of courage to change the system and that's something that's generally lacking in ballplayers here. . . . The players don't understand the system. They don't even try. All they want to think about is playing ball."

THE DEFECTOR:
THE STORY OF NOMO

The biggest weakness of Japanese players is that they don't have balls—with the exception of Nomo, that is. He has the balls and the heart of a lion. He is the only Japanese like that where his individual rights are concerned. The others . . .

MLB EXECUTIVE

What the Americans did in regard to Nomo was reprehensible. They knew what they did was wrong and Japan won't forget that.

NPB EXECUTIVE

JAPAN IN 1995 WAS A MUCH DIFFERENT PLACE THAN IT WAS IN 1965. For one thing, satellite TV was bringing the outside world into sharper focus. There were daily reminders in the Japanese sports media of the preferential treatment and special opportunities that major league stars enjoyed in North America. True, a debilitating lockout had wiped out the last half of the 1994 season and caused the cancellation of the World Series for the first time in history, but the players emerged wealthier and better protected than before. Moreover, the gap in pay and privileges between U.S. and Japan athletes had come to seem all the more disproportionate as the gap in the two countries' level of play perceptibly narrowed. In 1990, a Japanese all-star squad swept the first four games in a seven-game exhibition series against a visiting team that featured some of MLB's brightest names—like Cal Ripken Jr. and stringy-haired strikeout king Randy Johnson.

The protestations from the embarrassed major leaguers that they were not serious because the games were meaningless and that the postseason trip to Japan was just a vacation for them seemed like a poor excuse. In truth, they had been blindsided by a Japanese pitching corps that included a right-handed rookie pitcher with a weapons-grade forkball named Hideo Nomo. Randy Johnson buttonholed the 23-year-old at a private dinner one night during that visit and told him that he was wasting his time playing in Japan. "You belong in MLB," he declared. Nomo was not inclined to disagree.

He had been thinking about taking his ball and glove to the U.S. ever since he had dismantled the Americans in the 1988 Seoul Olympics. MLB had not signed a Japanese player since the 1967 United States-Japanese Player Contract Agreement went into effect. But Nomo's desire to play in the major leagues would change all that. In fact, so successful would he eventually be in attaining his goal that it would dramatically alter the baseball relationship between the two countries, creating resentment that would linger for years. As one NPB executive would later put it, "We will never forgive the Americans for what they have done to our game."

Nomo was born to a working-class family in the teeming section of industrially gray Osaka known as Honohanaku, in 1969. His father was a large, broad shouldered man from a remote fishing village off the coast of Hiroshima in western Japan, who had forsaken life on a deep sea trawler to become a postal worker in the big city. He and his wife, who also worked at various jobs, fed their son copious quantities of protein-rich boiled fish paste so that he would grow up to be big and strong, and, indeed, by the time young Hideo hit primary school, he stood head and shoulders above the rest of his classmates.

Father and son played catch together often and it was in these sessions that Hideo invented his bizarre twisting "corkscrew" style of throwing. It was a conscious effort, he said, a way of getting extra speed on the ball, as well as impressing his father.

"By twisting my body and by using this force," he explained later, "I was able to throw harder. And, at the same time, with that motion, it would be difficult for batters to pick up the ball."

As the ace pitcher on the baseball teams at *Ikejima Sho-Gakkō* (primary school) and *Minato-ku Chūgakkō* (middle school), he was known both for his speed and for a frightful lack of control. He would often walk the bases loaded, only to strike out the side.

Usually, an unorthodox motion like Nomo's, at such a young age, is the kiss of death in form-conscious Japan. Nomo, like his contemporary Ichiro, had been fortunate enough to play under a junior high school coach who left him alone. But the manager of the Kindai High School baseball club, one of the Kansai area's most famous big-time baseball schools and an organization that Nomo desperately wanted to join, pronounced him unfit.

"Young man," he sniffed, "with that tornado windup, you'll never make it."

Stunned at the cavalier rejection, Nomo turned to a small local school in the Osaka area, Seijo Industrial High School, that was not particularly distinguished for anything, let alone baseball. There were only 13 students on the entire squad (as opposed to more than 150 at behemoth Kindai), and the Seijo coach did not care how Nomo threw as long as he could get the ball over the plate. Nomo, growing into a bronzed 6'2" 200-pounder with meat cleaver hands, pitched exceedingly well for his school. In 1985, in a qualifying round for the national summer high school baseball tournament, he even pitched a perfect game. Still his pitching was not enough to take the team all the way to the Koshien tournament, and scouts who had watched him play in the regionals delivered the same verdict: "Speed: Good; Control: Bad."

Failing to attract any interest from the big university scouts, Nomo entered *Shin-Nitetsu Sakai,* one of the 300 companies that then sponsored baseball teams in Japan's semi-professional industrial leagues, which served as Japan's de facto, if defective, farm system. It was flawed because it was essentially an amateur operation, sanctioned by the *amateur* baseball association in Japan, and was closed to the participation of professional coaches, a restriction that stayed in place until the beginning of the 21st century. Moreover, its preferred system was tournament play, which tempted managers to overuse their ace pitchers, causing arm trouble.

Still, for Nomo, it proved to be a wise and providential move, because at Shin-Nitetsu, he was allowed to continue pitching with his corkscrew motion, and it was also there that he learned to throw his fearsome forkball, a pitch that dropped so much it looked like it was falling off a *kotatsu*—developing his grip by wedging a tennis ball into the webbing between his index and middle fingers and taping it in place at night when he went to sleep. The new addition to the Nomo arsenal elevated him to a whole new plateau as a pitcher.

Nomo's statistics in the rust belt league and his performance in the 1988 Seoul Olympics, where he led Japan to a silver medal, resulted in his being drafted by eight different clubs in the 1989 NPB draft lottery, a modern record. Nomo, however, was not the biggest story in the draft. That honor went, not surprisingly, to the Yomiuri Giants and their top draft pick, a nationally popular high school infielder named Daisuke Motoki who had starred in the summer Koshien tourney and who had vowed he would never play for any professional team except the mighty *Kyojin*.

As a result of the draft, the Kintetsu Buffaloes ultimately won the right to negotiate with Nomo and offered him a then record bonus of 100,000,000 yen (about a million dollars at the time) to sign with them. Nomo said yes, but only on condition that the Buffaloes promise *not* to change his form. It was the kind of demand that rookie pitchers in Japan were seldom presumptuous enough to make, but fortunately, the Buffaloes manager at the time was the easy-going Akira Ogi, the man who would later do so much for the career of another renegade of sorts, Ichiro Suzuki (see Chapter 1). He unhesitatingly gave his okay and Nomo responded by giving full expression to his skills in a rookie season that *puro-yakyū* fans still talk about.

With a forkball that was all but unhittable and a fastball that was often invisible, he led the league in wins, ERA and strikeouts (18–8, 2.91 and 287 K's in 235 innings, including 17 in one game), capturing the Rookie of the Year Award, the MVP and the Sawamura Award given annually to the best pitcher in the game. And he was just getting started. For the next three seasons, he led the Pacific League in shutouts, victories and strikeouts before being overtaken in 1994 on the leader board by another budding fastballer named Hideki Irabu, and his salary had inched up to $1.5 million a year. In all that time, he had only pitched in one nationally televised game, while Daisuke Motoki, the star of that 1989 draft and now a light-hitting utility infielder for the Tokyo Giants, was, of course, visible to the whole country every night.

Nomo was a shy, taciturn young man preternaturally gifted at hiding his thoughts and emotions, either on or off the mound. Reporters, whom Nomo was especially skilled at ignoring, joked that he had only one expression: inscrutable. Yet, he had an unnerving streak of independence that some journalists claimed came from years of being a latchkey child. As a boy Nomo had been known in the schoolyard for protecting weaker kids from school bullies.

Almost without realizing it, he became a poster boy for a new generation of rebellious youth. Nomo became the first Japanese player to wear Nike shoes in a midsummer All-Star series. Until then, all the players under a league-determined structure were party to a deal to wear Mizuno shoes and only Mizuno shoes in the mid-season classic. But, without asking permission, Nomo defied this policy and blithely sold his services under an individual contract, opening an unpleasant breach between him and Kintetsu officials who were getting a cut of the Mizuno deal and who were supposed to have say over *all* their player endorsements. It was a breach that would only grow wider in 1994 with the arrival of a new manager, Keishī Suzuki.

Suzuki was no ordinary figure. Unlike his more relaxed predecessor, Suzuki came in as a living god, a Hall of Fame pitcher whose career statistics occupied considerable space in the NPB record books. A barrel-chested, square-jawed left-hander who boasted a potent fastball and a world-class forkball of his own, he dominated the Pacific League in a 20-year career that lasted from 1966 to 1985, during which his record was 317–238, placing him fourth all-time on the list of wins. Only Masaichi Kaneda (404), Tetsuya Yoneda (350) and Masaki Koyama (320) were ahead of him. He led all of Japan in lifetime games pitched *without* having surrendered a walk, 340, which was about 340 more than Hideo Nomo had ever achieved. He also had lifetime totals of 71 shutouts, 3,061 strikeouts and 703 games pitched. He was so intimidating that after facing him in post-season exhibition play in 1968, St. Louis Cardinals catcher Ted Simmons declared that Suzuki was the "greatest pitcher he had ever seen anywhere."

Suzuki's philosophy could basically be summed up in four words, "Throw until you die." He had frequently pitched on two days' rest throughout his career and on more than one occasion had pitched in relief the day after throwing nine innings. During games he didn't pitch, he usually went to the bullpen to throw, ever honing his considerable artistry. Suzuki's regimen obviously had worked for Suzuki, but it was not one that Nomo, as hard a worker as he might have been, was prepared to follow. He had his own system. He had become a devotee of the philosophy of major league strikeout king Nolan Ryan (whose book on pitching and conditioning had been translated and published in Japan), which emphasized the more rational American system of abundant rest combined with a program of weight training.

Nomo did not mind throwing a lot of pitches in a game. He'd thrown over 140 pitches an arm-aching 61 times during his pro career (Ryan usually stopped at around 120). But he followed the Ryan canon of three to four days' rest after a start, believed necessary in order for the tiny muscle tears caused by nine innings of hard pitching to heal and for the tissue to regenerate. Under Ogi, Nomo had had his desired four days between starts, during which he only threw twice in practice, in light, leisurely sessions of 40 pitches each.

Such modern training ideas and methods disgusted Suzuki. He himself thought that 100 pitches every day in practice was about right and he pushed Nomo to do more. In one game in early July at Seibu Stadium, for example, Nomo had been having great difficulty with his control, but Suzuki left him in for the full nine innings. Struggling throughout, Nomo walked an incredible 16 batters, throwing a jaw-dropping total of 191 pitches, enough for a doubleheader, eventually winning 8–3. In another game, he threw 180. By refusing to

put in a reliever on such occasions, Suzuki was making a statement—
he was trying to build what he believed was the mental toughness
Nomo lacked, as well as put Nomo in his place.

Said Nomo's teammate, American Lee Stevens, who witnessed it
all, "It was clear what Suzuki was trying to do. But Hideo kept his
cool. Nomo wasn't about to give the manger the satisfaction of
showing that it bothered him."

By the midway point of that season, however, Nomo's shoulder
was ailing badly (an inevitable result, some said, of all those high
pitch counts). Suzuki dispatched him to the farm team to get back in
shape, which to Suzuki's way of thinking meant more pitching. "The
best way to cure a sore arm," he would say, "is to go out and throw.
Pitch through the pain." But this Nomo refused to do, choosing instead a program of calculated rest. Suzuki, who badly needed pitching for the pennant race, blasted Nomo to reporters as being "lazy."
To placate his manager, Nomo pitched in a few farm team games,
but that only worsened things. His arm became so painful that he
could only drive his car with his left hand. By the end of the season,
he would require surgery.

Nomo's secret desire to play in the major leagues had been
strengthened by several more pitching appearances in postseason
U.S.-Japan baseball matches. He kept baseball cards of his favorite
American players taped to his locker door in Fujidera and talked to
his *gaijin* teammates Ralph Bryant, Jim Traber and Kyle Abbot about
life in MLB. He had quietly hoped for an opportunity to present itself, but his troubles with Suzuki were making him think more and
more that time was running out. If he wanted an opportunity to go
to the U.S. before he completed the requisite 10 years to qualify for
free agency—with his arm still attached to his body, that is—then he
would have to create it himself. Thus, it was about this juncture that
Nomo began to meet with a man named Don Nomura.

Half-Japanese, half-Caucasian, a six-footer in his mid-30s, he had
recently made the shift to becoming a player agent. Sensing restless-
ness among the NPB troops, he had set his sights on the Japan market. Quietly asking around about potential candidates to defy the
system, he had come across Nomo, who himself had quietly been

asking around about finding someone who could get him out from under Suzuki's thumb. The two men began conferring secretly, concocting possible scenarios for a move to the States.

Nomura had a translated copy of the Japanese Uniform Players Contract and had employed the services of a Santa Monica–based baseball agent named Arn Tellem to look it over for loopholes that could be exploited. Tellem inspected the document and found something that had to do with the "voluntary retirement" clause.

The Japanese Uniform Players Contract, as we have seen, had been copied from a 1930s minor league contract in the U.S. It was quite similar to a U.S. major league contract. It had the same reserve clause, but there was one fundamental difference in the rules. Whereas under the terms of a U.S. pact, a voluntarily retired player who wished to return to active status could play only with his former team (unless he had become eligible for free agency under the terms of the basic agreement with the Major League Baseball Players Association), a voluntarily retired player under a Japanese contract was obligated to return to his former team only *as long as he stayed in Japan.* Going to the *U.S.* to play was an entirely different matter, it seemed. As would become devilishly apparent. It was thus Tellem's considered opinion that a player who went on the voluntarily retired list in NPB would thus essentially be free to play in the U.S.

The American and Japanese commissioners were still bound by the United States–Japanese Player Contract Agreement described in Chapter 4, a.k.a. the Working Agreement, which had been drafted and signed in the wake of the Murakami affair. It obligated both sides to abide by the rules as specified in the respective contracts and conventions and, as such, defined which players could be approached. However, because of the failure of the Japanese side, inadvertent though it may have been, to specify worldwide rights in regard to the ownership of its players, it was now becoming devilishly apparent that the U.S. side could go after Japan's stars without violating any of the conditions of the Working Agreement. The omission was, perhaps, understandable. Given the big gap that was believed to exist between the levels of play in the two countries at the time the document was signed (not to mention the social taboos that Murakami had come up against and which, most people thought, still existed), such a possibility was no doubt as far from the minds of the two signatories as a Japanese invasion of the U.S. auto market was in the minds of the then management at Detroit's Big Three—or as far removed from the realm of probability as a takeover of the Pebble Beach golf course by Osaka gangsters was in the daily thoughts of the residents of California's Monterey Peninsula.

The existence of this anomaly was confirmed and clarified in a series of letters exchanged between the U.S. and Japan baseball commissioners' offices—the exchange prompted by Don Nomura in a query to the U.S. commissioner. The operative instrument was a fax sent by Yoshiaki Kanai, executive secretary to the Japanese commissioner, on December 9, in response to consecutive faxes from William A. Murray, executive director of baseball operations in the Major League Commissioner's Office in New York, inquiring about the eligibility of voluntarily retired players moving abroad. Kanai's fax stated clearly and unequivocally in writing, "If a voluntarily retired player in Japan wishes to return to active status, he may sign only with his former team as far as he chooses to do so *within our country,* in other words, he would be able to contact [sic] with teams in the United States." That was about as concrete as Kanai could possibly make it. Although the relatively inexperienced Kanai (he was a former sportswriter) doubtless never intended his missive as an instrument by which Japanese stars could liberate themselves from the maximum security chains that bound them to their teams, nevertheless, that is exactly what it became. A "voluntarily retired" Nomo, wishing to play in the MLB, would, in fact, find the door leading out of Japan wide open.

In postseason contract discussions, Nomo made a pretext of negotiating. He asked for a three-year, $9 million contract, a demand he knew in advance the front office would never agree to. When, as he had predicted, they turned him down—"You're too young for that kind of deal," said one official. "You're ineligible for free agency and besides, you've got a sore arm"—Nomo said fine and declared his voluntary retirement from Japanese baseball. He was going to pursue other avenues of endeavor, he informed them.

It took more than one meeting for the powers-that-be on the upper floors of the staid corporate headquarters of the Osaka Kintetsu Railways, unaware of the existence of the Kanai-Murray letters, to fully grasp the fact that Nomo was serious. At one encounter, tempers flared and angry words were exchanged.

"Think of what you're doing to your career," exclaimed one official. "Think of the team."

"I am," said Nomo, "that's why I'm leaving."

When team president and general manager Yasuo Maeda angrily challenged him to sign his letter of retirement right then and there, Nomo readily complied. And just like that, he was free to play in America.

It was one of the most embarrassing incidents in the history of the franchise. The Kintetsu front office had been completely sandbagged, losing their best player without even realizing exactly what it was that had happened to them. In the following days, as word got around that Nomo and Nomura had put out feelers to West Coast teams, Maeda appealed to the commissioner's office for help, to no avail, however, because that institution had been caught off guard as well. League officials could only stand by helplessly as the Kanai-Murray letters surfaced in the press. At first, they tried to claim, somewhat lamely, that the documents were "private" and that they had been wrongfully made public, as if that somehow made them less valid. They also tried to claim that said letters referred to foreign ballplayers like Seibu's Orestes Destrade (a Florida-based Cuban who had also been mulling a return to North America). But no matter how they tried to spin it, a close inspection of the correspondence could not ignore its devastatingly clear wording. Kintetsu had no choice but to move into a face-saving mode.

"Do you want our permission to let you go to the States?" offered a rather desperate Buffalo official at a subsequent meeting with Nomo. "We can arrange to do that."

But Nomo was merciless.

"We don't need your permission to go to the States and play," he replied.

All Kintetsu could do was to grin and bear it and pretend they were being magnanimous. In January, their front office called a press conference and announced that Nomo would be released so that he could pursue an MLB career, with the blessing of the NPB commissioner's office (although, in point of fact, Kintetsu never did formally file the papers granting Nomo his *unconditional* release, meaning that they continued to hold on to Nomo's rights within Japan). Maeda also announced that he would take another look at the Kintetsu policy in regard to multiyear contracts.

In the wake of all this, the Japanese sports press went into its DEF-CON 4 mode, labeling Nomo an "ingrate," a "troublemaker" and a "traitor." Everyone had turned against him, baseball officials, fan groups and big names like Nagashima and Oh. Even Nomo's own father was against the move.

"Don't kick up sand with your feet," his father had admonished him, using an old Japanese saying. "You don't have to embarrass the Kintetsu front office like this. If you really want to go, you have to choose a better way. But why ruin what you already have here in Japan: wealth and status."

"It's my life," replied his son, aware that a "better way" did not exist. "I don't want to spend the rest of it regretting that I never tried. I want to see if I can do it."

Pere Nomo stopped talking to his son for quite some time.

It took an enormous amount of courage for Nomo to do what he did. But to hear him tell it, in his droll, laconic way of speaking, there was never any question as to the correct course of action. Whenever Nomura would begin to express doubts as to whether perhaps they had gone too far, it was Nomo who always straightened him out.

"Don't worry, Don," he would say. "We're doing the right thing."

To some people, it seemed fitting that the Chinese character for Hideo meant "hero."

Nomomania

When Nomo first left Narita Airport in February 1995 for interviews with major league teams he might join, not many reporters were there to cover his departure. Granted, there was an MLB lock-out in place, one that had begun the previous August and had forced the cancellation of the rest of the season and the 1994 World Series. But when that dispute ended and Nomo was offered $2 million to sign with the Los Angeles Dodgers—who had received an okay from the commissioner of Japanese baseball to pursue the ex-Buffaloes star—interest started to build. Those very same newspaper and magazine reporters who had accorded Nomo second tier coverage because he was playing for a lowly Pacific League team could now not get enough of him. There were 24 photographers and 15 TV cameras on hand to record his signing ceremony with the Dodgers at a Los Angeles hotel. And when Nomo began his preseason workouts, a squadron of video cameramen followed him like a heat-seeking missile, logging every microsecond of his new Dodgers existence and relaying it back to Japan by satellite. It was more press than he had ever seen in one place in his entire life, except of course when he attended a Giants game as a fan. Bothered by the intrusiveness, and the adverse effect it might be having on his new teammates, Nomo drew a line in the dirt near the dugout and announced that no one in the group was to cross it.

"If you come beyond this line," he warned, "I'll stop talking to you."

It did not seem like much of a threat because the recalcitrant Nomo seldom talked to them anyway. Yet when an NHK crew ventured forth across the line, Nomo, true to his word, initiated a boycott against them which would last for three years.

Some people back in Japan, still upset by what they perceived to be Nomo's underhanded ways, seemed to be rooting for him to fail. A Seibu coach named Haruki Ihara declared that Nomo could no longer be effective in Japan anyway because the opposition could read all his pitches. That was why he was leaving. "The key to beating Nomo," revealed the coach, "is not swinging at the forkball; his control is so bad, he'll eventually walk himself into trouble."

Another critic, a veteran baseball manager in Japan, told an inquiring Dodger executive they were making a mistake. "Nomo's arm is not that good anymore," said the man, who was a friend and contemporary of Suzuki, "and he's got a bad attitude."

It didn't take Nomo very long to prove them all wrong. He made his MLB pitching debut in San Francisco in early May and turned in a solid five innings in a no-decision performance. He went without a decision in his next four starts as well, often pitching before crowds filled with Asian spectators, but by the end of the month, he was leading the National League in strikeouts.

Then he switched into high gear. Setting up batters with his rising fastball, then finishing them off with his immaculate sinking fork, he won six of his next seven games, pitching two shutouts and setting a Dodgers rookie record when he struck out 16 Pirates in Pittsburgh on June 14. He was chosen the National League Pitcher of the Month for June. American hitters had never seen anyone pitch like him.

Said Barry Bonds, "It's really hard to pick up the ball with that corkscrew motion. Then he throws a forkball and the bottom drops out of it. The only way to win is to wait him out and hope his control goes south."

Through it all, however, he somehow kept his walks to a minimum. On the basis of a first half ERA of 2.05 with 109 strikeouts, he was voted the starting pitcher in the All-Star Game, which was, of course, an all-important first for a Japanese.

While all this was happening, a phenomenon called Nomomania had taken hold in Southern California. The gift shop at Dodger Stadium was selling Nomo Dodger jackets, T-shirts and sweatshirts faster than they could be manufactured in third-world sweatshops. More important, Dodger attendance rose 4 percent to an average of 38,311 per game when Nomo took the mound, thanks to the increased patronage of Asian spectators. The stands rocked to the strains of "Day-O," the old Harry Belafonte calypso standard in which "Hideo" was now substituted for the refrain. His popularity helped jump-start overall MLB attendance, which had initially slagged in the wake of the debilitating lockout of the previous year. Some people were calling him the "savior" of the U.S. game. Wrote *New York Times* reporter Claire Smith, "The 26-year-old contortionist from Osaka is causing a refreshing flutter of genuine interest in baseball. That is a welcome occurrence in a troubled sport too long preoccupied with depressing news about drugs, spousal abuse, strikes and lockouts."

The *Times* would also describe smog-choked Dodger Stadium as a "festival of Pacific Rim goodwill with Dodger pennants and flags of the rising sun fluttering through the stands." Even the festering bilateral trade friction and accompanying trash talk that had dominated U.S.-Japan relations in the early '90s seemed to abate for a time.

Nomomania reverberated all the way back to Japan where, in a remarkable turnaround that demonstrated the enormous flexibility of the Japanese, people had suddenly forgotten all the bad names they had been calling him. Foreshadowing Ichiromania, every game Nomo pitched was televised live in Japan, often on huge outdoor high-vision screens erected in urban centers amidst neon signs and billboards. This was a sight not seen since the 1950s, when the wrestling hero Rikidozan was body slamming American foes before an audience of millions watching on street corner TV sets. Meanwhile, Japanese fans young and old streamed across the Pacific by the jumbo jet planeload to watch Nomo pitch. They came in such great numbers that the Dodgers arranged for a Japanese restaurant to open in the ballpark solely to accommodate them.

The singlemindedness of the coverage was something to behold. One radio station started something called a Nomocast, broadcasting only those half innings of games when Nomo was on the mound, but returning to the studio when Nomo's teammates batted and Japan's hero sat inactive on the bench. An estimated 15 million fans, many of them standing outside at 10 A.M. in a light morning drizzle, watched the All-Star Game beamed to Japan via satellite. They continued watching even after Nomo was removed from the game because the camera continued to zoom in on him sitting in the dugout. "25 Dream Pitches!" said a headline in the evening edition of the *Asahi Shimbun,* summing up the game. Later in the season, one TV station ran an *eleven-hour* special on Japan's newest national hero.

As with Ichiro seven years later, Nomo became a bigger star and bigger media presence than he had ever been when he played in Japan, constantly pursued by a carnivorous pack of Japanese journalists. As with Ichiro, it was all so ironic because during the height of Nomo's years with the Kintetsu Buffaloes, hardly anybody came to see him pitch.

Also setting new standards for fickleness were those writers who called him cowardly and willful only months before, but now lionized him for his courageous independent streak. Whereas Nomo had been "sullen," he was now "serene." The "Shame of Japan," as he had been called by some editorialists, was now being put forward as a candidate for the People's Honor Award. Bushy-browed Prime Minister Tomīchi Murayama, a Socialist who oversaw a multiparty coalition dominated by conservatives, took time out from compromising his party's principles to fax Nomo a message of encouragement. In one of the more stunning turnabouts, the Pacific League president, who had earlier lambasted Nomo for his self-centered ways, now proclaimed, "He makes me proud to be a Japanese."

It was not all sweetness and light for Nomo, however. At the beginning of the season, he received his share of hate mail—not only from Japanese fans angry that he had deserted ship but also from racist fans in America, unhappy that a Japanese was playing big league ball. He received letters calling him a "yellow monkey," among other things, and demanding that he go home. "I could understand how *gaijin* ballplayers in Japan must have felt," he said.

There was one particularly ugly incident at Shea Stadium where a number of young white fans began shouting "U-S-A, U-S-A" and making derogatory gestures toward Japanese spectators in the stands, behavior which triggered a four-man fistfight. Eddie Kochiyama, a third-generation Japanese-American attending the game, was quoted in the L.A.–based *Rafu Shimpo* as saying, "Each time a group of Japanese fans wearing Dodger caps and shirts held up Nomo and K signs, standing for strikeouts, some whites sitting in front of them would turn around and give them the finger and chant U-S-A."

Kochiyama's companion at the game, a man named Steve Sandler, declared, "There's an atmosphere of anti-Asian and especially anti-Japanese feeling afoot in this country. There's a perception they're buying up the place and abusing trade privileges."

The Meaning of Nomo

Nomomania was also grist for a flurry of editorials on both sides of the Pacific as to "what it all meant." The *New York Times* saw Nomo's arrival on the scene as a sign that the "samurai culture" and Japanese penchant for exclusivity were receding. David Friedman, a fellow at the Massachusetts Institute of Technology, saw Nomo as a symbol or catalyst for rising Japanese nationalism. Writing in the *Los Angeles Times,* he said,

> The U.S. media cannot get enough of the unusual windup and delivery of Los Angeles Dodger pitcher Hideo Nomo. Cheering fans ignore nationality when rooting for Japan's strikeout king. In the United States, showcasing the world's most skilled athletes at the highest level of competition is what baseball—indeed, sports—is all about. But the beauty of top-flight baseball is largely lost on the Japanese expatriates filling National League ballparks wherever Nomo takes the mound. To them, Nomo is the latest in a long line of national champions doing battle for their country in enterprises—like autos, electronics and finance in the past—where foreigners once seemed invincible. Each ball and strike Nomo throws produces an exhilarating moment of national validation—or excruciating anguish.

Indeed, back on the other side of the Pacific, baseball traditionalists who had once heavily criticized Nomo's unorthodox corkscrew pitching motion were now saying that his performance showed the superiority of the Japanese baseball techniques. The august, if somewhat pompous *Asahi Shimbun* opined that the significance of Nomo's success was that it served as a "catharsis" for the Japanese public—a release from the "disgust" Japanese felt toward the U.S. over the constant carping by its government over trade.

Well-coiffed and articulate TV personality Tetsuko Koyanagi remarked in an interview with *Josei Jishin* (The Women Herself) that Nomomania was a lesson for Japan in that "America is a country that judges people on their talents and respects those with ability. . . .

whereas Japan is a country that tries to hold the talented back, instead of letting them succeed."

On the other hand, there were people like noted Japanese author Yasuharu Honda, who, in a jaundiced essay for *Views*, a popular monthly magazine, wrote that Nomomania demonstrated that Japanese fans were "the country bumpkins of the world" for their "unsophisticated, hysterical adoration" of a successful Japanese player, while virtually ignoring every other star in the U.S. major leagues. (The notable exception was the Dodgers' hirsute slugger Mike Piazza, not because he was one of the premier hitters in the majors, but because he was Nomo's catcher.)

When Nomo returned to an eagerly awaiting Japan that fall (having finished with a record of 13–6, a 2.54 ERA, 236 strikeouts and the Rookie of the Year Award), he gave them more raw material to analyze.

He and his agent Don Nomura responded to the barrage of media interview requests with unprecedented demands. For a one-hour TV appearance, he would require a minimum of 500,000 yen (then about U.S. $5,000), twice the average paid to Japanese celebrities. For simple print interviews, he wanted 50,000 yen for 30 minutes in a deluxe hotel room, with the exorbitant room cost to be paid by the interviewer. He signed endorsement deals with Kirin Beverages, Toyota, Nike, Sumitomo Life Insurance and IDC for a total of 480 million yen and eventually agreed to a 60 million yen pact with TBS for a series of exclusive appearances on that network.

This full-bore attempt to cash in on his name naturally rubbed some people the wrong way. One weekly magazine, the *Shūkan Jitsuwa*, ran a story sarcastically entitled, "Nomo's Back in Town. Pass the Collection Plate."

The hardest affront to bear, however, might have been his blunt attacks on Japanese baseball. Uncharacteristically talkative in his highly paid interviews, he described Japanese baseball as a closed world in which the players could not reveal their true feelings to the public and top echelon officials persisted in clinging to outdated customs. He was particularly critical of the way managers and coaches treated pitchers, abusing their arms in games and practice sessions, causing them to end up with shoulder and elbow problems that left them unable to pitch well, thereby putting an early end to their careers. He bemoaned the fact that so few pitchers had the gumption to refuse to pitch when their arm hurt. He noted that American pitching coaches like the Dodgers' Dave Wallace were consultants who solicited players' opinions, not just martinets who issued orders and expected blind obedience.

"Japanese don't think about money until it's too late," he complained. "In America, it's you pay, I play. Japanese have to be more aggressive."

It was not something that the officials in the NPB were accustomed to hearing, especially from a 26-year-old player.

By the end of Nomo's first month back in Japan, all his scheduled *taidan* (joint interviews) with other players had been canceled except for a meeting with former pitching star Yutaka Enatsu, fresh out of prison where he had served a three-year heroin rap. The word had gone out from the team owners that players were not to go near Nomo or his Americanized agent: Nomura indeed had become the Darth Vader of Japanese baseball for damaging the delicate tissue of the game's *wa,* and, it was generally believed, for infusing Nomo with greed.

One pundit writing in the *Asahi Shimbun* summed up the general feeling of the owners when he wrote, "Nomo will grow tired of U.S. baseball and start to miss Japan, but he will never be warmly accepted back into the fold."

Nomo's success provided one other important service. It offered contrary evidence to a set of views about Japanese baseball long held by many Americans who have played in Japan—namely, that Japanese players will never challenge authority, that they do not know how to be self-interested, that they fold under pressure, and that they would be unwilling (if not unable) to play hardball in the big leagues. Like a golfer sinking chip shots, Nomo had stepped up and, one by one, shattered each of these myths—at least as far as he was concerned. In the process, he became a symbol for a new generation of restless youth and a perceived harbinger for change. One report in 1995 estimated that 30 out of every 100 Japanese players, if asked, would say they wanted to play in the United States—although change itself, as we shall see, would come slowly, in baby steps.

Nomo, who once feared his career as a pitcher might end prematurely, went on to play longer in America than he had in Japan and pave the way for a host of other Asians to follow him, including several players from Japan and a few from Korea. He spawned a raft of magazine articles and books in Japanese about his accomplishments, many with titles in English. Examples included "Stair to the King," "Feel the Ecstasy," "Tornado in USA. We Need Nomo."

In Los Angeles, he set an MLB record of 500 strikeouts in his first 445 innings. On September 19, 1996, he pitched a no-hitter in Denver versus the Colorado Rockies, an accomplishment that many baseball people had believed impossible, given the mile-high thin air that sharply limited a pitched baseball's spin and movement. What made his feat all the more amazing was that he did it in near freezing rain, which made gripping the ball properly problematical and created perilous footing on the pitcher's mound as well. At one point, the rain halted play for 30 elbow-tightening minutes.

For a time, Nomo developed arm problems that reduced his effectiveness. He was released by the Dodgers and went to pitch for the Mets, then a Cubs minor league affiliate, undergoing elbow surgery in the process. Gradually, however, he regained his arm strength and returned to the big leagues, first with the Milwaukee Brewers and then the Detroit Tigers—where he became the first Japanese pitcher to start on Opening Day. From there he moved on to the Boston Red Sox, where, in 2001, he pitched his second no-hitter—becoming only the fourth man in history to throw one in both leagues—before finally returning to Los Angeles from where he had started.

The peripatetic pitcher reminded Japanese fans of the old masterless samurai known as *ronin*, who used to roam the land centuries past looking for temporary employment under local feudal lords. By the time Nomo had made his way back to L.A., he had added a change-up sinker and a curve to his repertoire. In 2002 and 2003, by sheer force of will it seemed, he became arguably the most reliable starting pitcher in baseball, leading L.A. in wins and innings pitched in 2002.

Dodgers manager Jim Tracy was so impressed he repeatedly described Nomo as a "warrior" to local reporters.

As popular as Nomo was, it might be added that he also made a number of enemies among the American as well as the Japanese sports press because of his reluctance to talk to them. The notoriously close-mouthed Nomo (in his unpaid mode, that is) habitually gave postgame "interviews" at Dodger Stadium consisting of sullen one- or two-word responses. In the beginning, many reporters accepted the explanation that Nomo simply couldn't speak the English language well and felt uncomfortable talking through an interpreter. Indeed, many reporters simply stopped going to the Nomo postgame press conference because they knew, whether he had won or lost, pitched poorly or well, he wouldn't say anything worth quoting, unless he insulted them for the poor quality of their questions—which he was apt to do.

"What kind of question is that?" was a standard Nomo reply, delivered in his unsmiling monotone.

Then, three years later, they witnessed the spectacle of Dodger Nomo interpreting for newly arrived New York Met Masato Yoshī in a spring training get together for the assembled press, translating easily from English to Japanese. For the onlooking members of the L.A. media, it was a stunning revelation.

"I felt like a complete fool," said one veteran reporter. "It also made me realize what a jerk Nomo was. He could have made our job in the press a lot easier with just a little bit more cooperation. A three-minute interview is enough for a decent story. Three minutes, that's all it takes, but he wouldn't even do that."

Sportswriters in Southern California much preferred the gregarious Shigetoshi Hasegawa, a former Orix BlueWave pitcher who was a reliever for the California Angels. Hasegawa, it is said, actually liked talking to reporters as well as studying and speaking English.

Among *Japanese* beat reporters, who were also given the cold shoulder more often than not, Nomo earned the contemptuous epithet of "*gaijin*"—a reference no doubt to notoriously uncooperative

American players like Clyde Wright and Willie Davis, who had played in Japan and were famous for their abruptness to journalists. (Wright once even urinated in a reporter's hat to express his views on a critical article the newspaper man had written about him.)

Among the Japanese media representatives was the aforementioned Murakami, who had made a second career for himself as a commentator on NHK telecasts of Nomo games. Murakami seemed a particularly suitable choice given what the two pitchers had in common. But Murakami had also made the mistake of seeming to scold Nomo in published interviews. Said Murakami, "He's going to be far, far away from making the major leagues as long as he depends on his agent and his interpreter all the time."

On a windy afternoon in August, 1995, before a Giants-Dodgers game, the San Francisco Giants honored Masanari Murakami a second time, 30 years after his last "Day." Nomo was asked to pose with Mashi for the benefit of the assembled media, which included both American and Japanese reporters and photographers. But, much to everyone's surprise and Murakami's embarrassment, Nomo refused. Murakami's seniority, something normally valued in Japan, counted for little, as it turned out, against Nomo's resentment over his predecessor's ill-advised remark.

Nomo told the *Los Angeles Times* of his distaste especially for the Japanese media. "They write about too many private things," said the intensely private man, who only on the rarest of occasions allowed photographs of his wife and children to be published. "They're like that paper I see at the checkout counter. You know, the one they call the *National Enquirer*."

That day, in front of Murakami, Nomo threw a one-hitter against the Giants, adding insult to injury.

The portrait of Nomo as a cold-hearted, self-centered egotist provided by some members of the press, however, did not square with the private one provided by his teammates, coaches and friends who described him as an honest, hard-working guy who was always trying to improve his craft, who never, ever wanted to come out of a game and who would often spend his free time, on his own, visiting orphanages and children's hospitals. To see him at one of these venues, shedding his normal reserve, signing autographs and warmly hugging his young admirers—some of them terminally ill—was, his closest friends said, to see the real Hideo Nomo. It was just healthy reporters he was reluctant to meet.

Summing it all up, Nomo's remarkable odyssey, his multitudinous wanderings, his incredible comeback from the brink of oblivion—all accomplished with a cultural burden heavier than a big *kanji* dictionary riding on his back—was testament he was someone special.

Said his pitching coach with the Dodgers, Jim Colborn, "You never know how well a Japanese player is going to do in the American game until he actually tries—the same is true with Americans going over there. You can have all the talent in the world, but if you don't have the character, you're not going to succeed. In Nomo's case, his is off the charts."

DARTH VADER, THE FAT TOAD AND ALFONSO SORIANO

I agree with what you say is wrong about the Japanese baseball
system. I just don't like the way you're going about trying to fix it.
KATSUYA NOMURA, ALL-TIME GREAT PLAYER AND MANAGER,
TO HIS STEPSON, THE TRAILBLAZING AGENT DON NOMURA

DARTH VADER

"Why did it take so long?" That is a question that has frequently
been asked in regard to the 30 years—from Murakami to Nomo—that
MLB waited before signing another ballplayer from Japan. Certainly,
the onset of free agency in 1975 had changed the status quo between
the two games—suddenly a higher level of U.S. player was available
to the Japanese side, a benefit that American owners did not enjoy vis
à vis their counterparts across the sea. In retrospect, MLB could have
used the extra talent Japan had to offer and in the 1970s they had the
capacity to wage and win a bidding war with NPB, where salaries
were comparatively low. So why the lack of predatory activity? Why
not scrap or revise that 1967 Working Agreement instead of continu-
ing to adhere to it?

Some published reports speculate that there was a "de facto" ban
in place, that as with the Murakami case, there had been pressure
from the U.S. government on major league teams to keep their
hands off the NPB stars—such pressure instigated at the behest of
the Japanese leaders worried that the Americans would hijack their

sacred game. As the argument went, the U.S. needed Japan's cooperation in matters relating to defense. Pressuring MLB with a threat
to take a second look at the antitrust exemption in the U.S. Congress
would be an easy enough favor to grant in return, and would certainly be enough to keep major league owners in line.

However, there is no concrete evidence that such pressure ever
existed. And no one in a position to know, in or outside the respective baseball commissioners' offices, believes there ever was. Robin
Berrington, a career diplomat in the State Department, had this to
say: "I was in the cultural office of the American Embassy in Tokyo
during much of that period—and was later, in effect, the cultural at-
taché. U.S. government–related sports activities were always carried
out through the embassy cultural office. Although there were several two- to three-year stretches of time when I was in D.C., I was
still involved in Japanese affairs and know of no efforts by the U.S.
government to pressure the U.S. major leagues to not sign Japanese
players. If there was anything like this going on, I suspect the embassy would have known about it." Marvin Miller, an active participant in and close monitor of the baseball scene for the last 40 years
of the 20th century, said, "I never heard even a rumor that there was
political pressure on the big leagues to keep their hands off the
Japanese." Added Miwako Atarashi, curator of the Baseball Hall of
Fame and Museum in Tokyo, and as knowledgeable as anyone
about contemporary Japanese baseball history, "That's news to me."
Scoffed one insider, "It's an intriguing theory, but the fact is there is
more evidence of aliens landing at Roswell than there is of this so-
called any 'de facto ban' on Japanese in MLB."

Aside from the novel concept that the MLB owners actually wanted
to honor the agreement they had signed, there are other theories
that present themselves, one of them being that the majors just were
not that interested in Japan, regardless of the rave reports they were
getting from Americans returning from the Far East. Said Don Nomura, "There was lots of discrimination in the States in the '60s and
'70s and it probably still exists to some extent. The U.S. never had a
vision of importing players from Japan—or from the Latin countries,
for that matter. Major League Baseball had no presence in Japan.

There was very little scouting there. Not like today, where they're picking up talent from all over the world." Added Bobby Valentine, who managed in Japan in 1995, "Despite what some people said about the high quality of Japanese baseball, there was just this idea prevalent in the States that the Japanese were not really good enough for MLB. It was insulting. But even the Japanese themselves bought into it."

Another theory has it that it just wasn't worth the hassle, even for those who understood the value of the Japanese player. The indomitable Bill Veeck, one of the true forces of nature in MLB, tried ardently to buy or trade for Yomiuri slugger Shigeo Nagashima when he was running the Chicago White Sox in 1968, seven years after Walter O'Malley made his unsuccessful offer. But, again, Yomiuri owner Shoriki and Nagashima, in the midst of winning nine straight Japan Championships, had their own agenda, having to do with national honor, and Veeck, exhausted, eventually gave up. So did the St. Louis Cardinals, who tried to sign Yutaka Enatsu, the San Francisco Giants, who wanted Lotte infielder Michiyo Arito, and the California Angels, who lusted after Hiroshima Carp left-handed ace Shinichi Ono. Either the athlete himself was reluctant to take such a radical step because of the language and cultural barriers involved, or if he was willing, his team, holding a firm grip on his services via the reserve clause, refused to part with him.

According to Buzzie Bavasi and MLB official Jim Small, as the Japanese economy exploded in the '80s, MLB owners indeed grew leery of a salary war with NPB, whose teams had been offering huge sums to free agent American players like Warren Cromartie. Their generosity reached a peak of sorts in the Bubble-era season of 1987, when the Yakult Swallows had outbid U.S. teams for the services of aging Atlanta Braves star Bob Horner, paying $2 million and offering him a then record $15 million package to come back for three more years. Horner, who discovered he did not enjoy living in a land like Japan, turned the offer down. But then, as big league salaries began to rise into the stratosphere, far outstripping what most NPB teams were prepared to pay for foreign talent, fear of a raid by Japan became unrealistic.

What ultimately changed the equation was the attitude of *some* of the Japanese players. The voluntary retirement loophole had always been there. It was just that no one was aware of its existence, because no one was trying to defect to MLB. Said Sadaharu Oh, regarded by many as the greatest player ever to play the game in Japan, a man who hit a record 868 home runs from 1959 to 1980, "In my era, if I had tried to go to the States to play, the public would have overwhelmingly turned against me. Feelings about such things were much more intense then."

In Nomo's era, however, Japan was not quite the insular country it was a generation or two earlier. Twelve million people now traveled abroad every year—up from a fraction of that number in Oh's playing days. Japan's foreign population (legal and otherwise) approached 1.5 million, triple what it was in the early '80s. On top of all that there was a new free-agent system in place and the ties of fealty that bound players to their teams had been loosened a notch—with the notable exception, of course, of the Tokyo Giants.

Thus, as one American baseball official put it, "It wasn't so much that the caliber of the players had greatly improved, but rather that the outlook of the players was different."

The new environment made it possible for someone like Don Nomura to come along and elbow his way through the door. Not that it was easy.

What Nomura did took a great deal of hard work and fortitude.

During the Nomo brouhaha, Nomura was bombarded with insulting phone calls and postcards, with messages like "You're crazy," or "You're greedy" and "You're a cheat to the players." He also received death threats from Japanese gangsters. The truculent Giants warlord Tsuneo Watanabe, foe of greed and chaos that he was, also zeroed in, saying, "If we recognize agents, they will be the ruin of Japanese professional baseball. . . . We can never allow agents, especially Don Nomura. He's a bad man."

An intelligent, well-mannered, if tightly wound individual, who neither smoked nor drank and exercised religiously, Nomura had a penchant for hard-edged candor that would win him the enmity of many officials on both sides of the Pacific. It was a penchant he first displayed during a meeting with Kintetsu Buffaloes president and general manager Yasuo Maeda, who in a desperate break with protocol had asked for a meeting with Nomura in the hope Nomura could somehow make Nomo see the light about remaining with the team.

In a meeting at the Miyako Hotel in Osaka, an island of deluxe, if artificial, comfort in the sea of endless concrete that was Japan's second city, Maeda complained he could not afford a multiyear deal because the club was losing so much money. Kintetsu had finished in third place, far out of contention, he complained. Attendance was sluggish, barely over a million. The team was in the red. In fact, the entire Kintetsu railway and department store complex was in the red. His hands were tied.

"If you don't have enough money then why do you have a ball club?" Nomura asked. "Maybe Kintetsu should sell the team to somebody who knows how to run one."

Maeda had never heard such insolence.

"Sell the club?!" Maeda retorted. "That's none of your business."

"That's right," replied Nomura. "It's none of our business that you're losing money. But then maybe you're not doing your sales properly. Maybe your marketing is no good. Don't take your inability to make money out on the players. They give 100 percent. They are very competitive out there on the field. It's not up to them to bring in customers. That's your job. If you can't do it, that is a problem."

Needless to say, the meeting did not last very long.

Japanese themselves often say that it takes *gaiatsu* (outside pressure) to change the status quo in Japan, given the atmosphere of rigid conformity with which certain established patterns are adhered to; in this instance Nomura-san was *gaiatsu* incarnate. If he had been a less willful individual, Japanese players might still be waiting for the golden gates of the temple of MLB to open to them. But being half-American and half-Japanese, and simmering with resentment at the way he'd been treated in Japan, he had all the qualifications to challenge the system head on. His story says a lot about the gulf that still separates the two countries.

* * *

Don Nomura was born Donald Engel on May 17, 1957, in St. Luke's Hospital in the Tsukiji area of Tokyo. He was the first child for Alvin George Engel, a 40-year-old civil service employee working for the Military Motion Picture Association, and his 24-year-old Japanese wife, Yoshie Ito. A younger brother, Kenny, would be born two years later. When Don was six, his mother walked out, leaving her husband to care for the children, never to return.

"I think that, for her, getting married in the first place had just been for purposes of survival, given her economic condition," he said later in a published biography about his life, "It wasn't that long after the war and things weren't easy. So she meets an American, marries him and has two kids, then realizes that she doesn't want it. . . . I guess in retrospect it wasn't a good time to have mixed blood or half-breed kids, because my mother always said not to tell anybody that she had been married to an American or that our father was Mr. Engel. I'd say to myself, What the hell is she talking about?"

At St. Mary's, a private Catholic school in Tokyo, Nomura showed signs of exceptional athletic ability as well as a penchant for untimely outbursts of temper (the latter, his teacher said, was typical behavior for children from broken, mixed-marriage homes). At the age of 16, he was kicked out of school for fighting and was subsequently enrolled at Chofu High in the suburbs of Tokyo, where he became an all-star baseball player and in his free time continued his activities as a rebellious social misfit. He was also seeing more of his mother, who had renamed herself Sachiyo and remarried. Her new husband was the playing manager of the Nankai Hawks, catcher Katsuya Nomura, who was finishing out a Hall of Fame career. His 657 home runs would be second in Japan only to Sadaharu Oh.

The next step was enrollment at California Polytech University, where he played baseball well enough to set his sights on a pro career, if not in the majors then at least in Japan. When he reached the age of 21, he was required by the Japanese Home Ministry to give up the dual U.S.-Japan citizenship he had been holding and choose one country or the other. His father, who had moved to Hawaii by then, had always told him to be proud of being an American—"The U.S. is the best country in the world," he would say. But the son opted for Japan instead. An opening at the Yakult Swallows had presented itself and he wanted to play there without being subject to the restrictions on *gaijin,* which at the time were two per team. He took the name Katsuaki Ito, after his mother, and in 1977, he also consented to being adopted by Katsuya, assuming then the name of Don Katsuki Nomura.

On the farm team, where he was sent, the daily drudgery was hard enough, but discrimination kept rearing its hydra heads. One of these belonged to the minor league team's bus driver, who made a habit of addressing Nomura rudely as *"Gaijin!"* poking fun at his rust-orange hair and, behind his back, referring to him as *keto* (hairy beast). One night, when the driver left his car at the team dormitory, Nomura decided to exact his revenge on the vehicle. He kicked it, dented it, jumped on it and then urinated on it. A crowd of his fellow players, which included Korean and other mixed-blood athletes, watched and cheered him on. "I'm doing it for you guys," Nomura cried, "because this guy is a goddamn racist—and worse." This drew more cheers. The police later charged Nomura with a misdemeanor. He was forced to pay a fine and issue a formal apology.

By this time, the multi-named Ito-Engel-Nomura (occasionally even he had a hard time remembering what his own *nom du jour* was) had come to some conclusions in regard to racial discrimination. From his time in California, he had come to think that there was indeed a difference between the U.S. and Japan on that score. In the U.S. proper, he believed, there were so many diverse non-white groups—roughly a quarter of the U.S. population was non-white—and there were so many laws to protect minority rights, along with a legal apparatus to enforce them, that you could have a decent, successful mainstream life there. In Japan, by contrast, he thought that if you were not 100 percent Japanese, you often had a more tortuous road to travel unless you had family wealth, special connections or somehow blurred your identity. It was possible to be shut out of the better universities and corporations because of your background, and it was much harder to take legal recourse, because of the relative paucity of lawyers and courts. Since less than 1.5 percent of the population fell into the non-Japanese category, discrimination was not the social issue it was in the States.

By 1981, thanks to a bad back, a bad batting average and bad relations with the coaches, Nomura was out of baseball and looking for a job. Worse yet, his father, at age 62, had committed suicide. Nomura had been sending him money from his not-very-substantial minor league paychecks to help him survive, but it was still not enough. After a business partner had embezzled funds from their joint enterprise and absconded to the mainland, it was more than Alvin Engel could take. He ran a hose from the exhaust pipe of his car into the driver's seat, locked the doors and started the engine. Neighbors found him sometime later. He had left a short letter saying, "I'm sorry."

"I went to Hawaii and picked up my father's ashes and brought them back to Japan," said Nomura. "I put them in the cemetery near our house. And I kept the letter. The sad thing is I couldn't relate it to anybody. Nobody really knew the existence of my father, because of the way my mother portrayed things to everybody. She lied to everybody about how she had never been married. She had all these different stories to explain the existence of her children. One, of course, being that me and my brother were from the orphanage and we never had a father. Or that they were never married. There were so many lies. It was just heartbreaking."

In 1982, Nomura packed up and moved to Los Angeles with a new wife, a former Tokyo-based dental assistant. There he worked a series of eclectic jobs: delivery van driver, minor league scout, Subaru car cleaner, travel agent, night janitor cleaning toilets in Little Tokyo, liquor store clerk in South Central L.A. and graveyard shift manager at a $10 a night flophouse, where the clientele consisted of drug addicts, ex-cons and prostitutes (of both genders). For a time, he was so poor he was forced to send his wife and new baby daughter back to Japan and to live out of his car.

By 1985, however, he had saved enough money to rent an apartment and bring back his family. Then in one incredible night at a Las

Vegas baccarat table, he converted $1,000 into $41,000. Showing uncommon discipline, he brought the money back to L.A. and invested in the real estate business. He put a down payment on a small house, built up enough equity to secure a loan, then bought an apartment to rent out.

Nomura rode the stock and real estate market booms of the late '80s. The small apartment he had bought, worth $250,000 at the time of purchase, shot up to $400,000 in value. With this kind of equity, he was now in a position to realize a dream he had long been nurturing: buying into a minor league club in the States.

He borrowed a quarter of a million dollars from the bank to purchase ownership of a California-based team called the Salinas Spurs—a Class A entry in the California League. This made him the second Japanese citizen to own a professional baseball franchise in North America.

The franchise was to serve as a supplementary farm system for Japanese professional clubs, a place where they could send their new high school draftees for seasoning. Nomura recruited four or five farm team players from Daiei and Yakult, barely out of their hormonal teens, and played them alongside equally hormonal American minor leaguers and a variety of veteran rogues and troublemakers not welcome elsewhere in organized ball. Among them were Steve Howe, banned from the major leagues seven times for drug abuse, and Leon Durham, a onetime MLB outfielder/first baseman who had been arrested for bringing a gun to the ballpark.

The Japanese visitors picked up a variety of habits from their idiosyncratic teammates—chewing tobacco, long hair, beards, periodic visits to Nevada's bordellos—some even developed a taste for the individualistic and infinitely shorter American approach to training.

A special member of the Salinas Spurs was the clubhouse boy, Mac Suzuki, who had been kicked out of an Osaka high school for fighting. Nomura had initially made the boy's acquaintance in the 1988–89 off-season during a baseball clinic in San Diego arranged by Tony Gwynn and Nomura's stepfather Katsuya. Suzuki, then 13, had one of the best natural arms Nomura had ever seen, and Nomura had taken him aside and told him, "Kid, whatever you do, don't ever quit playing baseball."

Suzuki's father, looking for a place to put his wayward son after his rudely interrupted high school career, had contacted Don Nomura for help and wound up sending the boy to Salinas, in the hopes his new surroundings would instill some discipline in him. Young Mac swept the clubhouse, washed the laundry, cleaned the spikes, pitched pregame batting practice and sold hot dogs during the game. He ate and slept with the players and pitched for a local American Legion team as well—all without speaking a word of English. Unable to read the labels on the boxes in the laundry room, he once unwittingly put Drano in the team washing machine, ruining all the uniforms.

Suzuki also had the best arm on the team. At Salinas, he grew into a 6′4″ 200-pounder who could throw the ball 95 miles per hour. He was an obvious pro prospect, and Nomura signed him to a personal representation contract and Mac Suzuki became his first client. He later negotiated a deal with the Seattle Mariners that earned Suzuki a million-dollar signing bonus.

Eventually, Nomura sold the Spurs to a group in San Bernadino for a million and a half dollars. Seeing the willingness of Hideo Nomo to make a stand and noticing the emergence of at least a handful of independent-minded players who were fed up with the plantation mentality of the Japanese system, Nomura became convinced that he could become a full-time agent in Japan. So he set up a company in Los Angeles, KDN Sports, Inc., hired an attorney, a bright, articulate young Berkeley graduate named Jean Afterman, and set his sights on his next target in Japan, an ursine young heat dispenser named Hideki Irabu.

Shuwozenegga

In the wake of Nomo's *shōji*-rattling debut, scouts from North America came pouring into Japan searching for more of the same. Officials in the Japanese commissioner's office, more than a little annoyed with themselves for having allowed the foreign invaders to slip through the gates, came up with the bright idea of unilaterally eliminating the irksome "voluntary retired" clause—now known as "The Nomo Clause" in Tokyo cocktail party conversation. They expanded the restrictions in the Japanese Baseball Convention by adding "voluntarily retired player" to the class of player prohibited from moving overseas, and they did this without informing their American friends, although they had clearly been obliged to do so.

The back-room maneuvering, however, did little to prevent a struggle for the services of the aforementioned Hideki Irabu, a 6′4″ 220-pound right-hander with a high-octane fastball, who joined the Lotte Orions of Kawasaki in 1991, a year before they moved across Tokyo Bay and became the Chiba Lotte Marines. It was a case that demonstrated even more vividly than *les affaires Murakami et Nomoaux* just how underdeveloped the concept of individual rights really was in Japan.

Irabu was born in 1968 to an Okinawan woman and an American GI, a young man who had then departed Japan without leaving a forwarding address. As Don Nomura had discovered, being racially mixed was not a great advantage in a country like Japan, and the difficult topic of his absent biological father was one that Irabu preferred not to discuss publicly (except to confide in one unguarded moment, to a couple of sportswriters, that he wanted one day to go to the U.S. and become so famous a ballplayer that his father could not help but notice).

Hideki was raised by his mother and stepfather—an Osaka restaurateur with the name (interestingly) of Ichiro Irabu. Hideki was an energetic child with a passion for baseball who displayed extraordinary athleticism before he had even entered kindergarten. On the advice of his stepfather, he enthusiastically adopted a routine of rigorous exercise to strengthen his body and his pitching arm—including one drill where he tied a rubber tube to a pole and tugged on it using his throwing motion to strengthen his arm and back muscles. By the time he was in the eighth grade, he threw such a hard fastball that classmates were afraid to play catch with him.

Throughout his school years, he would wake up every morning at

5:30 without fail and run. "I was just stunned by his ability to keep up with a lot of hard work," the elder Irabu later told a reporter. "Hideki would tenaciously hang onto things that a normal kid would have long given up. And that made me think that he might grow up to be an extraordinary man."

Hideki was drafted by Lotte in November 1990 at age 19. Because of his Terminatoresque physique, reporters dubbed him *Shuwozenegga,* after movie star Arnold Schwarzenegger. A simple, and for the most part congenial youth, he was also (unlike Ichiro) burdened with defective alpha waves. He had a temper that had surfaced often in his schooldays when fellow students were unwise enough to have made unflattering remarks about his slightly Western facial features, as well as in baseball games when he gave up too many hits. Playing for Lotte, he would break his toe kicking the bench after surrendering a ninth-inning home run.

On the other hand, he could throw the ball 99 miles per hour, which was a Japan speed record, clocked in a game in May 1993 against the Seibu Lions, and he would develop an intimidating forkball. By 1994, he had surpassed Nomo as the premier strikeout artist in the Japanese game and by the time he was 27 he had led the league in ERA (1995, 1996), strikeouts (1994, 1995) and wins (1994), among other categories. By this time he had also earned the nickname *kurage* (jellyfish) for the stinging effect his inside deliveries had on a batter's hands.

American manager Bobby Valentine, who managed Lotte in 1995, trumpeted his ace pitcher's talents far and wide. "Irabu is the Nolan Ryan of Asia," said Valentine in a typical bromide. "If he played in the U.S. he would do a lot to remove the fantasy that U.S. baseball is better than the Japanese." Valentine's pitching coach, Tom House, a Ph.D. who had in fact trained Hall of Famer Nolan Ryan for years, was equally effusive. After seeing Irabu throw over 100 miles per hour in practice numerous times, which was about as fast as anyone in the world could throw, he pulled him aside and said, "Young man, have you ever thought about playing in America?"

He had, not surprisingly. And it was about this time that Don Nomura appeared on the scene to start reinforcing that idea, while scouts from America had begun to show up in the Lotte stands. Valentine was fired in a turn of events worthy of Richard III (see Chapter 9) and control of the team was restored to a conservative Japanese faction. The Japanese Schwarzenegger now complained of being overworked and began to speak openly of his desire for a shot at MLB, preferably with the New York Yankees, a team he said he had loved since child-hood. The Yankees' dramatic triumph over the Atlanta Braves in the 1995 World Series was no doubt still fresh in his mind.

Irabu discussed his ambition with team officials on and off during that summer. In the beginning there had been much resistance. But, by season's end, when yet another new manager was named, it was clear that there was a dire need for more punch in the batting order. The idea began to take root within the organization that maybe a trade with an MLB team might not be such a bad idea after all.

At first, the San Diego Padres appeared to have the inside track. In early October they had formalized an agreement with the Marines calling for annual player exchanges and other forms of cooperation. There was also even talk, for a time, about a deal with the New York Mets, where Valentine would be taking over as manager. But Irabu had by then decided he would play only for the New York Yankees—and the Yankees, it soon became known, reciprocated his affections.

Irabu had hired Nomura, a man with whom he obviously had a great deal in common, and, who, as we have seen, was rapidly be-coming the Darth Vader of Japanese baseball. Critics suspected No-mura had somehow cast a spell on his client because Irabu had seldom before mentioned his love for the Bombers from the Bronx. There was talk of some sort of secret deal with Yankees owner George Steinbrenner for Irabu's services—a suspicion which, if true, would constitute illegal tampering. Nomura and the Yankees vocifer-ously denied the charge.

Lotte's chief operating officer Akio Shigemitsu, or "acting owner," as he was called, was reportedly outraged at Irabu's impudence. Shigemitsu was a Japan-born Korean but one with certain advan-tages other members of this particular minority group lacked—like an Ivy League education and a father (Takeo) who had founded the vast Seoul-based Lotte candy, chewing gum and hotel empire that had operations all across Asia. He was, in fact, used to total obedience. He threatened to keep Irabu out of baseball for the 1997 season—using the Japanese term *kaikorosu*, literally "keep and kill"—if Irabu didn't start being more cooperative. It was a threat that if carried through could represent a serious blow to Irabu's career.

In December 1996, there were meetings involving a number of Marines' representatives who were acting as intermediaries for Shigemitsu and Irabu. Nomura, in a nod to changing times, was even allowed to participate in some of them. Despite the front office warnings, Irabu and Nomura stubbornly refused to drop their insistence on the Yankees and Nomura even further suggested he might challenge the Japanese system in a U.S. court.

In the end, one Lotte official proposed a bizarre agreement which seemed like it might solve the problem. Under the proposal, the Lotte front office would promise verbally to do their best to deal Irabu to the Yankees, while in return Irabu would sign a "personal" letter, handwritten by a Lotte official, in which he agreed to follow the will of the front office. It just was a formality, Irabu was told, but one necessary to mollify Shigemitsu, who did not want a 27-year-old "employee" dictating terms to him. A Lotte official promised Irabu that the letter would never see the light of day.

Shigemitsu then offered Irabu to the Yankees, asking for, in return, the outfielder Cecil Fielder, who had hit 39 homers that year, with the further stipulation that the Yankees pay one half of the slugger's $10 million salary. The Yankees refused and they declined to offer any other players of Fielder's caliber either. In a meeting in January with Irabu and Nomura, Shigemitsu said that he had made his best efforts to grant Irabu's wish, but the New York Yankees would not cooperate. He then revealed that the "exclusive negotiating rights" to Irabu had been traded to the San Diego Padres for two second-tier players.

"You're no longer part of this club," he was quoted as saying.

Stunned at this turn of events, Irabu flatly refused to go. He and Nomura resolutely turned down the team's three-year $4.5 million offer, one which came with a $2.5 million signing bonus, and reiterated the pitcher's desire to go to the Yankees. When San Diego executive

Larry Lucchino told them that if Irabu didn't sign that he would have to sit out a year, Nomura countered that he and his client were going to bring San Diego before the MLB executive council and enlist the help of the MLBPA to do it. A close, fair reading of the U.S.-Japan Working Agreement, he argued, would force one to conclude that there was no clause allowing or governing or even pertaining to the type of trade that Lotte and San Diego had just made. Since the subject was not addressed, the trade had to be illegal and thus invalid. Nomura further complicated the matter by claiming that his client should now become a *free agent,* because of the cavalier way in which both sides had treated his player.

"What we have here is slave trade," Irabu told reporters in what amounted to a public declaration of war.

At hearing this, Shigemitsu was not amused and, signaling it was time to unleash the long knives, released the personal letter signed by Irabu to the press.

"This document shows that Irabu was willing to join any team in the major leagues," declared the acting owner. "I wish he would stop being so self-centered."

Fade to black.

In the end, a special session of the Major League Baseball Executive Council held in February in San Diego ruled against Irabu, this despite the fact that Lotte failed to refute Irabu's sworn affidavit about the personal letter and the verbal promise by the Marines front office of a Yankees trade. The council issued a written statement that said, "There is no violation of any major league rule or the basic agreement. The process which controls this is the U.S.-Japan 1967 Treaty which the Executive Council has followed to a T. We do not believe that the union has any jurisdiction in the matter." The rights of Japanese players were an issue, they allowed, but since the working agreement did not address that problem, nor did it *specifically prohibit* trades between the two countries, it was not a matter for the council to consider. The Padres retained exclusive negotiating rights and would keep them until Lotte withdrew them.

Had Irabu had been a different kind of guy—say, one like Ichiro, who didn't care where he played or how much he was paid as long as it was in the major leagues—he might just as well have given up and signed on with San Diego at that point. San Diego was a nice, clean town. The weather was good and there were lots of golf courses. What the hell. But Hideki wasn't anything like Ichiro. He had a sensitive streak as wide as Tokyo Bay. To his way of thinking, the San Diego organization had disrespected him as much as Lotte had by issuing that "sign or else" ultimatum. And he wasn't about to let that go by the boards.

"This player will never sign any contract with San Diego, ever," said KDN lawyer Jean Afterman. "When he does get the club of his choice, there will be a no-trade clause—no trade to San Diego. Not because of the players, but because the ownership and management treated him like a piece of property, a piece of meat."

That left the small problem of what to do with the rest of his career. In the off-season that year, free agent eligibility requirements had just been lowered to nine years. For a while, he toyed with the idea of rejoining his former team—which still retained "reservation" rights to him within Japan as opposed to the "negotiating" rights held by San Diego in the States, under the labyrinthine deal that had been struck. That meant he could put in his time and then qualify as a bona fide free agent under the new Japanese rules, which, according to the math involved, would be sometime in the middle of the 1997 season.

But Shigemitsu had his own twisted sense of pride. A Marines spokesman named Yugi Horimoto announced the conditions under which Chiba Lotte would take Irabu back. First he would have to *apologize* for his behavior in general, and, in particular, for his calumny depicting the Marines' business practices as "slave trade," a remark, said Horimoto, that had "gravely injured the Marines' reputation." But that was not all. Next, said Horimoto, demonstrating the grasp of civil rights that had long been the hallmark of NPB, Irabu would also have to submit a written statement to the major league and Japanese baseball commissioners, to all major league clubs and to the Lotte Marines that he had given up trying to play in the major leagues, promising that he would never, ever again in his entire life attempt to play baseball for a team in North America. It was an arrangement that, if agreed to, would make Irabu the oldest living reserved ballplayer in either country. The good news was that he would *not* be required to commit *hara-kiri*.

It hardly seemed possible that the situation could get any worse. But somehow, Don Nomura managed to pull it off by raising the specter of Manzanar. In an interview, he caustically remarked to a reporter that "Mr. Irabu is being kept against his will, as if he were a prisoner in a concentration camp. It is an internment camp to restrict him from playing where he wants. Is it because he's a Japanese?"

This comment immediately raised the hackles of Japanese-American groups all over the West Coast who failed to see any real correlation between the internment of more than 120,000 Japanese and Japanese-Americans by the U.S. government during World War II and the plight of a slightly overweight pitcher who made over a million dollars the season before.

Fortunately, fate intervened while the Irabu team was mulling the possibility of pursuing the matter in the U.S. court system, with the help of the MLBPA, whose leaders thought Irabu had been screwed. "If Irabu had had the name of John Smith, with blond hair and blue eyes," said MLBPA attorney Gene Orza, implying that discrimination had somehow affected the MLB Executive Council decision, "I do sincerely believe that all this would have never happened."

Luckily (for NPB, that is), legal action proved to be unnecessary. In the spring that followed, the Executive Council reversed itself and initiated a freeze on future transactions of the San Diego–Lotte type, producing a new rule that prohibited a Japanese player's contract or the exclusive negotiating rights to it from being sold or traded to a U.S. club . . . *without that player's permission.*

At the same time, San Diego, thoroughly disgusted with their Lotte experiment, gave in and traded Irabu to New York for three Yankee reserves. Irabu had finally won his pinstripes, signing a four-year deal calling for $12.8 million in bonuses and salaries, putting an end to the whole sorry chapter. It seemed that the soap opera that Irabu's life had become was finally over. But that was only a temporary illusion, for as we shall see, there was another act yet to come.

I-Rob-You?

Hideki Irabu would have his career with the Yankees, but it would not turn out to be quite what he had envisioned. Despite all the build-up, he found himself unable to live up to the promise of his NPB statistics.

He arrived on the continental mainland of the United States tenaciously trailed by a phalanx of reporters, many of whom he despised for the stories they had written about him during his struggle with the Padres. One printed story claimed that the real reason he refused to sign with the National League team was because his mother was of North Korean descent and the city of San Diego, as home to a major naval base, had figured significantly in military strikes against the Northern Korean peninsula in the past. At his Yankees contract signing ceremony in late May in Tampa, he grandiosely announced a list of offending Japanese publications.

He also took to insulting the members of the fourth estate with derisive names. "Goldfish Shit" was one. Another one was "Grasshoppers"—as in plague of locusts. "Let's say you have a rice paddy," he explained. "You are trying to grow rice. But the grasshopper comes in and eats up your rice plants. The press is the same way. They come to me and they eat me up with all this pursuit."

During a bullpen session at the Yankees AAA franchise in Columbus later in the year, Irabu unleashed an errant pitch that slammed into a photographer's thigh. Reporters present assumed it was intentional and the sports dailies back home headlined the news of this assault on their front pages, complete with photos of the bruised area and sketches of the "crime scene."

"Sorry," Irabu was quoted as saying. "You should watch where you're standing."

Irabu's relationship with the American media was not significantly better, despite a promising beginning. Flown to New York in owner George Steinbrenner's private jet for his first game as a Yankee, he was welcomed on the steps of City Hall by Mayor Rudy Giuliani in a widely covered event. His debut, a winning effort versus the Detroit Tigers at Yankee Stadium on July 11, in which he allowed two runs on five hits and struck out nine batters in six and two thirds innings, earned him glowing headlines in the city's notoriously bombastic tabloids.

However, this victory was followed by a string of bad outings in which his control and his fastball disappeared—along with his manners. In Milwaukee, the alpha-wave challenged Irabu spat in the direction of booing fans. Pitching in a subsequent game, he threw his glove at a batted ball. At Yankee Stadium, he punched a hole in the clubhouse door. Such outbursts, combined with the surly displeasure he frequently expressed at the umpiring, pitching mounds and other peculiarities of the American game, did not win him many fans and he quickly became a target for those initially supportive tabloids. They excoriated him with headlines like "I-Rob-You" and "Ira-Boo." A mistake became an "Ira-boo-boo." *Daily News* columnist Mike Lupica, noting Irabu's tendency to sulk when things went badly, called him a "big baby," while another scribe chipped in with "Ira-scible." Yankees owner George Steinbrenner also got into the act. Displaying a characteristic social sensitivity, he announced to a group of reporters, "I've got seven Hideki Irabu T-shirts I'm giving to the blind." It is not clear whether the reference to sight impairment had to do with his pitcher's problems in finding the plate.

One writer, noting Irabu's ever expanding midsection, his fondness for adult beverages and two-pack-a-day cigarette habit, later quipped, "Hideki never met a beer can or a cigarette he didn't like." Enduring a return stint to the minor leagues for "rehab," he finished the year with a mark of 5–4 and an embarrassing ERA of 7.09.

To veteran observers of Japanese baseball, such scoring was reminiscent of what many American players had experienced in Japan. Hard-working but hapless Dave Johnson, a former Orioles star, struggled in his highly paid first season with the Yomiuri Giants, earning the nickname "*Dame* Johnson" (No Good Johnson). Joe Pepitone, Rob Deer, Kevin Mitchell and Jeff Manto were among others whose sub-par performances met with similarly chilly receptions.

Japanese fans were somewhat discombobulated to see one of their own such an object of scorn. Said a Japanese kitchen worker at Obata's, a popular midtown Manhattan restaurant, "It's all very embarrassing. He makes Japanese people look bad." Back in Japan, ex-pitcher and ex-con Yutaka Enatsu, of all people, decried Irabu's lack of *hin* (dignity), while Don Nomura's opinionated mother went on nationwide television to declare that "Irabu is the shame of Japan."

But what bothered some Americans the most was Irabu's hiding the fact that his biological father was American. Thus when the *New York Times* published an article about Irabu's past and his attempts to hide it, the pitcher was singled out by many fans for his lack of candor and apparent shame over his biological makeup.

Irabu's mixed parentage was long rumored in Japan, a country which has always prided itself on its "homogeneity" and often looked askance at those of mixed heritage. Even in the 21st century, it is a society where people of mixed racial background can face social ostracism as children and, later in life, discrimination in finding jobs and marriage partners. Thus fans and local media had politely steered clear of the topic. In the American ethos, of course, where diversity has come to be regarded as a counterweight to prejudice and discrimination, one may be adjudged all the more interesting for having a mixed ancestry. As golfer Tiger Woods has said, mixed parentage is something to be proud of. Woods is part black, Thai, Chinese, white and Native American. Once, when asked which race he represents, Wood responded simply, "The human race."

The truth of the matter was, however, that Irabu did not know who his biological father was. And the thought that he had been abandoned as a child triggered a deep current of anger within him. The only way he knew to control that anger was to shut it in and refuse to talk about it with anybody.

Irabu was, in fact, not an unlikable young man. Cap pushed back, chewing bubble gum and talking about throwing his forkball, he seemed quite personable—not unlike any other baseball-playing youth. But he was also often morose and given to long fits of depression. Despite efforts by Yankees like Derek Jeter (himself of mixed parentage), David Cone and David Wells to help him integrate into the team, he spent much time alone, sitting by himself in the Yankee Stadium bullpen out in right center field. Irabu preferred the quiet of life in the New Jersey suburb of Fort Lee, where he lived with his new

Japanese bride, rather than bustling Manhattan, where many of his teammates lived and where irate Yankees fans had been known to throw stones and other things at him. On the road, he would shut himself in his hotel room, poring over anatomy books, trying to understand further how the phenomenon of body and muscle worked, and drawing pictures, something at which he became quite skilled. On occasions when he became particularly depressed, Nomura would have to fly in for a therapy session to buck up his client's spirits. Irabu would later experiment with religion.

The rest of Irabu's MLB career was as checkered as his first year. There was an incident in camp in 1998, when he kicked a Japanese photographer who had shot some video of him without permission and threatened to destroy his expensive camera if the lensman did not surrender the tape. Later he ripped up a reporter's name card and broke his pencil in two. That year, he had won six games by the beginning of June and was leading the A.L. in ERA at 1.98. He finished with 13 wins, but he had a spectacularly disastrous September, losing four of six and watching his ERA balloon to 4.06. He blew a 10-run lead in Oakland one night, sending Yankees manager Joe Torre into a yelling fit that could be heard in the stands.

Nineteen ninety-nine started with a disastrous spring camp, when, suffering from "private emotional problems," he made several mental lapses in the field. This prompted Steinbrenner, ever the one for delicate understatement, to label him publicly as a "fat, pussy toad." He rebounded with a 9–3 record and was voted the pitcher of the month for August. But then he collapsed yet again and finished with a record of 11–7 and an ERA of 4.84. If he surrendered a home run or two, he would suddenly lose his confidence in his fastball and shy away from it, which only made things worse. His maddening yo-yo inconsistency, his tendency to pitch brilliantly one game and horribly the next, led some to question his mental stability.

Yankees pitching coach Mel Stottlemyre, who worked hard to improve Irabu's tools, could not understand how a player could be so good one minute and so bad the next. "When Irabu is on, he has the best stuff of any pitcher I have *ever* seen *anywhere*," he said. "But when he is bad he is worse than just about anyone else."

Sports columnist Marty Kuenhert, who is well versed in the Japanese game, called Irabu a simple "nut case." Others cited drinking as the cause of his problems. But Jean Afterman, who went on to join the Yankees' front office in 2001, had another explanation. "He lacked psychological grounding," she said. "Because of his background, Hideki never really had a chance to figure out who he was, unlike other Japanese who came to the States. He didn't have a home or an identity. And I think that was the root of all his trouble. . . . That, plus the fact that the Yankees coaches kept trying to tinker with the way he pitched."

His former manager Bobby Valentine added, "He probably was in the wrong place to begin with. What he needed was a more sheltered environment. What he needed was not a 'show me' mode but a 'help me' mode."

Irabu was eventually shipped out of town—first to Montreal, where he underwent elbow and knee surgery and then went to the minors where he was suspended for getting drunk the night before a start. After that, it was on to the Texas Rangers, where he had a brief shining spell as a late-inning relief pitcher before developing blood clots that put him in the hospital and sidelined him for the rest of the season.

He completed a circuitous route back home, when he joined the Osaka-based Hanshin Tigers of Japan's Central League in 2003. Observers were worried at first that Irabu might have an attitude problem as an ex–major leaguer playing in Japan. But Tigers coach Tom O'Malley had flown to Texas in the off-season for a heart-to-heart talk with him and came away convinced that he was requisitely humbled, his head small enough to fit into a Tiger cap.

Indeed, back in blue-collar Osaka, rounding into what was perhaps the best condition of his life, Irabu enjoyed a revival, winning nine of his first 11 decisions, while leading the league in ERA. Players and coaches in NPB remarked how much he had matured as a pitcher. No longer was he just a thrower of two pitches. Instead, he was now changing speeds, planes and location.

Pundits said much of it had to do the Hanshin Tigers' popular and pugnacious manager Senichi Hoshino, a wiry, fierce ex-pitcher (nicknamed "Burning Hat" in his playing days for his intense will to win).

Hoshino was a hands-on leader, he would kick dirt on umpires, jump into fights with opposing players and scream at his own men—even slug them on occasion—to ignite their fighting spirit. But he also had a fierce devotion to his troops—he sent expensive presents (cashmere sweaters, kimonos) to his players' wives and mothers on their birthdays—and a preternatural talent for handling troubled young athletes. Hoshino had personally faced down gangsters who were trying to cozy up to his players, a job skill necessary in Osaka, which was notorious for its *yakuza* and illegal baseball betting in the stands.

Hoshino had taken Irabu under his wing and given him lots of personal attention—in one-on-one advisory sessions in the bullpen and private dinners in some of Osaka's most exclusive restaurants. In a preseason press conference, Hoshino took pains to praise his new acquisition.

"Hideki has a really gentle nature," he declared to reporters. "He's much nicer than the press makes him out to be."

Irabu's impressive start—on a consistent program of five days' rest between starts and a limit of 100 pitches per game—helped the Tigers take a huge lead in the first half of the season, sending Japan's economically depressed second city (which was hemorrhaging manufacturing jobs to mainland China) into fits of glee. Tigers goods flew off the shelf, helping to generate over 100 billion yen in total extra revenue for the region that year.

The Tigers went on to win the pennant by 14 games although Irabu slumped in the second half (as was his habit), finishing with a record of 13–8 and an ERA of 3.85. Hoshino announced to one and all that "None of this would have happened without Hideki." Indeed, so impressed was the *Tokyo Supōtsu* with the way that Irabu had interacted with the younger pitchers on the team, teaching them what he had learned in the big leagues, that the paper awarded him its MVP award, citing his "psychological contributions," even though Hanshin's left-handed ace Kei Igawa had won 20 games.

Irabu's successful season even inspired an article in the *New York Times,* by Tokyo correspondent Ken Belson, who cited the pitcher as an "example of a new breed of ballplayer in the NPB: Someone with outside experience who, rather than being shunned for the 'bad habits' he may have picked up overseas, can provide leadership on the field and in the dugout." In proving that a man can go to the United States and return intact, wrote Belson, Irabu may "convince even more players to try their luck in the major leagues."

In the Hanshin Tigers, Irabu had finally found a home where he felt welcome and in Hoshino, the father figure he had been lacking for all his baseball career. Said Hanshin's O'Malley, "Irabu has really fit in. Maybe he's more mature, more comfortable back here. He learned a lot in the States." Added writer Masayuki Tamaki, who covered the Tigers closely that year, "Hideki is back around people who speak Japanese and he's got a manager he can relate to. He's seems more relaxed than I've ever seen him."

Although some people wondered whether or not he should have left in the first place, it may also be said that it was his odyssey that transformed him from Steinbrenner's "toad" into a prince of Tigers (if you will pardon the expression).

Soriano

Before Alfonso Soriano became known as a New York Yankees prodigy, he was already historically important in Japanese baseball as the focus of a dispute which eventually led to the demise of the famous Working Agreement.

A tall, spindly-legged infielder, Soriano was a native of the Dominican Republic and a graduate of the Hiroshima Carp Academy, an institution established by the eponymous Central League franchise outside Santo Domingo as a means of cultivating cheap, local talent for use back home. It had one to two dozen members enrolled at any one time.

Soriano earned his first plane ticket to Japan in 1997 at the age of seventeen. Playing for the Carp farm team in the Western League, he hit .252 with eight home runs and 34 RBIs in 242 at bats, statistics that were hardly cause for excitement, but promising enough for someone who had yet to graduate from high school. Soriano, cheerful and outgoing, did not particularly enjoy the grueling practice sessions day and night, the bleeding and blistered hands from hours in the batting cage, the hectoring coaches yelling incomprehensibly at him in Japanese and the military-like dormitory life. He was homesick and sick of the Japanese-style game. "It's like a job," he complained, "there's no joy in it."

But he did recognize that the training he received had helped make him a more well-rounded player, better skilled at some aspects of the game—with the notable exception of his defense around the second base bag. He had also added several pounds of muscle, increasing his home run pop, and upped his speed down the line to first base by nearly half a second. He might have hung around Japan longer if the Carp had deigned to pay him a little more money than the $45,000 minimum he had been getting. But they refused to give him a raise and so he employed the services of Don Nomura.

Nomura, who had been prowling the ballparks looking for disgruntled ballplayers, had also been studying with great interest the Carp's practice of signing Dominican youths out of abject poverty and binding them to long-term low-paying "worldwide" contracts. Promising Academy players were asked to ink a bridge contract which bound them to the Hiroshima organization for seven years—whether they were in the Dominican Republic or Japan—then, if they made the Carp varsity, they would have to sign an NPB contract which obligated them for another nine years until free agency kicked in. Thus, it was entirely within the realm of possibility that a player recruited from the Dominican Republic could spend his entire career fulfilling contractual obligations to the Hiroshima franchise.

Nomura also discovered that the Carp had signed the underage Soriano without the approval of a legal guardian as required by Japanese law. A Carp attorney argued that because Soriano was a Dominican, Dominican law, where the age of consent was 18, should be applied, not the Japanese statutes, which put the age of majority at 20, even though Japan was, in fact, where Soriano was living when he signed his NPB contract. Nomura's attorney, Afterman, asked if that meant in the Japanese legal view a Saudi wife, living in Japan and committing adultery in Japan, would thus be beheaded in Japan, in accordance with Saudi law.

Ichiro Suzuki goes through his famous pre at-bat exercise ritual. Said one Japanese writer of the Seattle Flash, "Because of him, we've become Members of the World." (Photo by Brad Mangin/ Courtesy of *Sports Illustrated*)

Hideo Nomo: Japanese Braveheart. He opened the door to U.S. Major League Baseball for others from Japan to follow. (Photo by Chuck Solomon/ Courtesy of *Sports Illustrated*)

Hideki Matsui of the New York Yankees poses with a small detachment of the vast Japanese press contingent that covers his every move in North America. Cracked one American sportswriter, "I wouldn't mind having the Yankee Stadium film concession." (Photo by Heinz Kluetmeier/Courtesy of *Sports Illustrated*)

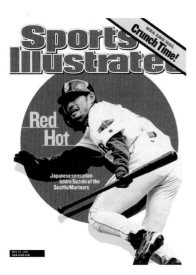

The first time *Sports Illustrated* asked Ichiro to pose for their cover, he turned them down: He didn't think he had proved himself yet. (Photo by Peter Read Miller/Courtesy of *Sports Illustrated*)

Hideo Nomo and his distinctive corkscrew or "tornado" windup, which he developed as a child. "I was trying to impress my father," he said. "It helped me throw the ball faster." (Photo by V. J. Lovero/Courtesy of *Sports Illustrated*)

The Journalist and the Samurai: Sports writer Steve Wulf extracts a rare comment from Japan's famously silent warrior. (Photo by Chuck Solomon/Courtesy of *Sports Illustrated*)

Hideo Nomo before his historic start in the 1995 All-Star Game in Arlington, Texas. This was the game in which Japanese baseball announced itself to the world. (Photo by Chuck Solomon/Courtesy of *Sports Illustrated*)

Kazuhiro Sasaki. They called him *Daimajin* in Japan, after a celluloid stone samurai that came to life to rescue imperiled Japanese villagers. As Seattle's ace closer, Sasaki regularly rescued his teammates from late-inning trouble. (Photo by Al Tielemans/Courtesy of *Sports Illustrated*)

Shigetoshi Hasegawa spends his free time writing bestselling books for readers back home. In 2003 he posted a 1.48 ERA pitching in relief for the Mariners. (Photo by Al Tielemans/ Courtesy of *Sports Illustrated*)

"I'm gonna be a part of it." Hideki Matsui takes on New York. (Photo by Eric Ogden)

"Scary" was the word
Hideki Matsui used to
describe riding in a
New York cab.
(Photo by Eric Ogden)

Playing in all seven
games of the Japan-
U.S. All-Stars base-
ball series, held in
Japan in November
2002, Kazuo Matsui
batted .423.
(Photo by
AP/WIDE
WORLD PHOTOS)

Kazuo Matsui signs
his first autograph
as a New York Met
in December 2003.
(Photo by
AP/WIDE
WORLD PHOTOS)

Ichiro Suzuki surrounded by pregame media: "Sometimes I wish I could make them all disappear." (Photo by AP/WIDE WORLD PHOTOS)

Sony Plaza in the Ginza. Watching live MLB broadcasts in the morning has become a national pastime in Japan. (Photo by AP/WIDE WORLD PHOTOS)

I said to myself, "I can do this." Ichiro hits a first-inning, first-pitch leadoff home run against the Oakland Athletics. (Photo by AP/WIDE WORLD PHOTOS)

"Don't call me Little Matsui." In the first game of the 2002 NPB-MLB all-star series, Kazuo blasted home runs from both sides of the plate. (Photo by JIJI PRESS/PANA)

During pregame warm-ups, a teammate asks Kazuo, "Where do you get your hair done?" (Photo by JIJI PRESS/PANA)

Ichiro and Orix BlueWave fans say sayonara to each other at Green Stadium, in Kobe, October 13, 2000. It was Ichiro's last game in Japanese professional baseball. (Photo by JIJI PRESS/PANA)

Several weeks later, wearing a new jersey, Ichiro appeared here at a Kyoto press conference with Howard Lincoln, CEO of the Seattle Mariners. (Photo by JIJI PRESS/PANA)

"Wassup, dude?" Ichiro communes with new teammate Mark McLemore. (Photo by JIJI PRESS/PANA)

Smiling in Seattle: Ichiro would go on to sign a new contract worth $44 million. Sasaki, however, citing "family reasons,"would suddenly return to Japan for the 2004 season, giving up some $9.5 million remaining on his two-year deal. Insiders would say the real reason had more to do with his declining effectiveness and the loss of 10 mph on his fastball than anything else. (Photo by JIJI PRESS/PANA)

Nomura took Soriano's case to arbitration, a hearing lasting several days that was adjudicated by the NPB commissioner and the two league presidents. Nomura was barred from attending.

The resulting ruling was, not surprisingly, adverse. So Nomura advised Soriano to take a page from Nomo's book and voluntarily retire. Soriano took this advice, left Japan for the U.S., and began taking part in tryouts for MLB teams.

The news of this defection was not well received in the Hiroshima camp. The Carp filed an injunction to block Soriano from playing anywhere else, claiming that he was still their property. They sent letters to all MLB clubs expressing an interest in Soriano, demanding that those organizations cease further attempts at communicating with him.

Once again the MLB Executive Council was convened to decide the matter, this time in New York. Among those attending was a delegation led by NPB executive secretary Yoshiaki Kanai, the ex-reporter who had no legal background, accompanied by several minions who were equally untrained in the law. Present on the U.S. side were MLB officials and a cadre of lawyers—men who had spent considerable time in federal courts fighting on behalf of human rights issues.

Until that time, everyone in the United States had assumed that the operative baseball agreement between the two countries was the one signed in 1967, the one which allowed voluntarily retired players to emigrate abroad. The Americans were unaware that the NPB in the post-Nomo era had unilaterally expanded the scope of their worldwide protections under the 1967 Working Agreement, because the Japanese side had failed to notify them and there was thus nothing else in writing to cancel out the Kanai-Murray letters. It was during this meeting that—surprise!—they first became aware of it, when the Japanese delegation began arguing that the Carp claim on Soriano was validated by the arbitrary amendment they had made in their own relevant Japanese-language documents.

One American official was said to be so irate at the Japanese side's unilateral attempt to change the rules that he had difficulty maintaining his composure. He faced his Japanese counterparts and said, "We in Major League Baseball simply cannot tolerate this kind of thing—you cannot keep trying to change the rules."

Director of baseball operations William Murray, of Kanai-Murray letters fame and a noted stickler for detail, said, somewhat testily, "For the past three years, we have been relying on this document for an interpretation of 'voluntary retirement' in Japan. Now you are asking us to give blind support to you for arbitrarily changing the system? . . . It's very difficult."

An American witness to that meeting actually found himself feeling embarrassed for the Japanese visitors over their lack of professionalism, lamenting, "These guys do not appear to have a clue about what the term 'human rights' means." Added another observer, "It was a joke that these guys were representing Japanese baseball. They might as well have sent Soupy Sales."

In a prepared statement, acting commissioner Bud Selig publicly criticized the Japanese commissioner's office for having unilaterally amended, in 1996, the conventions referred to in the 1967 agreement without going through proper channels.

A terse, pointed memo was dispatched to all major league general managers and scouting directors. It went as follows:

> After extensive communication with the Japanese Baseball Commissioner's Office, including recent meetings held in New York, we have come to the conclusion that Mr. Soriano was or should have been placed on the Voluntary Retired List of the Hiroshima Club. Based on earlier correspondence from the Japanese Baseball Commissioner's Office at the time Hideo Nomo was signed and the Japanese professional baseball rules, players placed on the Voluntary Retired List may only play for their former Japanese team should they choose to play in Japan. However, Japanese Voluntarily Retired players may play for any other team outside of Japan. The current U.S.-Japan Player Agreement does not restrict Major League Clubs' ability to sign a player on the Japanese Voluntarily Retired List.

Thus was history made. Soriano, now declared a free agent, signed with the Yankees. Also, in the wake of that meeting, the old 1967 Working Agreement was scrapped and a new protocol took shape, which forbade Japanese professional baseball from unilaterally making changes in its rules, and that such an attempt in the future would result in an immediate revocation of said agreement.

The Hiroshima Carp, understandably upset over the Soriano affair and Nomura's role in it, retaliated against the agent in a series of nuisance lawsuits that were eventually settled out of court, with no penalties levied. The Carp took no legal action in the U.S.

The Posting System

In December 1998, the new agreement, forged between the respective commissioner's offices of Major League Baseball and Nippon Professional Baseball, went into effect. It was called the Posting System and under this framework, there would theoretically be no more Nomos, Irabus or Sorianos. In the posting system, all 30 major league clubs in the United States would be allowed to bid for a Japanese player, made available by a Japanese club, with the exclusive negotiating rights going to the club which submits the highest bid. It thus represented a new, third path for Japanese players to go to the U.S. (The other two, of course, were the granting of an outright release or exercising one's rights as a free agent after playing nine full seasons.) The infamous voluntary retirement clause, or "Nomo Clause," would no longer be in effect.

Under the provisions of this agreement, Japanese clubs would post the names of players whom they were willing to make available (assuming, of course, the players involved were amenable) during the off-season period from November 1 to March 2. Within four days of posting, any interested big-league team would be permitted to submit a bid to the U.S. major league commissioner. The bid would be the amount to be paid to the Japanese club if the major league team did in fact wind up signing the player they had bid for. The MLB commissioner would then determine the highest bidder from all participating clubs wishing to acquire the services of said player and that lucky franchise would have 30 days to attempt to sign him.

In the event the Japanese club found the bid figure unacceptable (which it fully had the authority to do) or the U.S. club, for some reason, failed to sign the player in question after reaching agreement with his team (by, say, not offering enough money), the player's name would be removed from the available list and he would not be eligible to be posted again until the following November 1, meaning that the player would then have to play at least another season in Japan.

The posting system was obviously designed to benefit the Japanese team owners; it allowed them to maintain the integrity of their game for the time being and to control the flow of players to the U.S., and was thus in keeping with the long tradition of the professional game in Japan, whereby the front office wielded power over their players like feudal lords over their vassals. The man who devised the system, Shigeyoshi "Steve" Ino, then general manager of the Orix BlueWave, said simply, "Well, it gave the players something more than they had before. It was a way of meeting their needs as well."

That the system would not be very beneficial to the player went without saying. A U.S. team that wanted to sign a Japanese player had to pay for him twice, once to the team that owned the player's contract and once to the player—an expensive restriction.

Many American observers think the posting deal is a violation of U.S. antitrust law and an infringement of human rights, because the system prohibits a player from cutting the best deal possible for himself. MLBPA attorney Gene Orza questioned its legality "because it limits a player's freedom of choice; it totally ignores his rights." Nomura called it simply "a slave auction." Added Tony Attanasio, Ichiro's agent, "The player literally gets zero advantage from it. . . . the Japanese teams benefit by holding the players hostage."

Orza and many other knowledgeable attorneys believed that a lawsuit challenging the validity of the posting system in a U.S. court could, in fact, be won. All that was needed was a willing Japanese player with the patience and capital to pursue the matter in America's judicial system. The Japanese player would have to unilaterally leave his team, go to the States and sign with an American club.

Then, when major league baseball and Japanese baseball took their inevitable action to block the move, the player would have to file a lawsuit claiming price-fixing and market discrimination.

It is worth noting that the Japanese Professional Baseball Players Association never ratified the Posting Agreement. Nor, in fact, were they ever consulted about its imposition by the owners. The MLBPA offered to help the JPBPA fight the new system in court, but received a tepid response.

"Going to court," said union chief Toru Matsubara, "especially if the Japanese system is involved, simply takes too long, so the problem can't be helped."

"You can't force the Japanese players to stand up for their interests," replied Orza. "The U.S. players' union can only do so much."

Whether it remains in place or is dismantled, the Posting Agreement will certainly go down in history as a tribute to the efforts of Don Nomura to liberate Japanese players. For, whatever his real or imagined faults, it was he who found and opened up the loopholes that led to its creation. Had he not, who knows how long it would have taken for Japanese to make their mark in the major leagues.

GAIJIN

Baseball society in Japan is a strange beast. It would be too easy, and not entirely accurate, to say that it is as closed as some of the Japanese markets. Baseball in Japan is open to players and coaches from the United States, Taiwan and South Korea, but at the same time, the cartel nature of the game bottles up the competitive spirit.

The Japanese approach to the sport incorporates moral guidance, business management and company-based role assignments, making professional baseball a simple job for wages. Baseball in Japan has lost its passion and imagination.

YOICHI FUNABASHI, ASAHI SHIMBUN

I T IS NOT POSSIBLE TO WRITE THE HISTORY OF BASEBALL IN JAPAN WITH-out discussing the impact of the *gaijin*. It was an American professor from Maine named Horace Wilson who is generally regarded as being the one to have introduced the game—ahead of other Meiji Era American professors in Japan who exposed their students to the sport—when, in the early 1870s, he taught his students at Tokyo's elite *Kaisei Gakkō bēsubōru*'s basic rules and fundamentals. For this, Wilson was eventually inducted into the Japanese Baseball Hall of Fame.

In succeeding years, a long line of visiting college and professional players, and individual coaches, from North America have tutored the Japanese in a wide variety of skills and techniques, from the push bunt to the cut fastball. Ty Cobb, who spent several months at Keio University in the winter of 1931, was one of a number of Americans who taught baseball on Japanese college campuses in the early part of the century (although Cobb-san was unfortunately unable to teach Japanese to pronounce his name properly and thus went down in Tokyo history books as *Ty Kapp*).

When the prewar professional Japan League was established, players from the North American minor leagues like Harris McGalliard enthusiastically participated. The most prominent non-Japanese from that era was the pitcher Victor Starfin, mentioned briefly in Chapter 3, a stateless White Russian who won 303 games while playing for the Yomiuri Giants from 1936 to 1955, enduring enforced house arrest during the Second World War. The 6'4", 230-pound Starfin is the only non-Japanese besides Sadaharu Oh, Wally Yonamine and Horace Wilson in the Japanese Hall of Fame. Since 1962, when Don Newcombe and Larry Doby ended their careers with the Chunichi Dragons, former major-league stars have been an integral part of *Nihon Pro-Yakyū*. Daryl Spencer introduced big-league-style hard sliding, Clete Boyer taught modern infield defensive techniques and Jim Lefebvre introduced tee batting in pregame practice.

The *gaijin* also captured their share of titles and records. Leron Lee, who played eleven years with the Lotte Orions, had the highest career batting average of all players with at least 4,000 at bats in Japan with a mark of .320. Randy Bass set the record for highest single-season batting average in 1986 when he hit .389, and also won back to back triple crowns in 1985 and 1986. In addition, American Bobby Rose chalked up several extremely productive seasons, including 1999 when he led the league in batting average with .369 and RBIs with 153. In 2000 and 2001, in a remarkable sequence of events, first Tuffy Rhodes and then Alex Cabrera tied Sadaharu Oh's single-season home run mark of 55.

Overall, more than 700 foreign players have tried their hand in Japan in the first 70 years of pro baseball's existence there, but roughly half were not invited back for a second season. Among the more notable busts were Frank Howard, an amiable 6'8", 275-pound star slugger who played a total of one day in Japan before succumbing to a knee injury. Joe Pepitone received a record salary to play for the Yakult Atoms in 1973, but hit only .173, complaining all the while about his living conditions until he left in midseason to deal with a Stateside divorce. Rob Deer, a former Milwaukee Brewers and Detroit Tigers slugger, could only manage a batting average of .151 with eight home runs for the 1994 Hanshin Tigers, while Boston Red Sox star Mike Greenwell hit .231 in seven games for the same team in 1997.

The upshot of it all was that it took a certain type of individual to make it in Japan, and past success in MLB was certainly no guarantee of a similar result in NPB. In addition to different food and living conditions, a language barrier and a new set of cultural mores, a player had to be able to adjust to a heavier practice routine, tolerate more aggressive coaching and adapt to a different breaking-ball, control-oriented type of pitching. Although Japanese pitchers threw a few miles per hour slower on the average than their major league counterparts, they did have impressive control of all their forkballs, splitters, curves, sliders and *shōto*s, among others.

On top of all this, the *gaijin* had to deal with the ambivalent attitude Japanese displayed toward foreigners during much of the postwar era. Many real estate agents, landlords and night club operators, to name a few, have had "no-foreigners" policies, as did certain bath house operators.

Foreign membership on Japanese teams which, in essence, meant those players not born and bred in Japan, or those born to Japanese parents overseas, has been limited by rule. As this book went to press, each team in the Central and Pacific Leagues was permitted four imported players, including up to three pitchers or three batters—with unlimited numbers of *gaijin* allowed in the farm system. (A foreigner who plays more than nine years in Japan is no longer subject to these "*gaijin*" rules.) The Japanese Players Association defended such restrictions, arguing that without them Japanese baseball would be overrun by foreign imports, given the somewhat lower level of play in Japan, and that their presence would adversely affect the development of younger athletes by denying them opportunities to play. This system stood in contrast to MLB, where there were no such restrictions. It was, and is, possible for a major league team to field a starting lineup of players born outside the United States. In 2003, 28 percent of all big leaguers carried foreign passports and seven members of the starting lineup of the Florida Marlins in the final game of the World Series were born outside the United States.

In NPB, one still hears complaints about a "*gaijin* allergy" and the ideal of having so-called "pure-blooded" Japanese baseball has often been expressed by the sports insiders. For example, in 1984, Takezo Shimoda, the onetime ambassador to the United States who also served a stint as baseball commissioner in Japan, stated openly that "it was only natural that Japanese baseball be played by Japanese as the gap between the respective levels of the Japanese and American games narrows.

"Besides," he added, "Japanese baseball will never be considered first-rate as long as there are former major leaguers no longer wanted in their own countries in key spots in a Japanese lineup." In 1999, Giants manager Shigeo Nagashima announced to a group of supporters that his "ideal" for many years had been to field a purely made-in-Japan lineup.

Nagashima had been an illustrious member of the V-9 Giants (1965–1973), so-called because they had won nine straight Japan Championships and were themselves known as "pure-blooded" because all of their members were home-grown—with a couple of caveats. First baseman Sadaharu Oh, born of a Chinese father and a Japanese mother, carried a Taiwanese passport and needed a reentry visa whenever he left Japan; he had once been banned from playing in a schoolboy tourney because he was not a Japanese citizen. Left-handed pitcher Masaichi Kaneda, Japan's only 400-game winner, who finished his career with Yomiuri, was a naturalized Japanese, one of some 600,000 Korean residents born and raised in Japan. Many of them were the children of wartime laborers forcibly brought in from the Korean Peninsula, fingerprinted, forced to carry special ID cards and otherwise discriminated against.

The 1960s were a time when the Japanese longed particularly for heroes, as the country rose from the ashes of defeat and sought a new kind of national identity. If their laurel wearers turned out to have Korean or Chinese blood, the fact could be conveniently brushed aside. That Rikidozan was, in fact, born in North Korea was an unpleasant and inconvenient item of information that was unreported by the media in elevating him to national hero status.

The word "*gaijin*" (literally: "outside person") is considered demeaning by many foreigners living in Japan (and by some Japanese as well), but it was not always thus. Back in the Meiji Era, according to the *Asahi Shimbun*, the term was used simply to refer to people outside one's immediate circle of acquaintances. Before the Second World War, foreigners in Japan were referred to as *ijin* (different people) or *seiyōjin* (Westerners), then during the postwar occupation, in which several hundred thousand U.S. soldiers were stationed in Japan, many children began to refer to all Caucasian foreigners as *Amerikajin* (Americans), a practice that did not please the British, French, German and Australians living in the country. Gradually, *gaijin* became the word used for white people and *kokujin* or *gaijin* for blacks, but was not applied to other Asians or Arabs.

In the late 1980s, the use of the word "*gaijin*" fell out of favor in newspapers, on TV and in official government documents, replaced instead by the more formal "*gaikokujin*" (person from another country). It was more polite. In July 1991, the Office of the Commissioner of Japanese Baseball began using the "*gaikokujin*," in its contracts and official correspondence. Still, in daily conversation, *gaijin* remained a staple.

Another term used, incidentally, was *suketto*, literally, "one who helps." The implication is that one is there not as a member of the group but as an outsider with special skills or expertise to impart. A *suketto* is hired—indeed often overpaid—to raise the skill or technology level in his field, to refrain from any *wa*-damaging activities, and then to depart quietly so his pupils can practice what they have learned from him. The term had been applied not only to foreign ballplayers but to engineers, technicians, bonds traders and others in the long string of experts Japan has employed to raise its level of competition.

In baseball, the question of ethnicity was sometimes subjected to rather fine distinctions. Wally Yonamine, a second-generation Japanese-American who was born and bred in Hawaii and won a batting title for the Yomiuri Giants, was considered a *gaijin* under NPB rules, while Sachio Kinugasa, a Hiroshima Carp infielder whose mother was Japanese but whose father was a black American, was not. Kinugasa, holder of the consecutive-games-played record in Japan with 2,215 (more than Lou Gehrig, fewer than Cal Ripken Jr.), was born and raised in Japan, graduated from a Japanese high school and held Japanese citizenship.

Among home-grown players, there was also a sort of situational ethic which determined the extent of one's "pure-bloodedness." For example, Kinugasa had a big aggressive American-style swing, normally a no-no in compact form-conscious Japan, but it was reluctantly tolerated by his batting coach because, as he put it, "Kinugasa wasn't really Japanese, so it couldn't be helped." The great Kaneda (who soft-pedaled his Korean background) was notoriously short-tempered and combative; whenever he got into a brawl with an opposing player, writers would shrug and invariably whisper that it was his Korean blood that was causing his behavior because a "*wa*-loving" Japanese would simply never behave that way. The same was true with Hiroshima-born Isao Harimoto, the only player in Japan with 3,000 hits and one of the few Koreans in the game who didn't try to hide his background. Harimoto endured taunts about his ethnicity from his schoolyard days on up. There were more than a few Korean players in the NPB who assumed Japanese names, sang the praises of the Japanese way and did whatever else was necessary to stay safely in the closet, the better to get along with the crowd.

Said one knowledgeable sports writer, "I'd estimate that about 10 percent of 'Japanese' players are people of Korean descent residing in Japan. 99 percent of them hide the fact because, if they are found out, life is hard and troublesome. When you mention their background publicly, you should be prepared to be sued."

This made for some awkward situations. There were NPB stars who could not play for Japan's national Olympic team in 2004 because they were born in Japan of Korean ancestry and had deigned not to apply to become naturalized citizens—perhaps, because like many others in the same situation, they objected to Japanese government laws that awarded citizenship-at-birth solely on the basis of blood, not geography. Yet, at the same time, publishing their names in this context without permission could well result in litigation.

One of the more beloved players and managers in NPB in the latter part of the 20th century was a catacomb Korean, a man who frequently agonized over whether or not to "come out" as he grew older but has yet to make the big move as of this printing.

Pure-blooded Giants cleanup hitter Shigeo Nagashima continually surpassed his home-run hitting teammate Oh in favorite player polls among fans and media, despite far less spectacular statistics (he hit 444 career homers to Oh's 868), and retained his edge in popularity during all the years both men were managers—even though they both met with the same amount of success in that capacity.

Granted, Nagashima also had a more charismatic, bubbly personality than the shy, gentle, oft-morose Taiwanese, but Warren Cromartie, a former Montreal Expo who played for the Giants under Oh, saw his then manager as a victim of discrimination, noting Oh had once been barred from a high school tourney (but not the Koshien Tournament) because he was not a Japanese citizen. "Oh was a *gaijin* like me," he said. "That's the way he presented himself to me. And you could see it in the way some people behaved around him. The guys in the front office treated him like a lackey. But whenever Nagashima came around to visit, they would kiss his ass all over the place."

The concept of Oh's "foreignness," however, changed according to the situation. If Oh had trouble managing his players, then it would be suggested obliquely among insiders that it was because he wasn't really Japanese. However, if some interloper from the country that had defeated Japan in the Pacific War, as it was known, posed a challenge to Oh's single-season home run record of 55, then it was a different story.

Consider what happened to the Hanshin Tigers' American slugger Randy Bass in the last game of the 1985 season, against the Giants in Tokyo. Bass, with a total of 54 home runs, was intentionally walked four times, the Giants catcher uttering an apology in English each time: "I'm sorry." He avoided a fifth base on balls only when he reached out to slap a pitch that was wide of the plate into left field for a fluke single.

Oh, who as chance would have it, was managing the Giants that season, denied that he had ordered his pitcher to walk Bass, but American reliever Keith Comstock, who played for Yomiuri that season, claimed that the team's pitching coach had imposed a fine of $1,000 for every strike his pitchers threw to the Hanshin slugger.

Some Giants apologists tried to argue that the Giants were just protecting a hallowed club record. However, former Giants second base great Shigeru Chiba flatly declared that the team had acted out of good old-fashioned xenophobia.

"Of course, the Yomiuri group doesn't want someone from another team to break a Giants record, but there was a special aversion to an American doing it," he told a reporter.

Retired Tigers slugger Koichi Tabuchi, who, as a Tiger alumnus, should have been rooting for Bass, sympathized with the opposing faction.

"It was us against them." he said years later in a *New York Times* interview. "I played in the same era as Oh and we felt very strongly about his record. At the time, I would confess that people didn't want anyone other than a *Japanese* to break this record."

That incident also came to symbolize American frustration over the U.S.-Japan trade dispute, which was growing particularly intense at the time. MIT fellow David Friedman would later write in the *Los Angeles Times*, "Bass's predicament is perfectly consistent with Japan's fundamental industrial ideology, long enshrined in law and practice, of using foreign contacts to learn about and exploit others' knowledge for the benefit of domestic interests. In Japanese sports, as in technology and trade, buying the best for its own sake counts for little—that's an American conceit."

Ironically, Oh, the manager, figured in two other controversial assaults on his record by *l'etranger* from across the sea. In 2001, American Tuffy Rhodes, a former Houston Astro and Chicago Cub of little distinction—unable, it was said, perhaps unfairly, to handle a real major league fastball—found himself having the season of his life with the Kintetsu Buffaloes. In Japan, thanks to a rigorous weight training program, he was transformed him from a 5'11", 175-pound leadoff hitter into a 210-pound home-run hitting phenom. That season, he reached the 54th homer plateau with a full 12 games left in the season. It was a quest that received little attention in the Japanese press, partly because Rhodes played in the less popular Pacific League. The domestic sports media preferred to print front page stories about local Central League stars, like Giants slugger Hideki Matsui, accomplishing comparatively lesser feats—a sad state of affairs that Ichiro could have certainly sympathized with. There were none of the usual charts and graphs depicting Rhodes's assault on the record, although the sports dailies were full of them the following year when Matsui was on track to have his first 50-home-run season. And despite the fact that he was also hitting .336 at the time with 129 RBIs and leading the Buffaloes to a rare pennant, Rhodes had received not a single endorsement offer or appeared in any ads.

New York Times Tokyo bureau chief Howard French described the situation as "an unsightly reminder that for all the talk of the internationalization of the game, exclusionary provincialism still runs deep in Japanese baseball."

The friendly, outgoing Rhodes said he noted no real prejudice— "occasionally a wider strike zone," he told French. "But as far as the home run race, so far, so good. I haven't gotten any ugly fan mail or anything like that." But then Rhodes came up against the Daiei Hawks in a late-season weekend series in Fukuoka, with the Buffaloes' pennant triumph assured, and alls bets were suddenly off. The Hawks were then managed by Sadaharu Oh, following his tenure as Yomiuri skipper, and history was destined to repeat itself. Of the 18 pitches the Hawks mound corps threw to Rhodes in the Sunday afternoon game, pitifully, only two of them were strikes.

Afterward, Daiei battery coach Yoshiaki Wakana admitted it had all been his doing. "I felt bad because we couldn't win the pennant," he said, "and if Rhodes broke the record I would have felt sorry for Oh. I doubt Oh wants to see Rhodes break the record in front of him. I just didn't want a foreign player to break Oh's record."

Oh's response was, once again, that he had been left out of the loop, that it was been all up to the players to decide. But sportswriters who knew him believed that deep in his heart, Oh, the situational Japanese, wanted Matsui, a full-bore Japanese, to be the one to break his record—if anyone was going to do it. (It might be noted here that when Matsui joined the Giants he was given the uniform number 55, the significance of which absolutely no one missed.)

Observers noted, however, that the general mood appeared less xenophobic than before—perhaps because, it was speculated, Japanese fans had witness the magnanimous welcome accorded to Ichiro in North America, even as he was seriously threatening the single-season hit record of 257 held by George Sisler, as well as Shoeless Joe Jackson's single-season rookie record for hits. As the aforementioned Tabuchi put it, "Back then [i.e., in the '80s] the game seemed like Japanese versus the U.S. But now, with Ichiro and Sasaki, people are watching a lot of American ball and have gained a real appreciation for it. There's no prejudice anymore."

Buffaloes slugging third baseman, the rebellious, porcine Norihiro Nakamura, of the dyed orange hair, was especially livid. "What they did was rude," he said. "This is why Japanese baseball is no good." And whereas former baseball commissioner Takeso Shimoda had been largely silent on the Bass emasculation, the current NPB chief Hiromori Kawashima was quick to denounce the affair. "The decision of the Hawks to walk Rhodes," he declared, "was completely divorced from the essence of baseball, which values the supremacy of fair play."

Rhodes, frustrated at being unable to see anything resembling a strike, lost his rhythm, along with his usual discipline, and failed to hit another out-of-the-park blast. But, finishing at 55 homers, he did qualify for a share of the record. He was also accorded an interesting barrage of end-of-season publicity, thanks in part to French's article, which, according to one *Times* staffer, received a louder protest from the Japanese government than any other story on Japan that the paper ran that year. Although only one national sports daily, the *Tokyo Chunichi Supōtsu*, carried the story of Rhodes's record-tying 55th blast on page one, the *Asahi Shimbun* ran a photo of Rhodes on its front page, as well as on the cover of its weekly feature magazine *Aera*. What's more, Rhodes was an overwhelming choice for the Pacific League MVP and the city of Osaka honored him for his "contributions to the city," giving him a special award for being a "positive representative for the city of Osaka and for heightening sports awareness." It was not clear whether some of this gratitude was due to the fact that he had stopped at tying the record and not broken it.

One could say that the mood *had* indeed changed perceptibly, although not enough for Rhodes to be given the Matsutaro Shoriki award, doled out every year by the Yomiuri Group to the person who contributes the most to Japanese baseball. It was hard to argue there was a more deserving candidate, but the prize went instead to crowd favorite Tsutomu Wakamatsu, the manager of the Yakult Swallows, whose team had defeated the Kintetsu Buffaloes in the Japan Series in five games.

For his part, Rhodes did not forgive and forget. In an interview with Michael Murphy of the *Houston Chronicle*, in February 2003, he said, "I was so frustrated. I still can't speak to him [Oh]. At the All-Star game, if he's one of the coaches, I still couldn't shake his hand or say anything to him. He tampered with the game, which you don't do. But that's the way it is. Things are different over there.

"I just look at it like this: If Sadaharu Oh wants the record that bad, then he can keep it. The record doesn't make the man, the man makes the record. If someone takes that record from him, he's still going to be Sadaharu Oh. I mean, Babe Ruth is still Babe Ruth, right?"

In 2002, one year after Tuffy Rhodes's historic run, the big free-swinging Venezuelan slugger Alex Cabrera, the onetime Arizona Diamondback whose big-league career had been derailed by back problems and who was now playing for the Seibu Lions, made his own sustained assault on Oh's record, one which came to a similarly unsuccessful conclusion, thanks again to the Daiei Hawks pitchers.

Cabrera had hit his 54th home run with eleven games left in the season, tied the record on October 3 with five games left, then came up against the Oh-managed Hawks.

"My pitchers shouldn't think about the record," said Oh in a pregame interview. "They should just pitch like they usually do. It's only a record and I won't die if Cabrera breaks it."

Oh need not have worried.

In the contest that evening, Cabrera was fed a steady diet of un-hittable fastballs, inside high. He was walked twice and sent to first base in another at bat when a pitch caught him flush in the elbow. Cabrera was upset and so was his manager, who ordered him to re-taliate. Later, rounding third and heading home, he slammed full force into the Hawks catcher, elbowing him in the head and nearly knocking him out in the process. In the entire contest, Cabrera saw a total of six strikes, prompting a postgame outburst in which he let fly a string of invective at the Hawks manager.

"Oh didn't want me to break the record," said the voluble Venezue-lan. "It's not professional. He should have made his pitchers throw strikes."

Battery coach Wakana had departed the team in the previous off-season (and no one else in the organization had seen fit to make Delphic pronouncements about the sanctity of Oh's mark, or rather the mark he now shared with Tuffy Rhodes). Yet the hapless man-ager found himself yet again denying he had ordered his pitchers in any way to prevent the *gaijin* from breaking the record.

Oh's supporters rose to his defense.

"No pitcher wants to be the one to give up the record," said the aforementioned Harimoto, himself no stranger to discrimination, in a Sunday morning talk show, "It's understandable they don't want to pitch to him."

But such arguments were drowned out in a Greek chorus of boos by baseball fans who were beginning to feel embarrassed about the Hawks or their manager's inability to fight fair, especially when con-trasted to the outpouring of genuine affection for Ichiro in North America.

As the *Asahi Shimbun*, usually silent about such matters, bluntly put it, "[Oh] refuses to make a clean fight for the sake of an individ-ual record."

Added Seibu batting coach Koju Hirohashi, "I'm so sad if the rest of the world thinks this is Japanese baseball."

When the season ended and Cabrera, like Rhodes, had been stopped at number 55, *Yomiuri Daily News* columnist Jim Allen was moved to write, "From now on they should put an asterisk and a note next to Oh's name in the record book, saying that he repeatedly accepted the unsportsmanlike acts of his players to protect his record."

Some people might argue that America is not entirely a bastion of fair play and equanimity, either. Critics usually cite the hate mail Hank Aaron received while breaking Babe Ruth's career home run mark, or the chilly reception Roger Maris received when he passed the Bambino's single season mark of 60 homers. What would happen if Ichiro hit in 55 straight games, threatening Joe DiMaggio's great record, and then came up against the Yankees in Yankee Stadium, where he is perpetually booed? It is an intriguing question, but given the increased globalization and ethnicity of the U.S. game, the answer is, probably nothing. At the same time, it is also worth mentioning that the most popular sports figure in Japan, if commercial endorsements are any indication, is not Japanese, but an Englishman named David Beckham. Visiting Japan twice in 2003, he was mobbed each time by thousands of adoring fans.

The Gap

A former NPB commissioner named Ichiro Yoshikuni once said, "The teamwork involved in baseball fits in perfectly with the national temper of the Japanese. It did not always fit the temper of *Americans*." He was referring to the myriad of cultural and practical differences that have distinguished the two versions of the two games from each other and have frequently been the cause of conflict when Americans have joined NPB teams. This has been especially so where training and preparation are involved. As American Bobby Rose put it after his first season in Japan, "I ran a lot in the U.S. to get used to the Japanese way, but there was no getting used to it." A common refrain by Americans in their first spring camp is "I know how to get ready for the season and this isn't it." Said Darryl Motley, a former Kansas City Royals outfielder who joined the Chiba Lotte Marines of the Pacific League in 1992, "They don't enjoy the game. It is work to them. Work harder. That's the answer to everything for the Japanese."

Explained Koji Ishijima, interpreter for the Seibu Lions' American players, and later for Hideki Irabu when he was with the Yankees, "The way Japanese professional baseball has evolved is through college and high school baseball. . . . The school systems still stress form in groups, like the military, and baseball is just an extension of that, as are companies, ministries and government bureaucracies. When Americans come into this environment, of course, they get startled."

Americans regularly balk at Japanese-style training camp with its orders and whistles and drop-dead drills and find the games themselves generally overmanaged and slow-moving affairs full of 3–2 counts, sacrifice bunts and lengthy pauses for mulling strategy. The idea that all of this chess could end in a tie, a result that was supposed to send everyone home happy, was also hard for the Americans to swallow.

Warren Cromartie, reaching the end of the line after seven successful seasons with the Yomiuri Giants, summed up his career by saying, "I like Japan, my teammates and my manager, but I can't stand the way they play the game." Phil Bradley, who joined Yomiuri after Cromarite left, declared his team's style of play "incredibly boring." Said Mel Hall, who played outfield for the Chiba Lotte Marines and the Chunichi Dragons, "They practice the game so much that sometimes the enjoyment leaves them. Come late July and August, they're just going through the motions, some of them anyway. They burn out."

Matt Winters, an ex–New York Yankee farmhand who played several season in the '90s for the Nippon Ham Fighters, could not believe some of the things he saw, as he told the *New York Daily News:*

In 1992, we had this little left-handed pitcher on our team, a babyfaced kid. He got hit pretty good in one game so the manager takes him out, calls him down the bench and starts hollering at him. The next thing, he grabs a helmet and—boom—I'm not talking a little tap, man. He took the helmet and rapped the guy right on the head with it.

I was kind of watching, thinking, You've got to be kidding me, and all the Japanese players were just sitting up staring ahead like nothing was happening. I kept on watching, and, sure enough, he grabbed the helmet and smoked him in the head again. I looked at my interpreter and asked, "He's not going to try to do that to me, is he? Because if he comes up to me with a helmet, I'm going to grab a helmet myself."

But for a player to stand up to a manager in that case would have been considered inappropriate behavior and actually a sign of weakness. Players have to accept authority. It is the only way the team can achieve *wa*. At the same time, it is understood that foreigners, uninitiated as they are in *wa*'s Eleusinian mysteries, were to be spared such abuse. Serious injury to both parties might ensue, along with financial loss, since most ex-major leaguers came in with sizable guaranteed contracts. Thus, while his teammates are sweating through tortuous pregame drills, often the American import is off by himself, doing his own thing.

The fact is, a great many do not succeed, whatever their treatment, and the history of American participation in the Japanese game is dotted with spectacular failures. Not a few *gaijin* are in Japan because they have one or more defects in their game. Some can hit, but can't run or field. Big-swinging American stars often flop, while unknown reserves who work hard to adjust can succeed. Those who don't make the effort or are unable to adapt themselves to Japanese ways are prime candidates for early defections.

Don Money, a multiple Gold Glove winner, left the Kintetsu Buffaloes after 29 games in 1984 complaining of poor living conditions and a dirty locker room. Teammate Rich Duran soon followed suit, in protest over the harsh workouts the coaches put him through. That same year Jim Tracy, who went on to manage the Dodgers, left in disgust over the way his manager was, or rather, was not using him.

Ponkōtsū (Jalopy)

One of the more memorable cases involved former MLB star Kevin Mitchell, an ectomorphic slugger capable of titanic performances. In 1989, for example, playing with the San Francisco Giants, he was voted the National League's Most Valuable Player after hitting 47 home runs, driving in 125 runs and leading his team to a National League pennant.

He also had a history of violence and a reputation for being lazy, moody and indifferent. His MLB career statistics included 234 home runs, one suspension by the league president for disciplinary reasons and two arrests for assault. He was traded four times.

Prior to the 1995 season, his batting skills on the decline, Mitchell had declared his intention to retire. But then the Fukuoka, Kyushu-based Daiei Hawks offered him $4.5 million to play for one year. At the time, it was the highest single-season salary offer in the history of baseball in Japan, and Mitchell, who was not a complete fool, accepted.

In preseason media hoopla, Mitchell was hailed as the best *suketto* in the history of NPB. And in his first game, he seemed ready to live up to the billing, hitting a grand slam home run and sending Hawks fans into fits of ecstasy. In a postgame interview, he professed an undying love for Japan.

"I'm really enjoying this," he gushed. "Everyone here is so polite. I really admire the way the players carry themselves."

But it was all downhill after that. Within two months, Mitchell was on a plane back to the United States, now proclaiming that "Japanese are dirty. I really dislike them."

The problem ostensibly was an injury, or to be more precise, Mitchell's insistence that he was suffering from one and the inability of physicians to find it. After playing 28 games in which he hit six homers and drove in 19 runs, Mitchell had complained of a pain in his knee which he said he had twisted in practice going after a fly ball. However, an orthopedic physician at Fukuoka University commissioned by the Hawks performed an MRI and, unable to locate any afflicted areas, pronounced the Hawks' big *gaikokujin* fit to play baseball. Mitchell disputed the test results. He insisted that his knee hurt too badly for him to continue suiting up and demanded he be allowed to go home to the States for a second opinion. The Daiei front office rejected this request and ordered him to the farm as punishment for his intransigence. Mitchell refused to go, naturally, and an impasse resulted.

The folks at Daiei were not totally unaware of Mitchell's reputation as a troublemaker. They suspected that Mitchell had been jaking it ever since he arrived in camp three weeks late with well over 200 pounds on his 5′9″ puffer belly frame, but claiming that he was in tip-top shape and thus did not need to train with the rest of the team. They kept silent, but decided all the same to have him followed. They discovered that Mitchell had been out partying until the morning hours on the night before a game in Fukuoka. On another occasion in April, he had been spied drinking at a military club at Yokota Air Force Base before a game at Tokorozawa, home of the Seibu Lions, one he had sat out with a cold. The news of that latter episode was published in *Friday* magazine, accompanied by the screaming head-line "*4 Oku Yen no Ponkōtsū. Nameru na.*" (A 400,000,000 Yen Jalopy! Thumbing His Nose At Everyone!")

At this, Mitchell went ballistic. He accused the Hawks of spying on him, which was sort of stating the obvious because that was exactly what they had been doing. Daiei responded by refusing to pay him his salary for the month of May, estimated at nearly $400,000, upon which Mitchell packed up his suitcases—all several dozen of them— and returned to the United States. Both parties later sued each other, unsuccessfully.

Devil Man

The next American after Mitchell to give cross-cultural relations a black eye was Brian Warren, a late-inning right-handed relief pitcher who toiled for the Chiba Lotte Marines. He was guilty of a number of transgressions in his two years with the team, acts which earned him the nickname "Devil Man." He once described his own team to a reporter as "second rate shit." Another famous Warrenism was "I can't wait to get out of here." In 2000, in what many consider his crowning achievement, he became the first person in the history of Japanese baseball to be fined for giving the middle finger.

Warren had a habit of scuffing up the ball to make it break more sharply, a practice clearly forbidden by league rules on either side of the Pacific. Opposing players frequently complained about Warren's treatment of the baseballs they were trying to hit. One night in June 2000, a Seibu Lions coach spied Warren making a rather large abrasion on the cover of the ball between innings and demanded his head from the umpires, or at least enforcement of the penalty for scuffing or defacing a ball, which was ejection. However, since Warren had already been taken out of the game by his manager for strategic reasons, the protest was moot.

To the Japanese mindset, being caught cheating this way was no small thing. True, various forms of institutionalized cheating were, if not sanctioned exactly, accepted as social realities—witness the frequent political bribery, graft and violations of campaign contributions law; the regularity with which corporate agents stole industrial and trade secrets; and the fracturing of tax and accounting standards to disguise the extent of post-Bubble disasters in the corporate and financial worlds. But getting caught red-handed stealing signs was something worthy of front page headlines in the sports dailies. So was defacing a baseball, especially given the respect, if not reverence, for the equipment demanded by Buddhist and *bushido* tradition. It was especially unforgivable in an outsider who was supposedly there because of his superior skills.

In Warren's case, public contrition was the only acceptable remedy. The next day, however, rather than grovel in apology, he arrived at the ballpark with a glove he had fitted out with a screwdriver, a fork, and a tape cutter sticking out of various gaps in the leather. The joke worked, and Warren was temporarily out of hot water.

The next time Seibu and Lotte met in July, and Warren was put in the game, Seibu manager Osamu Higashio made repeated requests of the home plate umpire to check the balls that Warren had thrown, attempting in the process to disrupt his concentration. In retaliation, Warren ended his game-saving performance that night by stepping off the mound and flipping the middle-finger salute to Higashio in the Lions dugout.

Now, not all Japanese understand the seriousness of that gesture.

There is no taboo against its use in the media (nor for that matter is there against the word "fuck" and its *katakana* equivalent *"fakku"*; it's just a word they hear repeatedly in Hollywood movies). But Higashio understood what Warren was trying to convey and filed a formal complaint. Warren was subsequently reprimanded and his place in history assured.

Darryl May

Darryl May broke his share of taboos as well. May was a left-handed pitcher who had joined the Osaka-based Hanshin Tigers in 1998 at the age of 27, after a brief and unremarkable stint in MLB bullpens. Playing for what was hands down the worst team in baseball, perhaps in all of Central League history, May compiled a respectable enough record of 4–9 with an ERA of 3.40 in his first year, but became the subject of constant criticism when the new manager Katsuya Nomura—stepfather of agent Don Nomura (see Chapter 6)—took over the following year.

Nomura was Japan's greatest catcher. His 657 career home runs, while playing mostly for the Nankai Hawks in their tiny park (280 down the lines, 350 to dead center), ranked second only to Sadaharu Oh's total of 868. Nomura retired in 1980, after 26 years as a player, and went on to pilot the Yakult Swallows to three Japan Championships in 1993, 1995 and 1997. Nicknamed "Moose" for his hulking Berraesque physique and droopjaw mien, he had an almost disdainful attitude toward his players. His philosophy was common in Japanese sports: "Don't praise your players. Otherwise they will get big heads and slack off."

While his stepson Don was busy paving the way for Japanese stars to emigrate to MLB, the elder Nomura himself was not overly crazy about American players with big egos, fat paychecks and what he saw as a lackadaisical attitude toward practice and discipline.

Nomura axed many American players in his long managerial career. Perhaps the most famous axee was Larry Parrish, a former Detroit Tigers star who had played for the Swallows in 1989, the year before Nomura took over as manager, leading the league in home runs with 42 and finishing second in RBIs with 103. Parrish expected a fat new contract for 1990; instead he was fired by the incoming Nomura, who criticized the aging first baseman's defense, which, in truth, was not helped by a gimpy knee.

"I was completely stunned," said Parrish, who played every game. "I just had the best year of my life and they fire me. I couldn't believe it."

Then there was Tom O'Malley, who helped Nomura's Swallows win a Japan Championship in 1995, hitting .302 with 31 home runs and 87 RBIs in the regular season and winning both the Central League and Japan Series MVPs. He sparkled again in 1996, marking the sixth year in a row he had hit over .300, but then was suddenly given his walking papers, Nomura citing O'Malley's poor fielding, advancing age (37) and slowness afoot.

Rex Hudler, who in 1993 hit .300 with 13 homers in 410 at bats and played consistently good infield defense in his first year was also invited not to return. Hudler spoke for most Swallows foreigners when he told a reporter, "Nomura was one of the strangest managers I have ever played for. I said hello to him every day when I arrived at the ballpark for a solid month during one stretch. Sometimes, he'd grunt. But most of the time, he ignored me. He just stood there frowning."

Midway through the 1999 season, the Tigers were once again buried in last place, 14 games under .500. Nomura cited May's inconsistent pitching, which stood at 6–7 with a 4.25 ERA at the halfway point, as one of the primary causes.

Now, moderation of temper was not May's strongest suit. On July 18, 1999, he had been suspended for six games for bumping an umpire. And while serving his suspension, he took a brief team-approved trip to Guam to have a painfully swollen jaw treated by an American dental specialist living there. May's girlfriend Heather accompanied him, a fact not missed by the ever-vigilant sports press.

When May returned, Nomura sent him to the farm team. Nomura complained that because May was in Guam, he had missed two whole days of practice and was therefore not physically ready to pitch. Besides, Nomura said, the Tigers "didn't need any foreign pitchers."

May, who had been eager to return and claim his place in the starting rotation, refused to go. He appealed to the president of the Tigers, but when the executive sided with Nomura, May requested his release. When that too was denied, May took matters into his own hands. He wrote a letter to all Hanshin fans and had it published in a newspaper, handing out his own English release in the belief that his interpreter might water down any remarks in Japanese. It essentially accused Nomura of being a xenophobe.

On August 6, 1999, I officially asked the organization to release me. My request was denied by the Hanshin Tigers. This disappoints me greatly as I feel my request for my release was a valid one. I feel that our manager, Nomura, is against having foreign players as part of his team. I feel as though he had not treated me as a professional nor has he given me the same respect I have shown him. Due to this, I have decided if asked I will not return for a third season next year to the Tigers, as I feel it would not be in my best interests professionally or personally. Once again, I asked for my release because I felt it would be in the best interests of the ball club as well as myself. I want the fans to know that I thank them for their generosity and kindness and support towards me. I have truly loved playing in Japan because of them. It is going to be difficult to forget the Hanshin Tigers fans as they are the best fans in the world, but it is obvious to me now that the club does not have belief in my ability. Thanks again to the fans and the press that have been so supportive of me over the past two years.

That certainly got everyone's attention. One of the great sins for a player in Japan to commit is to publicly criticize team management. And May's criticism was about as public as you could get. Both English and Japanese versions of his letter were plastered across the front pages of all the morning sports dailies, while evening TV news programs gave them prominent play. It was an extraordinary public embarrassment for the Tigers and there were loud calls for May's head. The *Nikkan Supōtsu* ran a huge headline quoting a furious Nomura saying, "*May Yameru!*" (May Get the Hell Out). "*Gocha gocha iu nara yameru*" (If you're going to shoot off your big mouth, just quit), ran the subhead. A chagrined front office executive exploded at May for airing the team's dirty laundry in the Japanese media. It was something that just wasn't done. "If you don't want to play for this team," he said, echoing the sports sheet, "and if you can't keep quiet, just quit."

Unfortunately for all concerned, quitting was not an option for May because in the event he did turn in his uniform and glove, according to his contract, the Tigers would not be obligated to pay him for the rest of the season and that came to a considerable amount of money.

Although May had some sympathizers—Yujiro Fujiwara, a 59-year-old independent contractor and Tigers fan, was quoted by the *Nikkan* as saying, "Nomura should not be criticizing his players to the press. If I were May I'd do the same thing"—his actions amounted to the scandal of the year.

Hanshin suspended May and threatened to keep him in limbo for the rest of the season, purely out of spite for embarrassing the team, but they eventually wearied of having to deal with the matter and granted him the release that he wished for.

But May wasn't finished yet. A free agent, he signed on with the Yomiuri Giants, the Tigers' archrival. Under manager Nagashima, the man who had overshadowed Nomura in the press for so many years, he responded with his best season ever, beating the Tigers several times. He also made a point of praising Nagashima at every opportunity; the implied contrast was lost neither on Nomura nor the fans.

"Nomura said hello to me about three times all the while I was there," May told the Yomiuri newspaper's Ken Marantz, "But Nagashima is very friendly. He talks to me all the time."

May finished the year with a mark of 12–7 and an ERA of 2.95. (The following year he was 10–8 with a 4.13 ERA.) He also added injury to insult in June when he nearly beaned Tigers batter Yutaka Wada with a pitched ball (in retaliation for Hanshin batters repeatedly stepping out of the batter's box as he began his delivery)—earning himself a second suspension and a 500,000-yen fine. So infuriated was May at this that he lashed out at Japanese baseball and the media with a flurry of F-words, which were then printed in the headlines of several sports dailies by obliging editors.

May's relations with the press reached a nadir on March 8, 2001, when he left practice early complaining of a sore thigh. Emerging from the training room, he found himself surrounded by querying reporters who wondered if he weren't jaking it. He sprayed spittle on a photographer's camera and unleashed another flurry of *fakku* words, which also wound up in the dailies.

Enough was apparently enough. According to one report, May was offered a three-year $10 million contract by Yomiuri, and he turned it down to return to MLB with the Kansas City Royals.

"I didn't grow up wanting to play Japanese baseball," May told the *Kansas City Star*. "I was ready to come back home after the first season, but the money kept getting better. I just felt four years was enough."

Mike DiMuro

Not all the tales of woe involved imported players: Take the strange case of Mike DiMuro, a young American umpire headed for the big leagues, who was brought out to Japan by Central League officials to help raise the level of umpiring in NPB, which, it was universally agreed by all who had experienced it, was sorely in need of a boost. Unlike in the U.S., there are no umpiring schools in Japan and arbiters were hired on the basis of their performance in brief tryouts and their personal connections. They were often failed ex-ballplayers, which was perhaps the main reason for their humble place in the general scheme of things NPB.

Indeed, perhaps what separated Japanese baseball from its American counterpart more than anything else was the low respect accorded arbiters in Japan. There, umpires are regularly pushed and shoved around by the managers, coaches and players with impunity—or very light penalties: a 50,000 yen (a little more than

$400) fine, a three-day suspension, or, often, just a "severe warning" to the attacking parties. Given the right circumstances, they can be intimidated into changing their rulings.

Consider, for example, a game that took place in May 1996 at the Tokyo Dome between the Seibu Lions and the home team Nippon Ham Fighters. In the fourth inning, a Lions outfielder hit a drive to deep right center that cleared the fence, but popped back onto the field after striking a railing. When the second-base umpire signaled a home run, the Ham Fighter manager Toshiharu Ueda came running out of the dugout and, angrily man-handling the umpire, argued that the ball had hit the top of the fence. Perhaps, in part, because Ueda had once (in the seventh game of the 1979 Japan Series) pulled his team off the field for more than an hour to protest an umpire's call, all four arbiters conferred in midfield and decided to change the ruling from a home run to a double. This, of course, brought the Lions manager Osamu Higashio screaming out of the dugout to do some protesting of his own—which he punctuated with a stiff forearm to the chief umpire's throat.

Eventually, after considering which manager had more stature, who had argued the hardest and what the odds were that the cheering section would storm the field if they didn't like the ruling, the compromise was struck—in the true spirit of *wa*. The hit was adjudged to be a "ground-rule triple." There were no ejections, only a small fine, and a suspension dealt with later. The accuracy of the call never came into play—not even after Higashio stormed into the umpire's room to launch a postgame assault on one of them, an attack which included a swift kick to the shin. (When informed of the incident, Ham Fighters manager Ueda remarked, without a trace of irony, "*Shiai no ato wa ikenai*": "It's not acceptable to do that sort of thing *after* the game.")

Such an occurrence would have been unimaginable in the U.S., where the umpire's power is absolute. Any assault could result in a year's—if not a lifetime's—suspension.

Thus, it was inevitable, given this environment, that the first American umpire to work in the Japan pro leagues would meet with disaster. DiMuro, a 29-year-old AAA level umpire when he got the call in 1997, thought that working a year in Japan before its famously huge crowds in domed stadiums would be good preparation for the U.S. big leagues.

Yet, with typical obtuseness, no one in the league office saw fit to brief him on the differences in Japanese ball—to tell him, for example, that the strike zone in Japan was historically somewhat higher or that the phrase "Kill the Umpire" was taken more seriously than it was in the U.S. Worse yet, no one in the Central League offices sought to caution the managers and the coaches that violence against the umpires would no longer be tolerated. Perhaps they were afraid to, given the fact that they were ranked not much higher in the food chain than the umpires themselves.

Only days into the season, DiMuro found himself the subject of attack from Japanese managers like the churlish Katsuya Nomura, who did not like his concept of the strike zone. Said Nomura, "This man is ruining Japanese baseball." During one game in May, DiMuro found himself being rushed by a small group of Chunichi Dragons, angry over a called strike. The batter, a beefy first baseman named Taiho, led the charge, slugging DiMuro in the chest, pushing him back and nearly knocking him over. Dragon Leo Gomez was forced to come to the clearly shaken DiMuro's rescue. The penalty handed down by the league for the attack was, predictably enough, a mere letter of reprimand.

The incident highlighted again what were often gross differences in the disciplinary standards for foreigners and Japanese. One might ask why Benito Galvez was suspended for half a season for throwing a ball at an umpire and *missing*, while Taiho, who actually succeeded in making contact, received only a warning. Ditto for numerous other Japanese managers, coaches and players who have drawn blood from the umpires and received only light punishments. (We might also mention Kazuhiro Kiyohara, who once threw his bat at a pitcher and was barely reprimanded.)

However, when all is said and done, one or two things are clear. It is easier for the Japanese baseball establishment to punish outsiders than it is to discipline members of its inner circle. Foreign players dwell at the bottom of pro baseball's pecking order, right below the umpires. That means there is nothing lower in the Japanese game than a foreign umpire.

Dismayed by the lack of support, the American League, which owned DiMuro's contract, "ordered" him to return to the States because it was "not safe to umpire in Japan."

GAIJIN KANTOKU

I went there thinking I would be there for many years. Instead I wound up being the only manager to be fired in both the U.S. and Japan.

BOBBY VALENTINE, NOVEMBER 1995

A S A VEHICLE OF SOCIAL CHANGE, BASEBALL FELL SOMEWHERE BE-tween sumo and soccer in Japan. Sumo, dating back cen-turies, was the most inflexible. It was a world of feudal hierarchy where wrestlers wore top knots, scant *mawashi* in the ring and *yukata* outside of it. Foreigners who entered this world were ex-pected to thoroughly conform—to eat Japanese food, to master the Japanese language and to obey the ages-old rules of medieval servi-tude, which included tidying up the senior wrestlers after they had used the toilet. (Considering the girth of some of these behemoths, the custom was, in certain cases, of practical use.) Hawaiian wrestler Jesse Kualahula, known as Takamiyama, overcame such difficulties to forge a long career and in 1980 became the first Westerner to open up his own sumo stable or *heya* in Japan. He enjoyed contin-ued success with both Hawaiian and Japanese *rikishi*, while still ad-hering carefully to the age-old customs.

Soccer, introduced in the mid-20th century, had no discernible culture of its own in Japan. Numerous foreign coaches and players were imported to teach the game much as Western experts were imported to Japan in the early Meiji Era to help modernize the country. The coach of the Japanese national team, which had a good run in the 2002 World Cup, co-hosted by Japan and the ROK, was French; his successor Zico was from Brazil.

Baseball, imported from America in the 1870s, had been Japanized to a degree with its incorporation of the martial arts values of *doryoku* and *konjō*, as well as *wa*, but it was more flexible than sumo in dealing with foreigners. *Gaijin* players, especially those with big names in North America, were usually given special dispensation to train as they pleased and foreign managers were allowed in as long as they did not veer too far from the Japanese orthodoxy.

But while hundreds of foreign ballplayers have crossed the Pacific to play in Japan, only a handful of foreign coaches and managers have ever enjoyed gainful employment there. Although Japanese front office executives have long recognized that there may be something to be gained by employing *gaikoku shunojin* (foreign heads), they have also worried that the imposition of Western teachings might have a corrupting influence on cherished traditions, not to mention team harmony.

Familiar enough with the society to be keenly aware of the need for group harmony, two Japanese-Americans had reasonably successful careers as managers in Japan in the early postwar era: Yoshio "Kaiser" Tanaka and Tadashi "Bozo" Wakabayashi from Hawaii; the latter managed the 1958–59 Hanshin Tigers to consecutive second-place finishes. Wally Yonamine, a *nisei* from Honolulu who had played ten years with the Yomiuri Giants, managed the Chunichi Dragons and won a Central League pennant in 1974.

On the other hand, Joe Lutz, a former Cleveland Indians coach who was hired to manage the Hiroshima Carp in 1975, lasted barely a month amidst complaints he was trying to convert his players to American eating, bathing and umpire-baiting habits. Don Blasingame, ex-MLB star and longtime player and coach in Japan, lasted a year and a half managing the Hanshin Tigers, weathering constant caviling by the city's obstreperous blue-collar fans that he played the wrong people and did not hold enough team meetings.

Hanshin fans became livid when Blazer inserted an American

named Dave Hilton into his starting lineup over a Japanese rookie, Yukinobu Okada, who had been a nationally popular college star. Whenever Hilton came to bat, they showered him with abuse. Blazer and Hilton received hate mail and death threats and were faced with angry mobs outside the park. An enraged crowd of fans once nearly overturned a taxi carrying Hilton's pregnant wife. Hilton, who found himself unable to play well in such an environment, was released by the front office in midseason, while Blazer, upset over not being consulted on the signing of Hilton's replacement, resigned. Blasingame went on to manage the Nankai Hawks to two second division finishes, in 1981 and 1982.

Against this history, the news that the Chiba Lotte Marines had hired well-known MLB manager Bobby Valentine to run their team in 1995 was greeted by lovers of *Nihon puro-yakyū* with more than one set of raised eyebrows.

Valentine's Day

Valentine had a proven record of success in MLB. He was chosen by the Associated Press as American League Manager of the Year in 1986, when he led the Texas Rangers from the cellar to second place in the Western Division. He had been offered the job of helmsman for the Marines while he was working with the Triple A Norfolk, Virginia, franchise and waiting for an MLB managerial slot to open up.

A dyed-in-the-wool Pacific League doormat, Lotte had embarked on a radical rebuilding program under the leadership of new general manager Tatsuro Hirōka, one of the more respected thinkers in the Japanese game. A former shortstop who had a distinguished career with the Yomiuri Giants in the '50s and '60s, he had gone on to win several pennants as field manager for the Yakult Swallows, then later the Seibu Lions. A trim bespectacled man with a shrewd analytical mind—and the ability to physically mimic any player's hitting and fielding style and highlight its flaws—he had become famous for his own particular system of *kanri yakyū*, one in which he oversaw every facet of his players' existence, including their diet and sex lives.

His practices had been famous for their relentless season-long intensity—excessive even by Japan standards. He was a cold, hubristic man, loathed and feared by many of his players, but the bottom line was that his teams usually won. Said a former ace pitcher for the Lions, "I hated the SOB. But if you wanted to win, his way was the best way to do it."

Hirōka's appointment as general manager was something of a departure for Japan because most teams chose their GMs from pools of executives in the parent company, regardless of whether or not they knew anything about baseball. But Lotte's Akio Shigemitsu, the Ivy League–educated "deputy owner" of the team, was tired of always being on the bottom rung of the baseball ladder. So he had opted for innovation to extract his Marines from the morass of mediocrity in which they were mired.

It had been Hirōka's idea to import a *gaijin kantoku* to emphasize the fresh beginning Lotte was making. His master plan was to model the organization after an MLB franchise as much as was reasonably practical within the limits of the Japanese ethos, creating what he called a "revolution of change" within the organization. He had been studying Valentine for some time and thought he could use him to modernize certain aspects of his operation. He liked Valentine's track record and was particularly impressed with his philosophy for handling the pitchers, to wit: Valentine would not leave a pitcher in longer than 135 pitches per game and always gave his starters at least four days of rest between outings. It was a philosophy that had been adopted in the 1970s to cope with new levels of offense in the game and the vastly higher pitch totals this had caused. Hirōka thought it superior to the tired practice of many Japanese teams of using an ace pitcher in a variety of roles, without proper rest.

At the same time, becoming the first person with MLB managing experience to pilot a Japanese team appealed to Valentine's sense of history, as did the challenge of taking a weak franchise like Lotte and building it up. He agreed to a basic two-year pact, worth half a million dollars annually with special bonuses for fourth, third, second and first place. He would bring along his own personal staff to help him implement his program. Included were batting coach Tom Robson, who utilized a special stop-motion photo technique for analyzing a batter's swing, and Tom House, Nolan Ryan's pitching instructor, who was also the author of several important books on pitching published in the United States.

More important, Hirōka had given Valentine "full authority."

"If you don't like the coaches I give you," he said, "tell me and I'll have them replaced."

He added that, of course, Valentine would be expected to listen to the coaches' input, because they too had valuable experience and much to teach. That was why they were there in the first place.

After all, wasn't the idea to "blend" big-league baseball and Japanese baseball?

"Right," said Valentine.

"When Hirōka told me I could run the club my own way," he said later, "I just assumed that most things would fall under my jurisdiction or that once things started to jell, management would see the wisdom of a different way."

Those were, of course, famous last words.

Conflict

Almost from the beginning, despite good will and earnest intentions on both sides, there was conflict. Hirōka had arranged for the Marines to do their spring training in Peoria, Arizona, starting on February 1—instituting a no-drinking, no-smoking policy for the duration. Valentine had no problems with that per se, but he programmed an American-style day, which meant 10:00 A.M. to 1:30 P.M. on the practice field, allowing the players to spend the rest of their time at the golf course or swimming pool. Since they would train every single day, not four on and one off as most Japanese clubs did, three hours at a time in the blinding Arizona sun was quite enough, Valentine asserted.

This was something that was difficult for Hirōka's handpicked coaches to comprehend, accustomed as they were to working morning, afternoon and evening in camp back home. To them, Valentine's way, which was the way of every U.S. major-league team, resembled pregame warm-ups in Japan during the season.

One of the coaches was named Shozo Eto, who came with his own special pedigree. A graduate of Tokyo's elite Keio University in 1966, he had played and coached with the Yomiuri Giants for a number of years. Short, stocky, energetic and enthusiastic, his area of expertise was infield defense, which he had picked up directly from Hirōka, regarded as one of the best shortstops in NPB history. At Hirōka's request, Eto had spent six weeks in the autumn of 1994 drilling Marine players from morning to night in preparation for the next year's season, in sessions studiously (if skeptically) attended by Valentine. Eto, it was said, considered himself a "de facto" head coach, even though he did not actually have the title or the rank.

The other handpicked Hirōka assistant was Takao Obana, a tall, broad-shouldered former pitcher of some standing who had played under Hirōka with the Yakult Swallows when that team won the 1978 Japan Championship. Obana had left a comfortable job as a baseball commentator for Fuji TV's *Pro-Yakyū Nyūsu* to become a field lieutenant for his former boss.

Both men, who led a staff of six Japanese coaches, were confused by the abbreviated practice schedule under Valentine and relayed their concerns to Hirōka, who called Valentine to explain certain facts of baseball life in Japan.

"In the U.S.," he said, "you all have a farm system of several tiers, from Triple A on down. You have about 200 players under contract. By the time you get these players to the major leagues, they are already polished for the most part. But Japanese baseball is different. We have only one farm team, so we need extra time in camp to work on our various batting, throwing and fielding skills, not to mention team play."

Valentine, the impressions of autumn camp fresh in his mind, nodded in understanding and then he said no.

"If you increase practice time," he said, "the players will get tired. When you get tired, you pick up bad habits. I don't want to force them and I don't want to wear them out before the season begins.

Sometimes more isn't always better. They will round into form at their own pace."

"Well, then, what if they volunteer?" asked Hirōka.

"In that case, we'll give those who volunteer 30 extra minutes."

Perhaps Valentine was just being stubborn. But perhaps he had already learned that in NPB the word for "voluntary" was often a synonym for "compulsory" or "get your ass in gear or else." His refusal to allow any more practice signaled the start of Round One in what would prove to be a season-long battle. That evening, with Hirōka's assent and without telling Valentine, Eto and Obana began nighttime training outside the hotel where the team was staying. It took Valentine three days to notice the figures in the hotel garden. There, silhouetted in the desert moonlight, were batters taking hundreds of shadow swings and pitchers working on their pitching motion by snapping towels.

In the interests of team harmony, he decided to acquiesce and began participating himself.

There was also a problem with organization. In his meetings with coaches, Valentine would lay out a schedule for the next day, but then the next day would come and the manager would change his mind.

"I like to wing it," Valentine explained, "because conditions change from day to day." But to Eto and Obana, who were raised in a system where punctuality was king, inchoate planning a sin and every detail *always* planned out in advance from Day One, it was distracting and, they thought, inconsiderate. They tried to rationalize and shrug off Valentine's behavior as that of an outsider who was trying to establish his authority. At least, *that* was something they could understand.

Chiba was a city of 900,000 people on Tokyo Bay an hour's train ride from the capital center. Barely noticed by visitors on the way to and from Narita Airport, it was distinguished by its ocean winds, its gangsters and immigrant workers, and its proximity to the enormously popular Tokyo Disneyland. The nearby Makuhari Trade Pavilion, built on swamp land, had the distinction of being the venue where a display of American rice was once ordered removed by the Japanese government because its foreign taste was regarded as unsuitable for Japanese taste buds (as, no doubt, was its selling price, which was substantially lower than the government-run rice association would prefer to allow).

Chiba Marine Stadium, a cheap new windswept 30,000-seat structure on the outskirts of the city where the Marines played, was seldom filled, partly because of the oceanside chill that permeated the stands, especially in the early spring, but also because of the wretched baseball team that normally played there. The Lotte Chiba Marines, returning home with their new manager to start the exhibition season, were hoping that was all about to change.

The Japanese media had never seen anyone like Bobby Valentine. He eschewed the fancy cars and chauffeur-driven limousines preferred by most managers and bicycled to the park from his nearby apartment. In pregame practice one could often find him by the outfield stands chatting up the Lotte *ōendan*. Unlike most Japanese managers who stood imperiously on the sidelines during workouts, arms folded, watching silently, he would usually be out on the field among his players, encouraging them, teaching them, leading by example— all of which made for colorful photo opportunities.

Valentine seemed made for the Japanese media. He was a broad-shouldered and bronzed 45-year-old in excellent physical condition, with a full head of stylishly graying hair and a telegenic smile. He was *always* accessible for interviews. What's more, he was intoxicated with Japanese culture. He ate raw fish and noodles. He studied Japanese and spoke it as much as he possibly could, referring often to the dictionary he carried with him. It was not unusual to see him stop in the street on the way home to rap about baseball with fans and reporters.

"He's not aloof like other Japanese managers," gushed one Lotte fan in a typical bromide. "When he comes forth after a win, he's ready to talk." In fact, Valentine was one of the few foreigners to do the "1,000 fungo drill"—just to show that he could. And he did all 1,000, not one-third, or one-half, the way most modern players did. Moreover, he was still standing when he was finished. His interpreter, who had batted out all thousand balls, was overwhelmed.

"He was something," he said in amazement, "he really opened his heart to Japan," he said in amazement.

Known in Japan as *"Barentain,"* Valentine kicked off the season in an early-season commercial for Compaq Computers, which he planned to use to analyze the comparative strength and weaknesses of the opposition. One TV spot showed him sitting in his nondescript stadium office in front of his desktop with a message in gold letters appearing on the screen:

"WE WILL CHANGE BASEBALL"

Perhaps he was referring to customs like the 1,000-ground-ball drill, an exercise he privately believed to be "a colossal waste of time," despite the experience's salutary effects on his "spirit" and cross-cultural understanding. "It might be good for mental training," he said, but "after the first 500 balls, my fielding technique collapsed."

The new slogan, however, would not prove to be a self-fulfilling prophecy.

The team that Valentine inherited was not as bad as it had looked in the previous year's standings. In fact, coming as he did from MLB, where most people looked down on Japanese baseball, Valentine was surprised at just how talented his players were. He thought that Hideki Irabu could throw as well as anybody in the world and that the pitching in general was comparable to the major leagues. The men on his staff, he believed, had better control than most MLB pitchers and, in his estimation, they were all much better fielders. Moreover, the catchers didn't just block balls in the dirt, as MLB backstops did, they *caught* them, and although the outfielders generally didn't have the range or the arm power of major leaguers, they were technically more proficient. Valentine had also come to the opinion that his baserunners were better base stealers as well. Infielders Koichi Hori and Kiyoshi Hatsushiba, among others, he thought capable of becoming stars in the big leagues.

"There was this universal contempt for the Japanese leagues back home," he said, recalling his early weeks, "but I was truly taken aback at how good they were."

Valentine had also brought with him *gaijin* reinforcements in the form of left-handed pitcher Eric Hillman, smooth-hitting and smooth-fielding first baseman Julio Franco and hard-swinging outfielder Pete Incaviglia. He pronounced the '95 Marines as being "just two players shy of being like my Texas team." ("Unfortunately," he added, "those two players were Nolan Ryan and Ruben Sierra.") Valentine thought that two years was not an unreasonable amount of time to turn the Marines into champions of Japan. And so did Tom House.

The Marines got off to a miserable start of 8–14–1 in the first month of April, and quickly the sniping began. Some critics predictably blamed the team's poor performance on the low-key U.S. style training camp. But *inside baseball* had also become an issue. There were disagreements over when to steal, when to hit and run, when to swing away and, among other things, how much time to give a relief pitcher to warm up before coming into the game (not very much, according to Valentine, who was worried about preserving his pitchers' arms; a lot, according to pitching coach Obana, who insisted that because of the psychological makeup of the Japanese athlete, his relievers needed more preparation to get ready than Americans did).

Also, Obana could not understand Valentine's insistence that his pitchers throw a fastball away on a 2–2 count, when everyone knew that for the Japanese moundsmen, with their great control, forkballs and sliders shading the corners of the plate were just the ticket to tempt a batter fearful of being called out on strikes, especially if a big free-swinging *gaijin* slugger was at the plate. It was a strategy that succeeded time and time again in Japan. But Valentine, with logic that was equally difficult to refute, said, "What if the batter didn't swing? Why would a pitcher intentionally risk that happening and a ball being called, thereby putting himself in the hole with a count of 3–2? He'd just be hurting himself. A really smart pitcher wouldn't do something like that." (Obana could only reply, "He would if he was pitching in Japan.")

The most frequent arguments involved the bunt. With a runner on first and no out, for example, using the sacrifice bunt was a no-brainer to most Japanese managers. It was regarded as a vital offensive tool. They believed it created the best possible chance to score that all-important first run, which is why statistics showed that Japanese teams regularly sacrificed nearly three times as often as major leaguers did. To many American managers, however, sacrificing in that situation was just giving up an out to the opposition. They preferred to let their players hit away. It was also thought important for a manager to give his players room to maneuver, to display some initiative and creativity, to think and react spontaneously during the game, rather than blindly follow rote instructions. Be aggressive. That was American-style ball.

To Japanese coaches who believed that conservative baseball was gospel and who had lived and died by the sacrifice bunt their entire careers, it was dismaying to see a lead runner stranded after three routine outs—or worse, erased in a double play!

Valentine was not categorically opposed to the bunt. The sacrifice made more sense to him, though, when there were runners on first and second in the later innings. Otherwise, if you absolutely had to bunt, then do it for a hit, he said. Lay it down the third-base line, not toward first, to give yourself a better chance to beat the throw. Unless, as Coach Eto liked to point out, there was an aging out-of-shape *gaijin* on first, who probably couldn't make the play.

Valentine compromised on some things. He went along with the off-day practices. He allowed some extra throwing in the bullpen as the season went along, realizing that the 12-inning limit on games itself acted as a natural restraint on overuse of pitchers. He also attended, although with reluctance, the didactic pregame meetings, presided over every day by Eto. In MLB, meetings were usually only held before facing an opponent for the first time to go through an unfamiliar lineup. The daily meetings to analyze the opposition were presided over by Eto and were supposedly part and parcel of the famed Japanese attention to detail. However, Valentine took another view of them.

Since there were only five other teams in the league and you faced each one 28 times a year, not counting exhibition games, you quickly got to a point, he believed, where you did not need to watch any more videos; what else could you hope to learn from them? So it couldn't be the information that was important. It had to be the process—time-consuming though it was.

"I think the Japanese like doing what they do because they are used to doing it," he concluded. "Change is something that is really a foreign concept."

The Japanese approach to baseball, as to most things, was slow, cautious and conservative, based as it was on consensus decision-making. Some Western observers said this behavior pattern was a psychological crutch, one designed to reduce individual, personal risk and thereby minimize the possibility of failure and embarrassment. To Valentine, especially typical of that thinking was the pronounced Japanese tendency to extend every count all the way to 3–2. Everyone seemed to work unconsciously toward that end—the players, the pitchers, the coaches, even the umpires—because then all the strategic decisions would be played out and everybody would know that a strike was coming. Sometimes, he thought, it was to your advantage to swing away early in the count, even at a pitch outside the strike zone if you thought you could get a hit, especially if you were on a hot streak. To the Japanese, however, it was incautious, because you were also surrendering the chance of a walk and that was too much to gamble. Such dilatory tactics were one reason why their games lasted half an hour to 45 minutes longer than games in the U.S. "Outdoor Kabuki," some cynics called the Japanese game.

Perhaps the hardest burden of all for Valentine to bear, to borrow from Ruth Benedict, was the "help" of Hirōka's assistant general manager Masuichi Takagi, a man with no professional experience— only a journalistic background. Takagi often intervened in pregame practices, giving batters advice on how to position the head of the bat and dispensing other tidbits of wisdom.

"It was embarrassing," Valentine said, "to have somebody who had never played the game of professional baseball out on the field teaching."

The growing strains between Valentine and his coaching staff began to show. In May, Eto went to Valentine's office armed with a sheaf of data. He pointed out that Lotte's record in games where Valentine had failed to use the sacrifice bunt was an embarrassing 3–12, but 5–2 when he did. Did Valentine realize, he was quoted as saying, that players and coaches on the opposing bench were actually laughing at Lotte's bad moves? Valentine counseled patience; his tactics would pay off in time, he was convinced. Eto was not mollified. An argument ensued, which Eto lost, and according to one report, the meeting ended on a fractious note.

There was another disagreement about base stealing. Valentine had given the green light to five players, while Eto had opposed giving the green light to anyone. It was too reckless. On one occasion, Eto countermanded Valentine's order outright as to which base the fielders should throw to on an upcoming play. Another time, upset over some aspect of strategy, he threatened to quit. There were also reports of secret workouts conducted by Lotte officials, dismayed that Valentine was not working the players hard enough in practice.

Hirōka returned from a trip to the United States on June 13, to find the Marines in the midst of a seven-game losing streak and sinking deeper into the second division. They were a full ten games behind the second-place Seibu Lions. The rainy season was well underway, and the mold growing everywhere in the ballpark was an apt symbol of the rot that was disintegrating his little cross-cultural family. His coaches were bad-mouthing Valentine to the press and Valentine was complaining to the same reporters about his coaches' interference and the "dual policy" that was infecting the team.

"I want to manage my own way," he'd said. "I'm tired of all the interference."

In a meeting with his general manager, held at Hirōka's upper floor stadium office, Valentine said he had had his fill of being second guessed by Hirōka's crew. After a lengthy discussion, Hirōka reiterated his belief that they were on the same page as far as baseball philosophy went, with the possible exception of the bunt—the safety variety of which he thought was too risky because it was too hard to execute, while the sacrifice version he thought could not be employed enough. (There had been a game in which Valentine, down by three runs in the eighth inning with runners on first and second and one out, had neglected to bunt. Said Hirōka, "I would have bunted the two runners over, scored two runs, then got two more in the ninth inning." A dubious Valentine had replied, "I'll try it that way the next time I get a chance.")

He also complained about the intrusions of Hirōka's assistant Takagi. Hirōka replied that Takagi did know some things and that his position as Marines executive gave him a certain clout, but that he would see what he could do.

Valentine came out of the meeting convinced he had been given carte blanche to do things his way. "Excellent meeting," he beamed to reporters. "We're going to do things my way from now on."

However, Hirōka also met with Eto and Obana. Eto had presented his data and aired his grievances on other matters which Hirōka noted with concern. According to one report, Hirōka was dismayed that Valentine had reneged on his promise to hold practice on every single travel day of the year. He insisted that extra practice was imperative and that this should be accomplished with or without Valentine's cooperation.

In an attempt to tone down the vitriol, however, Hirōka brought up farm team manager Akira Ejiri to serve as head coach and act as a buffer between the two warring factions. It was a bold move because unbeknownst to Valentine, Hirōka had been planning to install Ejiri, a tall former outfielder of some note with the old Taiyo Whales, in the field manager's post, when all the changes were in place two years hence and Valentine's pact was up.

It was at this juncture, however—amazingly enough—that Lotte suddenly began to win. The team took six of its next seven games, even before Ejiri arrived in the clubhouse to unpack his bags, and continued to win as he was settling in at his place on the bench. By the halfway point the Mariners had reached the .500 mark and had begun to close the ten-game gap with second-place Seibu.

Both camps were eager to take credit for the sudden turnaround.

Valentine's adherents pointed out that he had developed a special rapport with his team that was now beginning to pay off. He had managed to wean his players off the by-the-numbers approach that they had been raised on. They had begun to comprehend and start playing Valentine's brand of aggressive baseball, which meant swinging away on 2–0 and 3–0 pitches instead of always trying to work a walk, and going from first to third on hits to the outfield of their own volition, whereas under previous managers they had been ordered to stop at second. Pitchers were throwing strikes on 2–2 instead of routinely advancing the count to the usual 3–2.

More than anything else, the players responded to Valentine's gregariousness and his enthusiasm on the field. He was like a cheerleader and that separated him from most other managers in NPB. He was a motivator and he had gotten his players to believe in themselves after years of mediocrity.

Said third basemen Kiyoshi Hatsushiba, a six-year veteran who was having the season of his life (he would lead the team in homers with 25 and make the all-star team for the first time), "Under Valentine, we became winners for the first time in my career at Lotte. It was fun playing for him."

A special key to the turnaround was the sudden blossoming of Koichi Hori, a lean-muscled young second baseman whom Valentine plugged into the starting lineup at shortstop, over the great opposition of the Hirōka camp.

It might be remembered that Hirōka was regarded as one of the all-time greats at shortstop, while Valentine had played the same position, among others, with somewhat less distinction. Neither Hirōka, nor his hand-picked protégé Eto, had considered Hori quick enough to start at short. Valentine's insertion of him there came over staunch objections, which had to have rankled.

Hori began, indeed, in a fashion that made his detractors look prescient. But, after making an embarrassing eleven errors in the first 55 games he played, he eventually transmogrified into one of the league's better shortstops—although not one with quite the range Valentine had predicted he would have. A big fan of the confidence-building batting clinics that Valentine's batting coach Tom Robson had conducted, he had also blossomed into a .300 hitter, winning the Player of the Month award for June. Asked later for the secret of his success, the shortstop said it was the manager's showing faith in him.

Still another addition that made a difference was rookie leadoff hitter Kenji Morozumi in center field. The latter had missed a lot of camp time due to the death of his father and was left languishing on the minor league team at the start of the season on the advice of farm team coaches. The defense up the middle improved considerably after Valentine called him up. Valentine remarked that he wished he had brought the youngster up earlier. Morozumi batted leadoff, hit .290 and stole 24 bases in 97 games. Julio Franco, a Valentine import from the Texas Rangers, was one of the top hitters in the league. He would bat .306 and win a Gold Glove at first base. (Less successful would be Incaviglia, who hit .181 with 10 homers in 71 games.)

Among the pitchers, Hideki Irabu, already a speedballer of the first rank, was on his way to leading the league in ERA, with 2.53, as well as strikeouts, with 239, for the second straight season in both categories, while mustachioed beanpole Satoru Komiyama would find his true métier, improving from a woeful 3–9, 4.24 in 1994 to 11–4, 2.60, his best year ever. Both had taken a shine to the instruction of Tom House, whose enlightened practice regimen between starts included throwing off level ground, rather than from the mound, a system which greatly reduced muscle tears. Among the MLB recruits, Eric Hillman would also be among the league leaders in ERA. All the pitchers liked the new team policy of not necessarily being obligated to throw a complete game, a departure from the system on other clubs. That year, Lotte would have very few arm injuries.

In Hirōka's circle, however, there was a different interpretation of events. Yes, Tom House had helped the pitching staff, but with the exception of Hillman, the pitchers had been there before him and their success was due as much to natural development as anything else. And had it not been for those Japanese coaches and their extra practice overseen by the Hirōka front office, Hori might not have developed into such a good shortstop, one who was now fully capable of turning the double play (and who would not make an error in his last 38 games).

In fact, after Hori made Player of the Month, Eto singled him out for a special pregame "Hell Week," making him field 150 balls a day to preclude the possibility of his developing a big head, before Valentine discovered what was going on and put a stop to it. (He was convinced they were punishing Hori for his success.)

After the first couple of months, Valentine had eased off his safety bunt strategy somewhat because it had become clear to him there were only two players on the team adept at executing the play. He gave both men the option of attempting to bunt for a hit or sacrificing depending on how they felt at the time. Here again, however, Hirōka's supporters gave credit for the change in policy to Ejiri, who had been instructed by the GM's disdain for that recondite tactic. In behind-the-scenes maneuvering, Ejiri had apprised the players of the possibility of their being swept under the Lotte *tatami* if they did not follow his instructions. Ejiri had also reportedly used similar tactics to rein in Valentine's so-called "green light" strategy.

Ejiri had been put on the team to serve as a buffer to ease the tension between Valentine and the other coaches, and, truth be told, Valentine genuinely liked the easy-going Hirōka ally. But it wasn't long before animosity developed between these two men as well. In addition to the usual objections to Valentine's strategy, Ejiri began protesting his manager's practice of making out the starting lineup without consulting him and the other coaches.

"We have input to give too," he said.

The rift became visible one time after Ejiri had gone into the manager's office to discuss strategy for the game that day. He sat down in a chair across from Valentine and the laid-back American, as was his habit, had leaned back and put his feet up on his desk, resting them next to his bank of phones and his Compaq computer, obscuring Ejiri's line of vision in the process. Ejiri found himself talking to the soles of Valentine's feet, and it offended his sense of decorum.

The next day, when he went into for the pregame discussion, he stood while he spoke.

"*Suwatte* [Sit down]," Valentine had said, clumsily, in Japanese.

"No thanks. I came to talk to your face, not your feet."

Valentine later wondered if his failure to use the polite form *suwatte kudasai* (Please sit down) had somehow offended Ejiri's finer sensibilities.

Then there was the time Ejiri lost his temper during a pregame meeting in August, when he noticed Pete Incaviglia listening to a Walkman, talking and laughing with Valentine in the back of the room.

After the meeting, he cornered Valentine privately and launched into an angry diatribe:

"I respect major league baseball," he said, "I respect major league managers. In a major league meeting, when a coach is talking and trying to help the team win, does the manager talk and laugh like that? Is that the major league way? If that is the major league way, I don't want any part of it."

"You've got it wrong," said Valentine, "I was just trying to explain to Incaviglia that he should listen to what you were saying."

"There wasn't anything funny about my remarks," Ejiri retorted.

"I felt bad about those incidents," said Valentine later. "I always sit with my feet up on the desk. And, in the latter case, I was trying to get Incaviglia to pay attention. I apologized to him afterward on both occasions. I wish they hadn't happened."

Amidst this imbroglio and the sauna bath heat of the Japanese summer, the Marines somehow kept on winning. In the month of August, they were downright torrid, winning 13 games, losing five and tying one. By August 29, they had moved into second place ahead of the Seibu Lions, a dozen games behind Orix, an impressive young team led by Ichiro Suzuki. Valentine was being lionized in the media for his rational use of pitchers and other game-winning strategies, like the delayed steal.

Up in Hirōka's stadium office, in postgame meetings that did not include Valentine, the GM was giving credit to his coaching staff, who apparently continued to insist that the team was winning in spite of Bobby-ball, not because of it. There has been speculation that the decision to give Valentine his walking papers had already been taken.

"I brought Valentine over," Hirōka was later reported as saying, "and I'm not going to shame him. I'll take care of things when the season is over."

In September, tensions between the two factions erupted yet again in a memorable, and for Valentine at least, a highly embarrassing incident.

After a victorious game against the Lions on September 10, Valentine had canceled a full-squad workout that had been scheduled for the following day, an off-day, ordering instead a special "pick-up" session for selected players whom he felt needed the work. His Japanese coaches were, once again, incredulous.

"How could he do that?" asked Ejiri. "Sure, we beat the Lions, but we also made three errors."

The Marines could not afford any more losses down the stretch. The team had six straight games starting on the 12th, three with the Daiei Hawks and then three with the first-place BlueWave, whose magic number for clinching the pennant stood at five, with 14 games left. It was imperative, the coaches believed, that *everyone* on the Marines practice—to be as perfect as possible the rest of the way. They regarded it as a point of honor, to hang on as long as possible even if mathematical elimination seemed inevitable.

Ejiri confronted Valentine and demanded a workout for the full squad. The American bristled. "The temperature is still in the 90s," he said. "It is incredibly muggy. Our players are tired. That's why they are making errors. What they need, in my opinion, is a breather."

Ejiri persisted. Valentine simply had to call a practice.

"If we have a full team workout tomorrow," Valentine replied, "can you guarantee me that we will have the same winning percentage the rest of the way? And will you put it in writing? Because if you're wrong about this, then I'll fire you."

Now it was Ejiri's turn to lose his cool.

"You're not in charge of personnel on this team," he cried. "We came here under a contract with Lotte to help strengthen this club. You don't have the authority to fire us."

The argument went on for about 40 minutes.

"I couldn't understand it," said Valentine later, "how those guys could talk the way they did to me. *I* was supposed to be the manager. The tail was wagging the dog."

Finally, the meeting ended, Valentine issuing what he thought was the last word. He was still running things and as far as he was concerned the full squad was not going to practice.

Ejiri headed for Hiroka's office.

At one o'clock the next day, Valentine appeared at the ballpark in summer shorts for his daily jog and started towards the outfield. Much to his surprise, he saw the entire squad assembled in uniform with general manager Hiroka addressing them.

"You're looking sloppy," Hiroka was telling them. "You're only about 70 percent of your best. In order to win more the rest of this year and challenge for the pennant next year, you have got to practice harder. You've got to gain that extra 30 percent."

And thus began an intense sweat-soaked four-hour workout. It was an awkward situation, but one that Valentine—other than to submit his resignation—had no choice but to accept and pretend not to notice as he went through his run and other ablutions.

The Marines won their next six games in a row, with Ejiri and company not hesitating to take full credit. Had it not been for that practice session, who knew what might have happened? On the other hand, they also lost three of their last five, an outcome Valentine attributed to their running out of gas.

The Resolution

The season ended with Lotte in second place and a record of 69–58–3. It was the best finish the team had had in eleven years. The pitching staff had an aggregate ERA of 3.27, down significantly from 4.50 a year before. Irabu had won the ERA title, with Komiyama and Hillman third and fourth. Hatsushiba won the RBI crown. Hori finished second in the league in batting. Franco was third. Hatsushiba was fourth. Three Marines were chosen on the postseason sportswriters' all-star team. Many reporters, fans and baseball people thought the Marines were the best team in the entire league in the second half of the season. In fact, in terms of winning percentage, they were.

Lotte deputy owner Shigemitsu expressed great satisfaction with the way things had turned out. Unaware of the internecine vitriol, he had been highly impressed with Valentine's bubbly, media-friendly persona and press support, which he thought was good PR for the company. He noted with satisfaction that attendance had increased nearly 20 percent and was of the belief that his eternally downtrodden baseball franchise was on the cusp of historic change.

For his part, Valentine was accepting congratulations for a fine season and basking in accolades from the press. He had been feeling so good about things, in fact, that before Lotte had played its final makeup games, he wrote a letter to Shigemitsu suggesting steps that could be taken to improve the team, which included seven recommendations about jettisoning certain members of the coaching staff and otherwise limiting outside interference. A shortened autumn camp was also on his agenda. What he didn't realize, perhaps, was that such a move was an enormous breach of etiquette in a culture that emphasized consensus and bottom-up decision-making, and where a lot of careful oral preparation (what the Japanese call *newamashī*, or laying the groundwork in advance) normally precedes the formality of committing such things to writing.

He attended a final, season-end meeting with Hirōka and Shigemitsu where he had expected an invitation to come back the following year. When one was not forthcoming, he adopted a more conciliatory tone.

"If you want to continue the same way next season with Eto and Obana and the rest that's okay with me. Let me be the one to suffer again. I don't mind."

"I want to talk with the other coaches before I decide," Hirōka told him solemnly.

"Does that mean you're going to talk with House and Robson too?"

"I don't need to do that," he replied. "They already favor you. I need a more objective opinion."

"Are you going to take a vote?" Valentine joked.

"Maybe," said the GM, never changing expression.

"What if it's a tie?" Valentine grinned. "Who casts the tie-breaker?"

Hirōka neither smiled nor responded, but Valentine had his answer soon enough.

In a subsequent audience with Shigemitsu, Hirōka reportedly said, "We could have won the pennant if we'd had a different manager. But we won't be able to do that with the one we have now. If you don't want to win next year, then don't make any changes. But, I warn you, there are three Japanese coaches who will resign if he stays."

Shigemitsu was persuaded.

At a press conference convened on October 17th, Hirōka announced the termination of Valentine's contract and the appointment of Ejiri as the team's new manager; he stressed "philosophical differences." Valentine's letter to Shigemitsu was also mentioned as a reason for the decision.

"Extra practice was needed so that the players could fully develop their potential which, in my mind, had not been completely reached," Hirōka declaimed. "But Valentine didn't want that. He wanted them to rest."

Later, a Marines spokesman, Kazuhito Maruyama, cited Valentine's "emphasis on winning games rather than training and building up the team," as a major factor in Valentine's firing, implying that the all-important *process* had been neglected.

The announcement was a huge shock to the baseball world at large, unaware that the internal squabble had become so serious. Back home, Valentine did not know what hit him. "I can't believe it," he said. "Here I was expecting champagne and flowers and they gave me the axe instead."

A survey showed that 70 percent of the team's fans wanted Valentine back. In fact, at a postseason event held at Chiba Marine Stadium—Fan Appreciation Day (where players got dressed up in funny costumes and frolicked with celebrities)—fans booed when Ejiri was introduced as the new manager, loudly chanting "Bobby, Bobby, Bobby." The head of Lotte's largest fan organization sent a petition signed by 14,000 fans to the front office, calling for Valentine's reinstatement. Julio Franco quit in sympathy.

Said center fielder Morozumi, speaking for many of his teammates, "I loved playing for Bobby. He did not require that we practice until we collapsed." Added Hori, "He taught me how to enjoy the game. I take baseball seriously, but Bobby's approach was fun. I wish I could play for him again." They had all come to believe that baseball should be fun, not simply work. A lot of players on Lotte liked this approach. In fact, they thought that Hirōka's way—the "way of the samurai," said one player dismissively—belonged in a different era. They wanted to enjoy themselves playing baseball and under Valentine, they could.

Some pundits, both Japanese and American, charged that Hirōka had fired his American because he was jealous that Valentine had been getting all the credit. As one associate put it, "Hirōka wanted to be recognized for his genius in bringing in a foreign manager. But when Valentine began to monopolize the limelight, he resented it. Valentine obviously presented a threat to Hirōka's image and authority, that was why he had to go."

In November, Valentine returned to Japan to "seek some answers," as he put it, to give interviews and to hold court at the Tokyo Foreign Correspondents Club of Japan. But Hirōka refused to let him monopolize the spotlight. Hirōka went on the popular Japanese television program "*Puro-Yakyū Nyūsu*" and intensified his criticism of his former charge.

He claimed that Valentine's "inept managing" had cost the team at least 15 wins during course of the season. He said that Valentine was the primary reason the team had finished last in the first three months of the season and that the Japanese coaches were the primary reason that Lotte was able to wind up in second place.

"We could have beaten third-place Seibu more often if Valentine had realized that they were stealing our signs," he insisted. Adding what in some circles in Japan is the ultimate insult, he said, "Valentine is a man who cannot keep a schedule.

"There was no compromise between U.S. and Japanese styles of baseball," he continued. "The manager cannot be everything. It should be the role of the coaches to train and bring the players along, but under Valentine's way there is no room for them. The coaches and I felt the same, but we did not want to shame our new manager. If we continued this way, there'd be a problem winning the championship. Valentine's philosophy simply doesn't fit Japan."

In Valentine's own press conference, held in front of 150 ink-stained wretches, assembled on the 20th floor of the Yurakcho Denki Building, overlooking the Imperial Palace Grounds, he reiterated his complaints about interference from the coaches and the front office, although he couched them in somewhat more diplomatic terms than Hirōka had. He said that while he really believed everyone was trying to do his best for the team, the gap between America's aggressive style of play and that of the older Japanese baseball traditionalists was just too big to overcome. He held out special criticism for the assistant GM Takagi, saying, "We were embarrassed to an extent to have a person who never played pro ball on the field teaching the player and sometimes teaching things that were opposed to what we the coaching staff were teaching. I had complaints from my players and I had ridicule from the opposition. I spoke to Hirōka about it, but nothing changed.

"To me," said Valentine, "winning is the best training you can give a player. I trained my players. I pushed them hard, but I also gave them time off to enjoy themselves and take it easy. Hirōka's idea was just to train. It was not related to winning. It was related to what they also do—the process—which to him, and the others, was as important as the result. More perhaps. Hirōka refused my request to send the young players to Hawaii over the winter where they could play in the league there and get invaluable experience. You cannot teach or practice experience. The only way is to play—to hit, bat, pitch and win games. Then you'll improve."

Valentine claimed that cultural differences were not a factor and stressed to the very end that Hirōka's way was extreme, even for Japan. "I talked to at least one American player from every team in Japan this year," he said, "and I can tell you, without a doubt, we practiced more days while I was manager than any other team in Japan." That may have been true, although it might be pointed out that not many people in Japan shared Valentine's philosophy on abbreviated spring camp schedules. Three hours a day in camp was just too short for almost all managers in Japan; it showed a lack of sincerity.

*   *   *

His attempt to keep things on the plane of civility did not last. Hearing of Hirōka's televised assault, Valentine declared in a subsequent interview that Hirōka was being "untruthful" when he claimed that Seibu was stealing his signs. He angrily refuted another report that by the second half of the season, he had so lost confidence in managing the team that his coaches had taken over issuing the signs ("Is that some kind of joke?" he said in response. "What do they think I did to earn my pay? Sit and watch?") and he reacted with vehemence to a pejorative magazine article published in the off-season in *Number* magazine by a prize-winning writer close to Hirōka that described "alarming" lacunae in his "baseball sense." Among other things, the article said that Valentine had an automatic hit-and-run called on all 2–2 counts, a "reckless" strategy that had appalled Hirōka when it was reported to him by his coaches. Because, as the article put it, "Japanese pitchers are so good that they could throw a forkball or a slider just outside the strike zone which would be very difficult for the batter to hit. The result was, all too often, a double play."

Valentine flatly denied that he had ever employed such a strategy, anywhere, anytime—not even when he was in the minor leagues. "There were a couple of times," he said, "when there was a steal on a 2–2 count, after a fastball had been thrown (which meant in Japan that a breaking pitch was coming). Sure, we got caught a couple of times, but that's the game. I can't imagine (the coaches) were that confused about what was going on. It really seems like they decided to lie to make the (managerial) change look good."

The similarities to the Akira Kurosawa movie *Rashomon*, in which four people involved in a rape-murder gave varying accounts, was striking.

Postscript

Indeed, at this stage, it may be impossible to get an accurate read on all the factors that caused the dismissal of a manager who had brought the franchise from bathos to respectability in a single season. Valentine himself was a controversial figure. In the States, like

Billy Martin, he could come in and turn a team around, then have it fall apart on him later. Although he was regarded as a very intelligent, knowledgeable baseball man, he was not universally liked by his players. His critics called him arrogant and a camera hog—a man preoccupied with self-aggrandizement. In 2002, an Associated Press article had even referred to him as the "most hated man in baseball."

While personality conflicts no doubt played a part in the melodrama, Valentine's (understandable) inability to grasp the subtext of his hiring was probably what sealed his fate—a fate shared by innumerable foreign hirees dating back to the Meiji Restoration. What his bosses might have made explicit from the beginning was this: "We want you to pass along certain things to make us better, but only within limits which we will define—that's what 'you're in complete charge but please listen to our coaches' means; you're only here temporarily and as soon as you succeed in giving us what we want, we'll replace you with a Japanese; we're not interested in you as a person, nor do we want you to inject American philosophy or culture into our game or our lives; and while we won't tell you any of this explicitly or explain the rules of engagement (that's not our way), you'll be expected to observe them anyway."

It is ironic in this context that Valentine was one of the few American imports into the game that made sincere efforts to bridge the language gap and learn to communicate with the people he worked with and for. He was determined to understand Japan as no other had before and to get the right blend of the two approaches. It turned out to be a more volatile mixture than anyone had anticipated.

By the same token, the Lotte front office's citing of "philosophical differences" may not have been that far off the mark, at least from their point of view. Critical in this philosophy was the mingled notion of authority and change. In Japan, continuity is seen as paramount: things have to change a little at a time, taking into consideration what has gone before and allowing the principals to make slow steady adjustments to new ways. Neither baby nor bathwater is thrown out, but incorporated into the new scheme of things.

Hirōka and company could not surrender real authority to Valentine and risk having him impose radical changes on the way things were done—on or off the field. By implication, that would have meant the old ways—*their* ways—were radically wrong, and this would have been unacceptable.

No doubt Hirōka's announced intention of hiring Valentine as a way of melding U.S. and Japanese styles was sincere. To this day, Valentine thinks the problem was with the coaches who "misinformed" the GM about what was going on. He voices nothing but the highest respect for Hirōka and insists that if he could have eliminated Eto and Obana and had direct daily communication with him, things would have been very different. We'll never know (although given the fact that both coaches were doing Hirōka's bidding from the start, that is unlikely).

None of this, however, can take away from what the lowly Marines accomplished under Valentine's stewardship. Whether or not Hirōka merited Valentine's esteem and whether or not he and his crew were smart baseball people, Lotte and the Japanese game in general had never lacked for long practices, knee-jerk sacrifice bunts, full counts and plodding conservatism that emphasized *wa* and consensus. The only variable in the 1995 mix was Bobby-ball, and it produced a turnaround that was astonishing. The idea that the players were maturing and the team was just coming around anyway, that they won in spite of him and all the behind-the-scenes conflict, that his bumbling strategy failures cost them 15 wins and the championship, might not look so absurd if the team had done anything the following season. In 1996, Valentine and his "mistakes" were gone, Hirōka and company were in full charge (one report said that Hirōka was giving instructions by cell phone to Ejiri in the dugout during games), the team *wa* that Valentine had supposedly disrupted was unthreatened—and they stank up the swamp! And, truth be told, no cool seabreeze has come along for years after to disperse the miasma.

Valentine's letter to Shigemitsu, telling him that canning his coaches would improve the team, may have been a gross breach of etiquette in Japanese terms, but the owner was nevertheless persuaded to act on the advice—only a year later.

* * *

For those who want the gory details, that odoriferous 1996 Lotte squad finished up at 60–67–3, fifth place and about a thousand kilometers behind pennant-winning Orix. The team's overall batting average plummeted—Hori, Hatsushiba and Komiyama, among others, had bad years—while the team's collective ERA ballooned. Tom House, who had remained with the team, explained the difference. "Valentine had us monitor pitch totals in practice and the games. The same with batting practice and ground balls. Hirōka/Ejiri went back to the traditional Japanese work ethic. The more you pitch, hit, practice, the better you perform. Hence, tired players with physical and mental deficiencies."

Hideki Irabu became embroiled in a very public tiff with Hirōka over his expanding pitch count and practice time. "Hirōka is really outside the pale," he actually said to reporters. In a highly unusual move, for the NPB that is, the Lotte players en masse filed a complaint to the ownership about Hirōka. Said Komiyama, "I really felt we could have won if Bobby had stayed as manager of the team."

By November, Hirōka and his entire staff had been fired.

Valentine, for his part, spent the season in Triple A back in the States, then took over as manager of the New York Mets. Shortly thereafter, he would lead them into the World Series. From time to time he met with Shigemitsu, when the latter visited New York, and Shigemitsu admitted that he had gotten some "bad advice" during Valentine's tenure as manager.

If there was anything positive resulting from Valentine's Japan experience, it was that he came away from it with an extremely high regard for the Japanese game. "I had seen the movie *Mr. Baseball*," he said, "and it was an embarrassment. The Japanese game I saw had a lot more dignity and class than that."

In New York, he would incorporate some Japanese practice routines—pregame soft toss, machines for bunting practice, fielding practice stations. He even half-joked that he might incorporate the 1,000 fungo drill into his system, as a kind of initiation test for rookies.

He said that while MLB had more power and was better at hitting and turning the double play than NPB, Japanese pitching was superior. "I don't really have a big awe of major league pitchers," he said, "but I am impressed with those in Japan. They have good speed and they can all throw breaking stuff on 3–2."

He predicted that if Ichiro Suzuki played in MLB he would hit .350 and win the batting title (about as accurate a prediction as a human being can possibly make). "Ichiro Suzuki is the best 21-year-old player I have ever seen, anywhere," he said at the time. "He can hit any pitch there is. And he can field too. He made a play I didn't think was possible. He caught a ball in right center, stopped on a dime and threw the ball 380 feet on a line to home plate to nail the runner. It was unbelievable."

And that wasn't all. In fact, he said, "Take 90 percent of the starting pitchers and top relievers in the NPB and they could make a big league roster in some capacity. Take the top 3–4–5 hitters on each team and they'd be in the starting lineup somewhere—maybe lower in the batting order, but they'd still be there. Daiei's Kokubo would lead A.L. second baseman in home runs.

"People don't believe me when I say this, but there are about 100 players in Japan who can play in the MLB in one capacity or another. Put a Japanese all-star team in an MLB division, let someone like Ogi or Oh manage them and they might wind up winning the World Series."

In addition to Ogi or Oh, the name Valentine might easily be added to the list of candidates.

It would be seven long years before another *gaijin kantoku* would make an appearance. His name was Trey Hillman, former manager of the Yankees' minor league system, and he was hired by another chronic Pacific League doormat, the Nippon Ham Fighters, to manage their team in 2003.

Before leaving for Japan, Hillman talked with Valentine, who offered him a basic introductory course on J-Ball and then said, "There will be times during the season when you will be standing in the field in the middle of a game in some weird situation and you'll ask yourself, 'What in the world am I doing here?!'"

Hillman, a clean-cut, straight talking Texan, said that never happened. But then he worked in a different situation (a less exalted GM) and indeed, a different environment, than had Valentine, suffused as it was in the warm new glow of international baseball good will, inspired by the American love affair with Ichiro. Acceptance was in the air. Thus, his general manager nodded in earnest approval when Hillman said he was going to have a camp that would be shorter than that of any other team each day by two hours and an evening session, that he planned to have the lowest number of sacrifice bunts in the Pacific League. He stood and watched without complaint as Hillman did just that, also setting a record for the fewest pregame meetings, as well as the shortest postgame meeting (41.7 seconds according to a coach's watch).

"I tried not to change too much, too soon," said Hillman, "because I understood what an emotional crutch that some of their institutions and rituals are. I let my pitchers throw a lot more than they should have, and I even sacrifice bunted on occasion in an early inning—something I wouldn't do in the States—because I realized how psychologically important it was to them to score the first run."

Hillman's team did not exactly set the league on fire, as Valentine's '95 Lotte squad had—finishing in fifth place—and he was often quizzed by reporters about his laissez-faire methods, but at least he got to keep his job for another year as the Fighters relocated from Tokyo to Sapporo. The same could not be said for Leon Lee, the former NPB star who was given the job of interim manager of the Orix BlueWave when their hapless manager Hiromichi Ishige was given the axe in May. When the BlueWave finished deep in last place, Lee was given his walking papers.

Both hirings had been surprising. But what really got everyone's attention were the events of November 1 that fall, when hundreds of well-wishers greeted Bobby Valentine's return to Japan at Narita Airport. The man who had once acquiesced in his dismissal, Aki

Shigemitsu, had just offered him a three-year pact for $2.5 million a year to come back and manage the Chiba Lotte Marines, who had not seen the sunny side of .500 since his departure. And Valentine would accept, thereby beginning Part Two of his Great Japan Adventure.

THE OTHERS

When I watch Japanese professional baseball, I root for my favorite team [Hanshin]. When I watch the major-league baseball
news, I look for the achievements of individual players over any
specific teams—like Shinjo, who moved from the Giants to the
Mets. I cheer him on.

TATEO SHIMIZU, *ASAHI SHIMBUN*, 2003

FROM 1995 TO 2003, 17 JAPANESE BASEBALL PLAYERS MADE THEIR
way from Japan to MLB. They went for the challenge of test-
ing themselves at a higher level and to break free from the sti-
fling strictures and wearying excesses of the Japanese game. They
went, as so many put it, "to see what it's like to have fun playing
baseball."

Americans liked them because of their belief, generally speaking,
in the team ethos and their commitment to the idea that playing
baseball was first and foremost its own reward—monetary considerations coming later. They were welcome additions to a game that
seemed increasingly consumed by greed and ego.

In Japan, however, they were admired for other reasons. They
demonstrated to their countrymen new and different ways of living
life, imparting lessons about bravery and self-reliance, something
that was not taught in Japanese schools. An Asahi newspaper reporter, Tateo Shimizu, touched on this when he wrote, "In American

school textbooks, the purpose is to teach individual responsibility and create strong individuals, as seen in the story of 'The Ant and the Grasshopper.' In elementary Japanese textbooks, however, such themes are largely absent; the most important thing is learning the value of smooth human relations and the group. . . . By not staying in Japan where they could have had a stable, secure and assured future and choosing instead a more difficult path, relying on skill and technique to test themselves, Ichiro and the others inspire countless young people to say, 'Okay. I can make it on my own too.'"

The Author

Of all the baseball émigrés who starred in these real life morality plays, perhaps none was as instructive as Shigetoshi Hasegawa, who demonstrated that a Japanese player did not have to be a superstar to make it in MLB. Hasegawa was the first draft choice of the Orix BlueWave in 1991 and went on to win Rookie of the Year honors. In six years, he compiled a solid, if not spectacular, record of 57 wins with an ERA of 3.11. Compact and muscular at 5'9", 170 pounds (and with a permanent five o'clock shadow), he compensated for a low octane fastball with a confusing array of breaking pitches that he could locate with remarkable accuracy.

His success was partly due to his willingness to try new things, such as the changeup he learned under American pitching coach Jim Colborn, who worked with Orix from 1990 to '94. Said Colborn, "The changeup is a great weapon. You throw it from the same motion as your faster pitches, but several miles per hour slower. It really fools the batters. But Japanese pitchers are notoriously resistant to learning it because it takes so much time to perfect and they have so many other pitches to master as well. Hasegawa was only one of two pitchers on the team to master it. He'd throw his fork and his slider and his fastball in the 80s, then come in with the changeup in the 70s. He wasn't afraid to use it in any situation and he was quite effective."

Born in Kobe, not far from historic Himeji Castle, Hasegawa had first learned about pitching from his grandfather, an amateur schoolboy baseball coach. He went on to star in high school where he pitched in the prestigious summer Koshien tournament (his team advancing to the quarterfinals) and then became a standout at elite Ritsumeikan University.

It was as a member of a touring college all-star team that he first saw the United States and he instantly fell in love with it. He liked the vastness of the U.S., the easily accessible golf courses, the freedom and the looseness of American society.

"I decided I wanted to live there," he said. "But, I couldn't see driving a cab or being a gardener. So that left baseball. I made up my mind to be the first Japanese in the majors, after Murakami. But Nomo beat me to it."

After Colborn had left the team, Hasegawa began asking the Orix front office to let him go. As he was still years from free agent eligibility and the posting system had yet to be established, the only way for Hasegawa to realize his dream—(other than to copy Nomo's m.o.)—was through the cooperation of Orix ownership.

Now, Japanese teams did not always make decisions based solely on economic considerations. Other factors, such as *ningen kankei* and *ninjō*, sometimes came into play. In Hasegawa's case, Orix arranged a deal with the Anaheim Angels, involving a substantial amount of cash.

"Sure, we wanted to keep him," said GM Steve Ino. "But at the same time we wanted to accommodate his wishes." (It should be remembered, however, that this act of human charity also came in the wake of Hasegawa's worst season ever—4–6, 5.34 ERA, 87 IP—and was one Orix chose not to repeat when Ichiro Suzuki was the player asking to be sent to the United States.)

Hasegawa's move to MLB was regarded as something of a gamble for him and the Angels, given that he was not an overpowering stud pitcher like Nomo or Irabu. If he flopped, it could very well have had a negative effect on other Japanese aspiring to play in the majors. And, in fact, his debut did not exactly set him on the high road for Cooperstown. While he showed enough talent to make the California roster, it was not as a starting pitcher, as he had hoped. Failing to impress in several starting assignments, he was banished to the bullpen by Angels manager Terry Collins, who undiplomatically announced, "It's quite clear that Shigetoshi is no Nomo."

Hasegawa's new slot as a middle-inning reliever was not considered very prestigious back in Japan and the number of reporters following him dropped accordingly. This was fine with Hasegawa and finer still with Collins, who had both grown tired of answering questions about why he was not in the starting rotation. Absent the distractions, Hasegawa was able to focus on becoming a good setup man. After an initial period of adjustment, he finished the season with three wins and seven losses and an ERA of 3.93. In July of that year, he relieved in the sixth inning of a game versus the Los Angeles Dodgers, which the Angels lost. Pitching for L.A. was Hideo Nomo. It was the first MLB matchup of pitchers from Japan.

Hasegawa studied the weaknesses and strengths of the batters in his league, as well as the habits of different American League umpires. In 1998, he compiled a record of 8–3 with an ERA of 3.14, and by now Collins was singing a different tune. "This guy's outstanding," he was heard to say after a particularly impressive relief appearance.

In 1999, "Shiggy," as he had also come to be known, slumped to a record of 4–6, 4.91, but still managed to pitch a remarkable streak of 27⅓ scoreless innings. In the year 2000, he had his best season. He led the Angels in games pitched (66), wins (10) and ERA (3.48). Along the way, he had taken Angels relief ace Troy Percival's advice to embark on a full-fledged weight training program. Hasegawa would spend two hours after every game in the weight room and by his fifth year in the majors, he was throwing his fastball at 93 miles per hour.

Recovering from a tear in his rotator cuff which sidelined him for part of the following season, he signed on with Seattle as a non-tendered free agent in January 2002. When Kazuhiro Sasaki went on the disabled list, Hasegawa became the team's closer, producing an eye-popping ERA of 0.77 over the first half of the year. His performance earned him a spot on the A.L. All-Star team, making him the third Japanese to have played for Akira Ogi to join that distinguished squad. This statistic prompted one *Asahi Shimbun* reporter to quip, "Ogi has played a bigger role than the Foreign Ministry in diplomatic relations with the U.S."

Hasegawa's own contributions to trans-Pacific relations indeed extended beyond the realm of baseball. Bright and disciplined, he shunned the use of an interpreter and made a concerted effort to learn to speak English (although sometimes he would hide out in a restroom for a time, "just to get away from English-speaking people"). His performances on American television were perhaps more famous in Japan than the games he pitched.

Although millions of educated Japanese study English in secondary schools, their conversational skills are limited, thanks to a grammar-oriented curriculum, designed for college entrance examinations, that focuses almost entirely on reading and writing. Thus, many Japanese can make sense of a *Hamlet* soliloquy but are terrified of actually saying hello to a live native speaker.

"We're afraid of making a mistake," one is often told. "That's why we're hesitant to speak."

Hasegawa, however, did not suffer much from such insecurities. He fearlessly babbled away, sometimes in broken English if need be, to anyone who put a microphone in his face. His interviews in English were so fascinating to the folks back home that a publisher asked him to write a textbook about English. The resulting tome, entitled *My Way to Study English*, became a best-seller in Japan and spawned a host of imitators. Hasegawa also wrote a book about baseball called *Adjustment* in which he stated his belief that the heavy workload he had endured during his early years in Japan and the lack of a sophisticated weight training program for pitchers had indirectly contributed to his shoulder injury. Following that, he authored a book on self-management that also hit the best-seller lists.

Hasegawa reveled in life in the United States. He bought a house in Newport Beach and became an off-season golf junkie, spending only an average of two weeks in Japan. While his wife sometimes complained of little discriminations, living as a Japanese among Americans, Hasegawa never did. "I learned to speak English well enough to tell people off if I have to," he said.

Hasegawa was popular with his Seattle teammates, who liked his

open, gregarious manner, and the writers, who appreciated him because, unlike the other two Japanese on the team, he was always
willing to talk. His locker in rain-soaked Safeco Field revealed evidence of a man who was also busy improving his mind. Stacked on
one shelf, alongside uniforms and street clothes, was a mini-library
in both Japanese and English, including several tomes on business,
along with books on mental training. One of his favorites was James
E. Loehr's *The New Toughness Training for Sports: Mental, Emotional
and Physical Conditioning from One of the World's Premier Sports
Psychologists*. Another was *Das Capital*, by Karl Marx, which Hasegawa had read in the off-season.

Hasegawa's Boston-based agent, Ed Kleven, paid his client the
ulimate compliment when he said, "I'd gotten out of the business of
handling baseball players and had turned to media people. I never
thought I'd represent a ballplayer again but then a former client of
mine, Jim Colborn, came along and introduced me to Hasegawa. If
Shige had a twin brother I'd take him on in a second. That's how
highly I think of him. There's just something pure and sincere about
the guy."

Hasegawa talked to a reporter in 2003 of one day coaching or
managing, of taking what he had learned back to Japan, or, con-
versely, staying in the U.S. and teaching what he believed the Japanese
had to offer. While he echoed the other Japanese players in his admiration of MLB's freedom, dynamism and aggressive approach to the
game, he also harbors reservations about the prevailing work ethic.

"Americans don't do enough," he said flatly. "If I was a coach in MLB,
I'd make a young pitcher throw more in camp. A hundred pitches every
three days. I know the Japanese overdo it with *seishin yakyū* and hurt
their arms, but what Americans do isn't nearly enough."

The Salaryman

The next Japanese player to make the big leap across the pond
was a chunky, well-fed, right-handed finesse pitcher named Masato
Yoshī. A veteran of ten years with the Kintetsu Buffaloes and three

with the Yakult Swallows, he had a reputation as a reliable, unpretentious salarymanlike performer, one who politely waited until his 13th year in baseball, 1997, to have his best season. In that campaign, he won 13 and lost six, with an ERA of 2.99, and was instrumental in the Swallows' drive to a Japan Championship.

By this stage of his career, Yoshī was, of course, eligible to become a free agent, but when he was approached by Don Nomura to exercise that right, he was initially reluctant. At age 32, with a personality as unobtrusive as his pitching, he found the pull of tradition difficult to resist. (Acquaintances said his main concern seemed to be that people not dislike him.) The Swallows had offered him a two-year contract with a big raise and he was inclined to take it. If he declared free agency, what would the people in the Yakult organization think of him?

"It doesn't matter what they think of you," Nomura told him. "They're not going to pay you on the basis of your personality or your good manners. If you couldn't pitch, do you think they would they be offering you a two-year contract?"

But, Yoshī asked, didn't he *owe* something to Yakult?

"What you *owe*," said Nomura, "is allegiance to your fellow players. You have to claim your rights. You have to do this for the younger guys. Make a stand for the next generation."

It took a while but Yoshī finally came around to Nomura's way of thinking. He asked Yakult to tack on two more years. The team refused, so Yoshī declared free agency. At a press conference that resembled a wake, a solemn Yoshī made a public apology to Katsuya Nomura, his manager (and his agent's stepfather), for leaving the team. "This is just something I have to do," he said. Then he sat back and watched in amazement as the offers rolled in. The Seibu Lions and the Hanshin Tigers were both willing to pony up five million dollars over four years. The Yokohama BayStars upped the ante to seven million. Then the Yomiuri Giants stepped in and offered nine million dollars over the same time frame. Yoshī was flattered. He had always wanted to play for the Giants. In fact, Giants manager Shigeo Nagashima had been his idol as a boy. It was a dream come true.

"Fine," said Nomura, "if that's what you really want. But tell them you want an extra four million to put you in the top salary tier. Also insist on having the right to determine your own routine in spring camp. Tell them you refuse to do the 100-pitches-a-day routine that all other Giant pitchers have to go through. And tell them you're not going to take part in their autumn training camp at the end of the season. Make all these demands nonnegotiable."

Since it was the Giants' hard and fast policy under Tsuneo Watanabe not to allow the use of agents, Yoshī would have to do his own negotiating. It was something he was loath to attempt because it was regarded as such an honor just to be invited to wear the uniform of the proud *Kyojin*. Giants players simply did not make such demands—unless they were foreigners, that is.

Nevertheless, Yoshī memorized Nomura's talking points and practiced saying them in front of the mirror. He paced the floor nervously for half an hour before summoning up the courage to dial Nagashima's number. The baseball legend listened to Yoshī's demands and said that although they were no problem for him personally, he would have to discuss the matter with the front office. There, as it turned out, they *were* a problem. Summoned to a meeting with the Giants' general manager, Yoshī was given a tongue-lashing. The upshot was that he could either take their initial offer or they would find someone else. While trying to figure out his next move, Yoshī suddenly received a call on his cell phone from an old friend and former Kintetsu teammate, Hideo Nomo. It would change his life.

"Masato," said Hideo, "why are you wasting your time with teams in Japan? Do you really want to stay there and then in five years look back and have to admit to yourself that you didn't do what you know you really wanted to do in your heart? Stop and think about what you're doing."

Yoshī stopped and thought. And when he was finished, he did a remarkable thing. Turning down millions at perhaps the only stage in his career where he could command such offers, he accepted a deal with the New York Mets for only $200,000, plus performance bonuses. It was an incredible risk and it represented a remarkable transformation for the conservative Yoshī, one that astonished sports fans all across Japan. Hideo Nomo could not have been prouder.

In New York, Yoshī played for Mets manager Bobby Valentine, who had managed in Japan three years earlier and seen him pitch. Used exclusively as a starter in New York, Yoshī finished with a record of 6–8 in 29 games and a 3.98 ERA. The Mets rewarded him with a two-year deal for $5.25 million and the following season he demonstrated that he was worth even more. In what would prove to be his best year in MLB, he won 12 games, lost eight, and led the Mets into the playoffs. Down the all-important September stretch, he logged five wins, compiling an ERA of 1.68 for the month.

Valentine was effusive. "He's the most reliable pitcher we've got," he said. "Yoshī keeps us in every game."

Yoshī later moved on to the Colorado Rockies and then the Montreal Expos, putting in a total of five years in the majors, before returning to Japan in the 2003 season.

The Stone Samurai

Among the many ripe morsels to fall from the NPB tree in that era was Kazuhiro Sasaki, hands down the best relief pitcher in the Japanese game. Playing in the '90s with the Yokohama BayStars of the Central League, he won an unprecedented five Central League "Fireman of the Year" awards and was so imposing he was nicknamed *daimajin*, after a feared feudal era deity based on the "Legend of Haniwa."

Popularized in a 1966 Daiei Film Studios trilogy, *daimajin* was a 50-foot stone statue of a samurai; brought to life out of a cold, deep sleep in an island forest by the prayers of peasant villagers, he went forth to fight marauding bandits, evil warlords and other villains. The physical resemblance of the 6′4″, 220-pound Sasaki to the statue, from the hard, squared shoulders to the etched facial features, was eerie, although the respective m.o.'s were slightly different. *Daimajin*, the deity, saved the day by trampling his foes, impaling them and flinging them against the rocks. *Daimajin* the reliever achieved the same results with a stomach-churning forkball.

Growing up in bucolic Miyagi Prefecture, several hundred miles north of Tokyo, a region known for its rice paddies, picturesque pine tree islands and *kokeshi* dolls, Sasaki was a sickly child who was frequently hospitalized with high fevers, an experience which may have accounted for his habit of bringing home stray animals to be nursed. With the help of his mother, who made him drink large quantities of milk, and his father, who played daily games of catch with him, he gradually built up his strength, developing into a big and brawny but good-natured specimen of Japanese manhood. He went on to play big time high school baseball and secretly taught himself the forkball in defiance of his manager's orders, throwing hours every day on his own. After attending *Tohoku Fukushi* University, where he sat out three baseball seasons with chronic back problems and twice underwent surgery for a slipped disc, he was drafted by Yokohama in 1989. Wearing the number 22, which he considered lucky because he was born on February 22, at 2:22 in the morning, he became the Central League's premier bullpen ace within three years.

In 1998, he had the season of his life when he led the BayStars to a rare Japan Championship. He set a record for saves with 45 (in 51 appearances over a 135-game season), another record for ERA with 0.64 and was selected as the MVP of the Central League. Sasaki was so difficult to hit that opposing managers plotted game strategy versus Yokohama as if they only had eight innings to play. Once he came on in the ninth, it was virtually impossible to score.

Sasaki had thought about leaving Japan for MLB more than once. He gave the idea serious consideration when Hideki Irabu was trying to join the Yankees in 1996 and again at the end of his epic '98 season, but both times he decided to stay—out of loyalty to the organization.

"I've always dreamed of playing in the major leagues," he said on each occasion. "But right now, I can't betray the Yokohama fans, because they have cheered me in such a great manner."

He was also having too good a time. At his peak, Sasaki was making $4 million a year, the highest salary in the C.L. His slew of endorsements included Kirin Beer, a beverage he reportedly consumed in copious quantities to complement his two-packs-a-day cigarette habit. According to the tabloids, which spared few details, he also enjoyed a fully active social life.

Sasaki especially liked playing for his manager, an unconventional soul named Hiroshi Gondo who disdained forced group practices, meetings, sacrifice bunts and other such accoutrements normally associated with Japanese-style baseball. He had good reason to.

In 1961, as a whippet-thin pitcher for the Chunichi Dragons, Gondo won 35 games, pitching an astronomical 429 innings and—not surprisingly—ruining his arm in the process. By the age of 24, he was finished as a top-line hurler. "Many times my fingers and arm hurt," he would say of that era, "but I pitched anyway. If I had refused the manager the fans would have said, 'You're not a man.' The *bushido code* was very strong."

Now, however, Gondo's motto was "Think for yourself," a philosophy that raised many eyebrows.

"Amazing," said a fan named Takeshi Yokozawa who had followed Yokohama for 40 years. "I always thought that Japanese athletes were usually treated lower than pigs by the coaches. They are expected to do what they're told, but nothing else. So Gondo's thinking for yourself is a splendid departure, but it [i.e. thinking for himself] must be incredibly hard for the athlete."

Unfortunately for the BayStars, Gondo's success was short-lived. Yokohama finished the next season in third place; Sasaki underwent midyear surgery to remove bone chips from his elbow. Team officials were reportedly so unhappy with the lack of discipline on the team that that they fired Gondo and hired a veteran manager famous for his strictness and his affinity for long, hard practices. It was at this juncture that Sasaki decided to make his move.

Through a third-party introduction, he hired agent Tony Attanasio, who negotiated a contract with the Seattle Mariners for the same amount of money Sasaki had been making in Yokohama. In 2000, under the watchful eye of about 80 reporters from Japan, he broke the Mariners' team record for most saves in a season with 37 (in 40 opportunities), winning the A.L. Rookie of the Year Award. He followed that with 45 saves in '01. What made these achievements all the more remarkable, to Americans at least, was the fact that Sasaki threw 50 warm-up pitches in the bullpen before every appearance, about four times as many as the other relievers on the team. In a first for a player from Japan, Sasaki also appeared in a Mariners commercial, along with fellow relievers Jeff Nelson and Arthur Rhodes. Dressed as a Musketeer, replete with cape and sword, he seemed a thoroughly Westernized version of his old *daimajin* persona. A favorite of Nintendo owner Yamauchi back in Kyoto, he signed a new two-year contract worth $8 million a year, much to the shock of others in the organization, thus becoming the first Japanese player in history to earn more than one billion yen in a season.

In Seattle, Sasaki lived alone in a Mercer Island condominium. His wife, a former TV singer, reportedly remained in Japan so their two children could attend Japanese schools. He bought himself a silver Porsche, frequented local Seattle watering holes and was spotted hanging out at the University of Washington student union. On the road, he was often wined and dined at expensive Japanese-only nightclubs by wealthy Japanese businessmen residing in the United States.

Sasaki found himself the subject of media scrutiny early in the 2002 season when he made a 24-hour *kamikaze* trip back to Japan. "Concern over his wife's health," he told reporters at the SeaTac arrival lobby, contradicting what he had said before his departure, when he denied that illness was involved. There was much speculation in the Japanese press about what the real reasons could have been. The *Shukan Posuto*, a popular weekly magazine with a nose for scandal, guessed that a divorce might be imminent. The writer cited Sasaki's past reputation for womanizing and reminded readers of women who had spent the night with Sasaki and told all in the media afterwards. As the *Posuto* put it, "His rumored extramarital liaisons are too numerous to count." Sasaki, for his part, denied a split was imminent and as of this writing he was still married.

That trip back to Japan, it might be noted, made Sasaki the only

Japanese in the major leagues ever to leave his team in midseason for personal reasons. Although granting leaves for births and deaths and other emergencies in the family is a common practice in the U.S.—Barry Bonds left the Giants twice in 2003 for several days each, first when his father fell ill and then when he passed away—in NPB such conduct was extremely rare. Duty always came first.

In 2003 tongues began wagging when Sasaki went on the DL twice. The first time, he said the problem was his back, which caused the velocity on his fastball to dip to 85 miles per hour. The second time, it was fractured ribs, an injury incurred, he said, when he slipped and fell while carrying his suitcase up the stairs into his house. It was a story that few people believed.

Tokyo Supōtsu, in an article entitled, "This is an $8 million closer? Give me a break," mused that there were other factors involved; the subtitle of the piece, *yopparatta ue de no akushidento* ("Inebriated Accident?") made it clear. If there was no substantiation, the story did quote one local Seattle-based reporter who noted that "Sasaki is famous for drinking a lot."

However, nothing could spoil the legacy that the pitcher had created in Japan. As Fusakazu Hayano, a longtime baseball fan and resident of Kanagawa Prefecture, in which Yokohama was located, told a reporter, "What he did was amazing and truly inspiring. I remember the days after World War II, when major league ballplayers who visited Japan like Joe DiMaggio were gods. Now we are reversing the situation. Who could have ever thought that possible?"

At the end of 2003, Ichiro's contract came up for renewal and he was naturally due a huge raise. There was also talk in the Mariners front office of adding a fourth Japanese star to go along with Sasaki, Ichiro and Hasegawa. This reportedly caused a certain amount of grumbling among the other Mariners that the players from Japan were going to take all the money. There was a special irony to this turn of events, for it was the sort of complaint that Japanese players in NPB had long been voicing when their clubs signed high-priced talent from the major leagues. But now, for once, the tables had been turned.

Who could have ever thought *that* possible?

The Unknown

Lost in all of the media attention directed toward Sasaki were the adventures of an obscure farm team player in Yokohama named Tomokazu Ohka, who, ironically, would beat his more famous teammate to the major leagues.

Born in templed Kyoto—the ancient capital of Japan—Ohka was raised in semi-poverty with his two brothers by his single mother, who eked out a hardscrabble existence delivering *bentō*. Growing into a sturdy six-foot, 180-pound right-handed pitcher, he was drafted by the BayStars on the basis of a strong curve ball and a 92-mile-per-hour fastball. He sparkled in minor league appearances, but after a series of lackluster performances on the first team, BayStars management lost interest.

The feeling was mutual. Ohka could not stomach the tight, hierarchical restraints that characterized life on an NPB team where the *kōhai* or junior players had to kowtow to their senior *senpai*—notwithstanding the liberal policy of manager Gondo. *Kōhai* were still expected to pick up the balls at the end of practice, run errands for the *senpai* and generally behave like lackeys. What's more, Ohka had been dreaming about the major leagues ever since junior high school when he read a translation of *Nolan Ryan's Pitcher's Bible: The Ultimate Guide to Power, Precision and Long Term Performance*, by Tom House.

He appealed to the club's longtime foreign department director Tadahiro Ushigome for help. Ushigome was a an ex-interpreter, a man who knew as much as any of his peers about baseball in the United States, knowledge acquired over a lifetime of scouting and signing players from North America for his team. It was he who had first brought ex-Yankee third baseman Clete Boyer to Japan back in 1972 when the BayStars were known as the Taiyo Whales. He had regaled people in the organization with many a story about life in America and young Ohka had been an eager listener. Ushigome arranged a stint in the Florida Instructional League with the Boston Red Sox entry there. Over a winter of play, Ohka showed enough for

the Boston front office to express some interest in him. He begged
Ushigome to arrange a deal.

"Are you sure you can handle a full season of life on a minor
league team?" asked Ushigome, "There are no Japanese interpreters
at those levels, you know."

"I'll learn English," replied Ohka.

"What about Japanese food? There are no Japanese restaurants in
most minor league towns and you've got to eat on $30 a day."

"I don't care about that. I'll eat cheeseburgers every day if I have to."

One thing led to another and eventually the BayStars granted
Ohka free agency so that he could sign with the BoSox. (Yokohama
would later receive cash and a player in return.) Before Ohka left, he
came to say goodbye to Ushigome and told him, "Even if I don't succeed in America, I'm never coming back to Japan."

In America, Ohka played in places like Pawtucket and Trenton.
Under the tutelage of a pitching coach named Bob Shaeffer, he
learned to throw the two-seam and the four-seam fastball. When the
1999 minor league season was over, he was suddenly called up to
the Red Sox, where he appeared in eight games in relief. He thus became the ninth Japanese to play in the major leagues, beating *daimajin* to MLB by a full seven months.

After that, Ohka bobbed up and down between the majors and
the minors. On June 1, 2000, at the Triple A Pawtucket franchise, he
became the third pitcher in the 117-year history of the International
League to pitch a perfect game. He displayed his fighting spirit in
other ways as well. During a rain delay in Durham, North Carolina,
he got into a fistfight with Korean teammate Sun Woo Kim. The next
day, at the risk of reinforcing popularly held views about the Japan-
ese-Korean relationship, the two athletes picked up where they left
off, coming to blows at the team's hotel and making it necessary for
the police to intervene. When it was over Ohka needed six stitches
to repair a cut mouth.

In 2001 he was traded to the Montreal Expos and began to flour-
ish the following season when Frank Robinson took over as manager
there. Under the quiet, patient stewardship of the former baseball

great, who took a personal liking to Ohka, the young man from Kyoto became one of the better pitchers in the National League, with a record of 13–8 and an ERA of 3.18.

That fall, the youth who wasn't good enough to stick with the Yokohama BayStars as a second-tier pitcher returned to Japan as a starter for the visiting major league all-star team that featured Barry Bonds and Ichiro Suzuki.

It was the first time that most fans in Japan had ever seen him play in Japan. But by then, of course, thanks to NHK and the Japanese sports dailies, most people in the stands knew who he was.

The Spaceman

Tsuyoshi Shinjo had always been known as being a little off-center. A four-time all-star, a seven-time gold glove winner and one of the most recognizable players in Japan, thanks to his ten-year affiliation with the Central League Hanshin Tigers, Shinjo was as far from the traditional image of the buzz-cut all-business Japanese ballplayer as one could find in NPB. With his sharply handsome features, his gleaming white teeth, and his outré fashion sense, which featured leather suits, orange wraparound sun glasses and eyebrow makeup, he looked more like he belonged in a rock band than in center field. After a peek inside Shinjo's locker, one visitor wryly noted, "He's got more hairspray in there than my wife does in her bedroom."

He was unconventional in other ways as well. In 1994, his fourth year in baseball, this native of Fukuoka, Kyushu, recorded a love song (entitled "True Love"), which sold a grand total of 8,000 copies. By the time he reached 28, he had written his autobiography, entitled "Dreaming Baby." And he had become so famous for making outlandish statements that a collection of them were published in a book entitled, appropriately enough, *The Analects of Shinjo*.

A sample for your reading enjoyment:

"I am one," he said, "who wants to be adored by others instead of admiring someone else. I don't want to follow others, but rather start something new and have others follow it."

And:

"What I want from life is to drive a really cool sports car and dress nice."

Chided by his managers for his casual attitude towards baseball, he was frequently in hot water. In the spring of 1995, while rehabilitating a sore ankle at the Tiger's minor league facility, he showed up for practice late, an infraction of the rules for which he was punished by being forced to sit in the painful *seiza* position (legs folded under the hips) for a full hour, while his teammates practiced around him. After batting only .225 in 87 games that year and being heavily criticized all season long by Tigers manager Taira Fujita for his lack of a work ethic, he temporarily retired, saying he would rather go into show business than remain under Fujita's thumb. When Fujita told reporters, "Shinjo's behavior must be due to bad upbringing by his parents," his comments ignited a bizarre public name-calling match with Shinjo's mother, who was angered by his comments. By the time voluntary training rolled around the following January, however, Shinjo had decided to return to active duty.

Shinjo could run like a Nara deer on speed and his arm was almost as good as Ichiro's. Although he was a .249 lifetime hitter who could not hit the outside breaking pitch, he rose above himself in 2000 when he batted .278 with 28 home runs, 85 RBIs and 15 stolen bases. Becoming a free agent, in his ninth year, he unexpectedly turned down several multimillion-dollar, multiyear offers from Central League teams and, seemingly on a whim, signed with the New York Mets for a reported league-minimum $200,000.

Already dubbed "Airhead" and "Spaceman" by detractors, Shinjo's decision caused even supporters to question his common sense. When Shinjo first revealed his plans at a family gathering, a favorite uncle jumped up out of his chair and cried, "What the hell are you thinking, you idiot?"

"I want to test my abilities," Shinjo replied, "and I want to have fun playing baseball."

His unexpected jump to the U.S. reportedly annoyed Ichiro, who, having just signed with the Seattle Mariners, saw his dream of standing alone as the first Japanese position player in America being usurped.

"What on earth did the New York Mets sign a guy like that for?" he was quoted as saying. "If someone like him can go over there, the major leagues must not be anything much these days. Putting me and Shinjo together is a joke."

Shinjo liked the major leagues from the very first day in spring camp when he was told, much to his delight, that the workday was finished at 1:30. At times, he showed flashes of real talent. He had several important hits during the season and made some fine defensive plays in center field. What impressed baseball savants the most was the way he always hustled in on ground balls to the infield to back up in case of an error, something that not all American outfielders could be bothered to do. In a moment of unguarded enthusiasm, Mets manager Bobby Valentine called Shinjo the best center fielder in the major leagues after Atlanta Braves star Andruw Jones. Evidently, though, it wasn't enough. After a first season in which Shinjo had hit .269 with 10 home runs in 123 games, he was traded to San Francisco.

Playing in different leagues, Shinjo and Ichiro did not have their first MLB meeting until March of 2002, when Seattle hosted the Giants in an exhibition game in Peoria, Arizona. Witnessing this historic event was longtime San Francisco fan Steve Eisenberg, who described it thusly: "It was like two street cats eyeing each other for supremacy. Ichiro and the Mariners came out on one side of the field, while Shinjo and the Giants were on the other, both principals trying hard to ignore each other. Eventually, at the urging of the battalions of reporters that were glued to them, they met each other briefly in center field, reluctantly shaking hands, before beating a retreat. It was all over before you could say *Sayonara*. You could tell that neither one of them wanted to stay and chat."

Twenty or so reporters from Japan formed what was dubbed the "Shinjo Patrol." First in New York and then San Francisco, they followed their man everywhere. They were required by their organizations back home to file stories on Shinjo every day whether he did anything newsworthy or not, and since he was spending more and more time on the bench, their daily task became increasingly more difficult.

Their constant quest for printable information, however useless, began to wear thin on Giants manager Dusty Baker.

"I'm not used to being asked every day about the same person," Baker sighed, after watching his outfielder hit in the low .200s for most of the first half of the year. "How much can you say in a 24-hour period?"

In the eyes of the reporters from Japan, everything that happened on the Giants had to be run through the Shinjo filter in their dispatches or else the people on the desk back in Japan would spike it. Thus, two key hits by Giants outfielder Kenny Lofton, who had taken away the center field position from Shinjo after joining the team in a midseason transaction, were reported in the Japanese papers as "Shinjo's rival gets two hits, scores three." A homer by Barry Bonds might be described as "a blast by Shinjo's friend and teammate." Reports of Giants games would be headlined "Shinjo Starts" or "Shinjo goes hitless" but often fail to give any non-Shinjo-related details such as who won the game.

With Shinjo languishing on the bench for extended periods of time, one enterprising member of the Shinjo Patrol became so desperate for a story angle, he took a photograph of his subject to the various strip joints and gay bars in the Castro District, asking bartenders and patrons alike if the good-looking young man in question had ever patronized their establishments. Hearing of this, Shinjo became so upset he stopped talking to the Japanese press for a time, instituting a ban on reporters from Japan entering the Giants' locker room.

Rival players thought Shinjo a bit of a hot dog, or as Tokyo-based sportswriter Dave Wiggins put it in one of his *Asahi Shimbun* columns, "*le grand frankfurter.*" On the rare occasions when he hit a home run, for example, he would fling his bat in the air, or touch home plate with one hand—just "to be different." Such acts earned him an occasional pitch in the ribs.

Younger fans took to Shinjo's flashy style, in particular, the trademark orange wrist bands he wore extended all the way back to his elbows. Shinjo jerseys, T-shirts, sunglasses and other paraphernalia sold well in New York and San Francisco. But their hero simply couldn't hit MLB pitching. It wasn't just outside breaking pitches he had trouble with, it was also the high inside fastball. Back with the Mets in 2003 and batting .198 in midseason, he was sent packing to the organization's Triple A franchise in Norfolk.

Shinjo's career did have one bright spot in it. In 2002, he became the first Japanese to play in a World Series, when he started Game 1 of the 2002 fall classic for San Francisco against the Anaheim Angels. In the order of status-ranking feats back home, that counted for a lot. It was something that Ichiro had yet to do and that perhaps made all the other sacrifices worthwhile.

Shinjo had left his wife and child behind in Japan so he could remain "hungry" in the U.S. Although he never expressed regret at giving up all that money back home, he did complain of the loneliness of being a "*gaijin*" in MLB, and the lack of restaurants serving food he could eat. His advice to others who would follow him: "Bring along a DVD player and lots of movies from Japan."

Shinjo became the benchmark for every run-of-the-mill Japanese position player in NPB who was toying with the idea of trying his luck in the U.S. "Look at what happened to Shinjo" became the watchword—which perhaps convinced some players to stay right where they were.

The Solipsist

In 2001, Kasuhisa Ishī was one of the premier lefthanded pitchers in Japan. In nine years with the Yakult Swallows, he compiled a record of 78–46 with an ERA of 3.38. At six feet and 185 pounds, his strengths were a fastball in the mid-90s and a knee-buckling curve to go with a slider and a splitter he could throw with great efficiency when he was on. At his best, he was untouchable—a money pitcher who helped his team win three Japan Championships. At his worst, he was a complete disaster—a pitcher who would suddenly walk the bases loaded and literally hand the game over to the opposition. Typical of Ishī the Good was 2001 when he won 12, lost six, and captured the ERA title with a mark of 2.61, helping lead his team to a Japan Championship. Typical of Ishī the Bad was 1999, when he won eight games, saw his ERA balloon to 4.81, and led his team to a miserable second-division finish.

To hear Ishī tell it, playing baseball was the last thing he had ever wanted to do. His father, owner of a Chiba-based private construction business, had pushed him into playing the game as a boy to help him strengthen his lungs and overcome a childhood case of chronic asthma. Ishī continued to play baseball through high school and when the Yakult Swallows offered him a huge bonus to turn professional, he accepted.

"I'm not that crazy about baseball," he would say, even as he achieved stardom. "I'm interested in becoming a film director."

Said a reporter who followed him closely, "I suspect his attitude is just a pose. He knows he can't make the kind of money he's making doing something else. He talks that way because he thinks it's cool. If you're a young guy, it's hip these days to be cool and detached."

His attitude confused his coaches. Ishī did not seem to care whether he was taken out of a close game in the late innings or not. While most other pitchers on the team wanted to stay in as long as humanly possible, Ishī was always ready for a hot shower after 100 pitches, which was a problem for the Swallows' coaching staff, who preferred much higher pitch counts and, if at all possible, complete games. To make matters worse, Ishī frequently complained of shoulder and arm pains, and skipped many starts as a result.

His sense of physical conditioning was almost nonexistent. Like many of his young contemporaries, he smoked three packs of cigarettes a day, habitually consumed Coca-Cola and junk food, and liked to go out and spent more time soaking in Tokyo's bars and clubs than in the trainer's whirlpool. He once made the news when an alert magazine photographer snapped him climbing over the fence around the house of his girlfriend, a famous fashion model named Uno Kano, in defiance of her father's orders that the two stop meeting.

In the fall of 1996, after a season in which Ishī had appeared in only eight games because of arm surgery, the Yakult front office announced they were denying him permission to move out of the team dormitory into an apartment of his own. They deemed Ishī, 23 years old at the time, "incapable of managing himself." (To this Ishī replied, "It's okay with me. I like the dormitory.") He also got into hot water with the team's notoriously strict manager, Katsuya Nomura, who was particularly exercised about a trip Ishī took to Australia over the subsequent New Year's holidays with Uno. Since his shoulder was bothering him, said Nomura, he should have stayed home.

A famously sloppy dresser (baggy shorts and T-shirts), who wore a perpetually morose expression, he appeared often on TV celebrity shows. In the first game of the 2001 Japan Series, he pitched eight innings of one-hit scoreless ball against Tuffy Rhodes and the Kintetsu Buffaloes, striking out 12 batters and walking five in a 1–0 victory. The Swallows won the Championship in five games and then Ishī declared free agency. He signed a four-year contract with the Los Angeles Dodgers worth $12.3 million. He picked Los Angeles at the urging of his new wife, a TV announcer with Fuji Television, who had lived in L.A. and spoke fluent English. The Dodgers had selected Ishī hoping that the fans might take to him the way they had to Hideo Nomo. It turned out to be a false hope. Had they watched a documentary on Ishī filmed by NHK that spring, they might have toned down their expectations in this regard. In it, Ishī is seen unwrapping a gift from Sammy Sosa, an autographed bat. He looks at it, lays it down, shrugs and is heard to say, "I'm only interested in myself."

Ishī was impressive in the first half of the year when he got off to a 10–1 start. Dodgers catcher Paul La Duca claimed no lefthander in the National League had better stuff. But then Ishī inexplicably (or perhaps *predictably* would be the better word) fell to a 4–8 record over the next half of the season. His ERA ballooned to 4.27 late in the season before a batted ball hit him in the forehead and put him in the hospital with a concussion. (He was lucky he wasn't killed.)

Ishī's critics complained that the speedballing solipsist was more interested in beach ball and other off-the-field activities near his beachside digs than he was in the goings-on at Dodger Stadium. His coach Jim Colborn found himself in the unusual position of urging Ishī to mingle more with teammates and do more to win their trust. "Try to come earlier," he suggested, "spending time getting to know these guys. It will pay off in the long run on the field." It was something coaches in Japan had long been prompting their foreign charges to do.

In the weeks after the All-Star break, Ishī had become an object of derision in the Dodger Stadium press box. In late August, he was kayoed yet again, this time in the first inning of a game against the Atlanta Braves, and was booed loudly. This came on the night after a team from Louisville had defeated a Japanese squad 1–0 in the Little League World Series final, telecast on ESPN. A suggestion by an American reporter that Ishī be traded to the Little Leagues in return for the 12-year-old Japanese ace drew laughter and nods of assent by other writers. Cracked the reporter, "At least this one would have better control."

Recovered from his concussion, gratified by the show of concern over his welfare by his teammates—"The letters and the visits and the words of encouragement really moved me," he was quoted as saying—and concerned about his future perhaps for the first time in his career, some people said they thought they detected a new attitude. (He also had a new son to take care of.) He improved his conditioning routine with extra time on the treadmill each morning in Dodgertown camp.

Said his pitching coach Jim Colborn, attributing Ishī's second-half slide in '02 primarily to his inability to adjust to the longer American season, "When you redline your effort from Day One without any sense of where the finish line is, you're eventually going to peter out. Certainly, that was the case with Ishī. He's got it now, I bet you. You watch."

We watched.

And Ishī came through with a record of 9–7, 3.86 ERA and 147 IP—which included a stint on the disabled list with an injured knee.

GODZILLA

Japanese fans are finally standing up to Japanese sports, which for so long have resisted internationalization by using every trick in the book to hold on to its popularity like a desperate dictator. And the Giants have been the biggest offenders. To wear a *Kyojin-gun* uniform is no longer every schoolboy's dream. The stars of the future are looking to follow in the footsteps of their heroes Nakata and Ichiro—to become soccer stars in Europe or baseball stars in America. Giants' owner Tsuneo Watanabe may continue to do his utmost to reverse this trend. Yet, Watanabe and the Giants are fighting a losing battle. They can not reverse the tide of Japanese people finding the confidence to succeed on an international playing field.

YO TAKATSUKI, *ASAHI SHIMBUN*, 2002

Of all the players to come to the MLB, Matsui was the one who most represented the Japanese personality. He was the most normal.

YUSUKE KAMATA, PRODUCER, FUJI-SANKEI COMMUNICATIONS

Matsui reflected a wider spectrum of Japanese society than Ichiro and Nomo who, while excelling at what they did, were somewhat alienated and unhappy because they really didn't fit in anywhere.

MARK SCHREIBER, LONGTIME TOKYO-BASED AUTHOR

IT WAS FINALLY TIME TO FACE THE CAMERAS. BASEBALL SLUGGER Hideki Matsui looked at the battery of reporters in the banquet room of Tokyo's plush Imperial Hotel and cleared his throat.

Into the breathless silence, he delivered a grim-faced, 40-minute monologue. His words were unrehearsed and he occasionally stuttered with the emotion of it all. He had consulted with scores of family members, friends, teammates, former teachers; he had even asked God for guidance. He had tried to tell himself he needed to stay for the prosperity of Japanese baseball. But in the end, the nine-time all-star's love for his team had given way to a stronger personal ambition. He was opting to become a free agent and go to America to play.

Although others had preceded Matsui to the majors, he was special. A left-handed hitter with 332 career home runs and three MVPs under his belt, Matsui had batted cleanup for most of his career on the legendary Giants, a spot occupied by some of the greatest names the Japanese game had produced: Tetsuharu Kawakami, the "God of Batting"; Shigeo Nagashima, "Mr. Giants"; Sadaharu Oh, who hit more lifetime home runs than the great Hank Aaron; and matinee idol Tatsunori Hara, Matsui's manager in 2002. It was a sacred trust and Hideki Matsui had been the latest keeper of the flame. Abandoning such a prestigious post, not to mention leaving the proud *Kyojin*, simply wasn't done.

Until now, that is.

Matsui bowed his head and apologized profusely to Giants management, teammates and the fans. But then, after expressing more contrition for his selfishness, he said, "I have to do this. Even if people think I'm a traitor."

It was hard to envision an American superstar like, say, Barry Bonds making such a speech, but fans of Hideki Matsui would have expected nothing less. For nine years, the 6'2", 210-pound hero toiled industriously for the Giants, never missing a game despite a plethora of injuries. His streak of 1,250 consecutive games played was the second longest in Japan. With an unparalleled work ethic and unglamorous ways, he was a diligent poster boy for the Japanese everyman, an empathetic hero for those who wondered if their endless, anonymous toil as salarymen, or office ladies, might ever pay off. In an era where Japanese heroes tended to be pop stars with spiky hair and equally spiky personalities, he was reassuring evidence that the old ways still survived.

An unabashedly nice guy, always ready to accommodate his adoring Japanese fans with an autograph and reporters with an interview, Matsui had never been known to complain about anything to anyone—not even to an umpire. He was a living monument to the words of Yomiuri founder Matsutaro Shoriki, whose deathbed wish several decades earlier was "May the Giants always be strong and may they always be gentlemen."

So respected, in fact, was Japan's iron man that when he announced his seismic move to MLB, the daily *Nikkan Sports* noted that it was the first selfish act Matsui had committed in his 28 years.

Mercurial Yomiuri Giants honcho Tsuneo Watanabe had done everything he could to keep his star. He had lashed out at players like Ichiro for abandoning their country and had accused Ichiro's team, the Orix BlueWave, of "selling out Japan" when they accepted $13 million for Suzuki's rights via the newly instituted posting system. He even equated MLB's invasion of Japan to the arrival of Commodore Matthew Perry and his Black Ships a century and a half before, prying open that closed island nation to world trade after two and a half centuries of isolation.

In May 2001, Watanabe had appeared at the Giants' home ballpark, the Tokyo Dome, with his crony, the former prime minister and noted right-wing hawk Yasuhiro Nakasone, symbolically at his side, imploring his fellow owners, in an impromptu press conference, to exhibit a little more "sports patriotism." (The irony of such a plea surely did not escape these other 11 men, who for some years now had watched him raid their teams.)

In light of this PR offensive and the likelihood that the departure of a star of Matsui's magnitude would cause the Yomiuri fan base to further erode, most fans had assumed that the Giants cleanup hitter would be loath to go against his powerful boss's very public wish that he stay put. Thus, at the end of the year, when Matsui turned down a $64 million, six-year offer from Yomiuri—the highest in NPB history—the nation was collectively astonished. Japan's most obedient salaryman had stood up and the country was forced to take notice.

Bio

Hideki Matsui was born in snowy Ishikawa prefecture on the Sea of Japan on June 12, 1974, the second of two sons, and was raised in the small industrial hamlet of Neagari. His father, Masao, worked for a computer software company and also managed a private church founded by Hideki's grandmother Ruriko Matsui, a shaman faith healer who specialized in sick children and who reportedly had the gift of second sight. It was called the *Ruri Kyōkai* (Church of Ruri) and was affiliated with the 50,000-member *Tenso Kōkyō*, a nationwide religion that attempted to consolidate the teachings of Christianity, Buddhism and Shintoism, admonishing its followers against greed, anger, gluttony, dishonesty and other evils proscribed by all three.

Athleticism ran in the Matsui family. Hideki's mother may have been so traditional that she kept her opinions to herself in the presence of men, but she had also been a star volleyball player in her school days—the daughter of a kendo expert and younger sister of a third-degree black belt holder in *aikido*. Young Matsui, always a head taller than his classmates as a boy growing up, was himself a multi-sport phenom, earning a first-degree black belt in judo and winning a city-wide walk-on sumo tournament.

It was *yakyū*, of course, where he really blossomed, participating in competitive playground games with his older brother (who eventually gave up the sport to join a rock band). A natural right-hander, he was so good at *bēsubōru* in primary school, even when playing against boys several years his senior, that he was forced to handicap himself by batting left-handed, which is how he came to be a portside hitter.

In junior high school, a baseball coach gave young Hideki a copy of Sadaharu Oh's famous book on hitting, *Daunsuinngu* ("Downswing"), in which the great slugger described how he practiced his batting form with a sword, attempting repeatedly to slice in precise halves a piece of paper suspended from the ceiling. The only way to accomplish this extremely difficult feat was to angle the swing down and snap the wrists, which also happened to be extremely useful in developing bat control. After reading the Oh opus, Matsui adopted the downswing dictum and practiced it with uncommon zeal, often staying up until three or four in the morning to work on it, according to his father. Hideki spent so much time swinging that his hands were perpetually covered in blisters and calluses, while his favorite bat was stained with blood at the grip end. Able to hit the ball harder and farther than any other middle school student in memory, he destroyed so many balls in practice that his team had to ask for an increase in its baseball budget to purchase more.

As a junior high school standout, Matsui was recruited by Seiryo High School in Kanazawa. Seiryo was a Western Honshu powerhouse, a regular participant in the national championship tourney at Koshien Stadium and an institution that was known for its Spartan training.

As one former player said of its rigorous regimen, "You didn't feel as though you had a real practice until the manager had slapped you in the face two or three times."

Matsui moved into the Seiryo dormitory and began year-round practice that included numbing workouts before and after school, as well as intensive summer and winter camps. On days the ground was covered with a thick blanket of white snow, colored balls might be brought out for increased visibility in practice or else the manager might simply suspend normal drills and order everyone to make a lung-bursting run through the snow up and down a small nearby mountain.

It was at Seiryo that Matsui, who pitched and played third base, was first nicknamed "Godzilla"—a moniker which, at the time, was as much for a severe case of adolescent acne as it was for his tape-measure blasts. Legend has it that the young athlete once launched a ball in batting practice that cracked the tiles on the roof of the Seiryo manager's house, nearly 140 meters (430 feet) away. In Matsui's three year career at Seiryo, he hit 60 home runs in toto and made four appearances in the hallowed National High School Baseball Championships. His seven RBIs in the opening game of the 1992 spring invitational tournament tied a record, as did his tourney total of three home runs. He was the only schoolboy player in Japan with his own tailor-made long ball sign. In addition to the usual instructions of "swing" and "take" that were normally flashed from the bench, Matsui's manager at Seiryo had devised one which stood for "Hit a home run."

Matsui's outsized reputation was clinched in the final game of the summer tournament when he was intentionally walked an unheard-of five times by the opposing team, *Meitoku Gijuku* High School, with a capacity Koshien crowd of 55,000 fans and a nationwide TV audience watching openmouthed. The actions by Meitoku, which went on to win the tournament, were regarded as unsportsmanlike by many observers and prompted uncharacteristic catcalls from the stands as well as heavy criticism in the media the next day.

However, Matsui's stoic, emotionless conduct during those at bats drew great praise from tournament officials and reporters alike. Said the manager of Ikeda High School, another Japan powerhouse, "He was wonderful. You wouldn't know he was a high school student. That settled, calm attitude. You can't achieve a state like that without a lot of practice." Beamed an admiring sportswriter who had witnessed the game, "He was magnificent. Just like a samurai faithful to the code of bushido." At the end of the tournament, a representative of the High School Federation stood up and officially declared, "All students should learn from Matsui's attitude."

Matsui credited his restraint to a severe public slapping he had received from his junior high school manager, the punishment delivered after Hideki had thrown a bat in anger at an opposing pitcher who had similarly refused to challenge him.

"It was a valuable lesson for me," he said, recalling the encounter as an adult. "From that day on, I resolved never to lose control of my emotions in a game again."

The manager's behavior, which resulted in his ejection, was triggered in part by the actions that season of Seibu Lions hitting star Kazuhiro Kiyohara, who had hurled his bat at a pitcher in retaliation for being hit in the side by a fastball in a nationally televised game. Matsui's mentor was concerned that his star pupil was emulating what he believed to be highly disgusting behavior. But equally important, he was alarmed over Matsui's careless treatment of his bat.

"Players have to show respect for their equipment," he said, echoing what baseball leaders had been saying in Japan since the Meiji Era.

Matsui was the most coveted player in the 1992 draft lottery and as luck (or, as some paranoid participants believed, a fixed draw) would have it, the Yomiuri Giants won the right to negotiate with him. Upon formally signing with the Giants in a nationally telecast event, Matsui received the first of thousands of unsolicited medicines and letters of advice from Giants fans who had been shocked to see close-ups of the savage boils on his skin. (It was a problem which, in fact, took several years to clear up, leaving him with a leathery, pockmarked face.)

Matsui was given uniform number 55, highly symbolic in that it stood for the single-season home run record held by Sadaharu Oh, a mark that everyone fully expected Matsui to challenge one day. Like Oh, Matsui had not been a naturally gifted hitter. It had taken Oh three years of hard work and effort after turning pro to emerge from mediocrity and the same would prove true for Matsui. In his early seasons with the team, he was known to swing the bat as many as 800 times in two-hour batting practice sessions, working hard to develop even more discipline at the plate. He frequently reported to the home of his manager Shigeo Nagashima for morning batting instruction sessions in Nagashima's basement gym.

"Concentrate all your nerve endings on the sound of the bat when you swing it," Nagashima would say cryptically. A "whish" was no good. But a "whoosh" *was*.

In 1996, after three years of steady, if unspectacular growth as a pro, Matsui had his breakout season. He batted .314 with 38 home runs and 99 RBIs, and won the Central League's Most Valuable Player award.

Said his admiring batting *sensei* Nagashima, "He got so he could sit on the fastball and still hit the breaking pitch. He could slap the curve to the opposite field or pull the inside speedball down the line. His bat speed was something."

Matsui repeated his 1996 performance the following year, swatting 37 homers, batting .298 and driving in 103 runs, as he settled in for a long run as the Central League's marquee player. (For those who want the details in black and white, here they are. He batted .292 in 1998, leading the league in both homers [34] and RBIs [100] for the first time. In 1999, it was .304, 42 and 95; in 2000, it was .316, 42 and 108. In 2001 he won his first batting title with a .333 average, hitting 36 homers and driving in 104 runs.)

Matsui had also polished his defensive skills, evolving into a gold glove centerfielder who compensated for his less-than-spectacular throwing arm and foot speed with all-around baseball sense and an unparalleled work ethic

Matsui's pregame workouts were a model of *doryoku*. In addition to sweat-inducing sessions at a batting tee and in the batting cage, they included an exhausting fly-ball-chasing routine in the outfield—30 balls hit over his head, to his left, to his right—and then 20 wind sprints from foul pole to foul pole. Visiting San Diego scout Gary Nickel, who witnessed one of these tiring midsummer displays, could only shake his head in admiration. "Here is the best player in Japan in a pregame situation working his butt off," he said. "How often do you see that in our game?"

In 2002, Matsui elevated his game to a higher plane. In that season, with a slightly shortened, line-drive-producing stroke, he hit 50 home runs and batted .334 with 107 RBIs. It was one of the best all-around performances in memory and he barely missed a triple crown when Chunichi Dragons Hiroki Fukudome edged him out for the batting title by nine points. Matsui also led the Giants to the Central League championship and a successful sweep of the Seibu Lions in the Japan Series, marking the Giants' third national title and fourth pennant in the Matsui era. By this time, his annual salary had risen to nearly $5 million a year, the highest, for a Japanese player, in NPB—a figure which he doubled with bonuses and endorsement fees, donating substantial sums to various charitable organizations.

Through it all—the awards, the adulation, a life constantly in the limelight—he remained almost unnervingly low key. He should have made more money. Some foreign players were making over $8 million. But Matsui humbly continued to accept modest raises throughout his career. (As he put it, after one particularly unproductive contract negotiation when he failed to get the huge raise everyone had predicted—finishing up his fourth year in the pros, the one in which he had hit .314 with 38 home runs and 99 RBIs—"Team officials told me that I'm actually worth more than my salary, but that they had to keep it low in line with those of other players. It's doesn't bother me."

Moreover, he wore no earrings, no rock star sunglasses, no outlandish hip-hop togs of the type favored by contemporaries like Ichiro Suzuki and other luminaries of the new Japanese consciousness. Flash and youthful irreverence were just not Matsui's style, even if the conservative Giants hadn't frowned on such outré displays. Instructed to stay in the team dormitory and refrain from dating during the first several years of his career, so as to devote all his concentration to baseball, Matsui complied, without a whimper, his manner a model of proper deportment.

He liked to tell people of the vow he had made to his father at age 14—occasioned by the bat-throwing, face-slapping incident—never to say or do a hurtful thing to another living human being ever again. It was a vow he insisted he had kept. And it was a measure of the respect he commanded in his own country that most people believed him.

Trailed constantly by a scrum of Japanese reporters eager to record any Matsui moment for the devoted and insatiable Japanese media machine, Matsui invariably wore a smile—unlike the prickly Ichiro. "I asked for this life," he would say. "Nobody forced it on me and I have a duty to the people who put me here." He refused to charge admission at the Hideki Matsui House of Baseball back home—a practice which stood in marked contrast to the Ichiro Museum in Nagoya, where a ticket costs $8. It just wouldn't be fair, he explained.

Some cynics called Matsui simpleminded, a workhorse without the brainpower to comprehend what all the attention really meant or the sophistication to mimic Ichiro's studied cool. But Matsui, who in fact had been an attentive student with high marks in math (one who actually sat in the first row of the classes he attended), would shrug and say, in his coarse baritone, "I'm just an ordinary guy." He liked to have an occasional beer. He liked to shoot the breeze with the security guards and maintenance personnel, and he liked to trade tapes from his extensive library of adult videos with reporters. (His reply, when asked about his eccentric hobby, was a droll "Doesn't everybody do this?")

Said one Japanese journalist, describing Matsui's affinity for such unique Japanese cultural institutions as no-panties *shabu-shabu* and hostess nightclubs, "Matsui is very unpretentious. All of us are horny guys more or less. But Matsui doesn't attempt to hide the fact. That's a refreshing attitude which is one reason, I guess, why fans took to him so much."

As the end of the 2002 season approached, Matsui endured public and private appeals from new Giants manager Tatsunori Hara and others connected to the Giants, all orchestrated by Watanabe, calling on Matsui to stay for the sake of team and country. There were letters from Yomiuri officials to Matsui's parents asking them for their cooperation. Shigeo Nagashima, the just retired "manager emeritus," even took the unusual step of writing an op-ed piece in the *Yomiuri Shimbun*'s archrival, the *Asahi Shimbun*, urging his former charge not to desert. His teammates needed him, the nation of Japan needed him. If Matsui left the proud *Kyojin*, then would nothing be sacred anymore? It could very well mean the end of Japanese baseball, not to mention the civilized world as the Giants braintrust knew it.

But Matsui was feeling other pressures as well. With the whole country buzzing about Ichiro Suzuki, if Hideki Matsui, the jewel of the Central League, did not try his hand, people would say he was a wimp, that he had no guts, no *konjō*. It was a double bind. No matter what he did he would either be called a traitor or wimp. In the end, his manhood—and his curiosity—won out, although he looked like a man on the way to the gallows, when he delivered his sayonara speech, rather than one about to realize baseball's biggest dream.

Freedom

Despite whispers among Yomiuri management that Matsui was a deserter, the star's decision was largely applauded by the Japanese baseball-viewing public. The affection baseball fans held for Matsui was evidenced by the thunderous standing ovation he received at a postseason exhibition game at the Tokyo Dome following his final appearance in a Tokyo Giants uniform—and this from a crowd not known for such spontaneous displays of emotion.

They were also responding to his sincerity and the fact that he truly seemed torn between his affection for his fans and teammates and his desire to go to the U.S. But the ovation also showed how much things had changed in Japan. (As Oh had put it when he heard the news, "In my era, if I or Nagashima had said we wanted to go to the major leagues, 90 percent of the fans would have been against it. Now, it's reversed, 90 percent the other way.")

The public's feelings were summed up by Prime Minister Junichiro Koizumi, who told TV reporters, "It's sad he won't be at the stadiums in our country anymore, but on the other hand, more and more Japanese sportsmen are making their mark on the world stage. I think that is admirable."

Public interest in Matsui's migration to the U.S. was, if it can be imagined, higher than that for Ichiro. For one thing, Matsui would be the first full-fledged power hitter from NPB to make the trans-pacific leap. As the first Japanese to go bicep to bicep with the andro-enhanced musclemen who had come to dominate North American baseball, it was hoped that he could single-handedly erase the image of Japanese as practitioners of "small-ball." Then there was the fact that he ultimately decided to play for the New York Yankees, whose owner George Steinbrenner had been lusting after a Japanese star of his own after seeing what Ichiro had done for the Seattle Mariners' winning percentage and subsequent bottom line. After the Yankees had lost in the first round of the 2002 playoffs to the Anaheim Angels, Steinbrenner's scouts had told him that Matsui was just the man to revivify his team.

The Yankees already had great name value in Japan, thanks to Babe Ruth, Lou Gehrig and Joe DiMaggio, all of whom had played in exhibition games there during their careers. DiMaggio had even come to Japan on his honeymoon with Marilyn Monroe. Yankee Stadium, with its great tradition, was special to the Japanese and so was the city of New York. Seattle was one thing, but the Big *Ringo*—hey man, that was the top of the heap. If Hideki Matsui could make it there, that would mean that Japan would, in a very real sense, make it there as well.

However, even after declaring free agency, the process of extricating himself from the grip of the Giants to join the Yankees had not been a simple matter for Matsui. Although on the surface it appeared that he had cleanly severed his ties with his former team, in reality, it wasn't quite so. Japanese society was in great measure about personal relationships, about *on* (obligation) and *giri* (duty) and *mentsu* (face). These were concepts that meant something to Matsui, and because it was his desire not to displease anyone more than he already had, he continued to let the Giants participate in and influence his future—actually allowing them to act as a go-between in negotiating with MLB and choosing which team he would play for. Thus, although many MLB teams had expressed interest in the slugger's service, when Watanabe announced to reporters that if Matsui absolutely had to go to the U.S., then he should go to the Yankees, the only team in the United States deemed to occupy a social stratum equivalent to that of *Kyojin*, the matter appeared to be settled for all and good (which was fine, by the way, with Matsui; he had been a Yankees fan for a long time).

However, there was, as usual, more going on than met the eye. During 2002, officials from the Yankees, including vice president Jean Afterman, had been invited to Japan several times to discuss a working arrangement between the two organizations, to discuss players exchange and development, among other things. Yomiuri was especially interested in a tie-up between NTV and the Yankees' cable sports network YES, whereby the Yomiuri Group would be first in line to obtain the rights to telecast the New York Yankees games in Japan—once the old MLB contract with NHK had expired at the end of 2003. This would naturally have enormous appeal if Japanese slugger Hideki Matsui were in the Yankees lineup and would make for an ideal sports viewing schedule: Matsui/Yankees games in the morning and Yomiuri games in the evening, with Yankees game highlights flashed between innings. They also wanted to convince YES to televise Yomiuri Giants games in North America, which, indeed, was something that could come in handy in the event of another MLB strike.

The Yankees, for their part, were interested in player development and training, and, of course, Matsui. Related to this was the presence of Yankees stars Bernie Williams and Jason Giambi on an all-star squad of major leaguers that visited Japan for a goodwill series of games against Japanese competition in the fall of 2002, a tour that was sponsored by the *Yomiuri Shimbun*. (The *Yomiuri Shimbun* and the *Mainichi Shimbun* had been alternating sponsorship of the event on a biannual basis for years.) Not once had Yankees owner George Steinbrenner ever allowed any of his players to participate in such tours. This time, however, Steinbrenner sent over his two stars as emissaries to woo Matsui and smooth relations with Watanabe's people.

Incredibly, the Giants introduced the word "rental" into the negotiations—another bizarre indication of how differently the Yomiuri group interpreted the term "free agency." The Giants wanted an option clause put in Matsui's contract whereby the Yankees would "rent" Matsui for a period of, say, three years, after which he would be sent back to the Tokyo club, against his will, if necessary. Said one involved official, "The Yomiuri people did not seem to understand how the U.S. system and option clauses worked, because such an arrangement under MLB rules was not possible with a Japanese team without Matsui's consent, which he was in no position to give at the time. I found it amazing that they would try to set conditions like that."

In the end, the Yankees and the Giants did cobble together a working agreement for player development, but one which did not include rights to Yankees games (which, in any event, New York was forbidden to sell overseas without permission from the MLB commissioner's office) or rights to Yomiuri games in the States or any quid

pro quo involving Matsui. In December, after the agreement had finally been signed, Matsui hired Jason Giambi's agent Arn Tellem to
negotiate his Yankees contract, one which set no conditions on the
Japanese star's future availability to his former team.

Yanks

Just exactly how Matsui would do in his new milieu was a subject
of much discussion in Japan during the postseason winter months.
Numerous big-league scouts had praised his patient, disciplined approach at the plate and his skill at running the count to 3–2. This,
combined with his natural power, they believed, would enable him
to make the adjustment to big league pitching. They saw him benefiting from hitting in a lineup that included an unusually high number of batting stalwarts like Derek Jeter, Jason Giambi and Bernie
Williams, not to mention the Stadium's famously short right-field
fence. Said Sammy Sosa, who had given Matsui batting instruction
in 1996 while visiting Japan on a postseason tour, "Man, that dude
will hit .300 with 25 to 30 home runs."

Others were not so sure. Succeeding as a power hitter in the
biggest of leagues was a different proposition, given that the unfamiliar assembly of pitchers Matsui would have to face (nearly four
times as many, in toto, as he saw at home in his six-team loop) generally threw at a greater velocity than those in the Japanese leagues
and were not afraid to intimidate a rookie batter by throwing high
and inside. Moreover, many of them threw a two-seam fastball, a
pitch rarely seen in Japan, that breaks or slides down and away from
a left-handed batter when thrown by a right-handed pitcher. Ichiro
Suzuki was able to succeed against such formidable opposition because of his speed. Even when he only managed to get a piece of the
ball and send it spinning on the ground, he could leg out infield hits.
However, a power hitter like Matsui had to hit the ball squarely or
else watch his outs climb. And Matsui would no longer have the luxury of playing in the atmospherically challenged Tokyo Dome (modeled after the Minnesota Twins Metrodome), where the ball traveled

farther. Among the skeptics was Sadaharu Oh, who was quoted as saying that it would likely take Matsui the better part of a year to reach his stride.

Some fans even questioned whether or not Matsui had the right personality for success in MLB. In a worrisome precedent, he had performed miserably in that 2002 goodwill series with MLB all-stars. Playing under intense media scrutiny, he failed to hit a single home run, batting an embarrassing .161 in the process—this despite the fact that his less heralded Japanese teammates pummeled top pitchers like Bartolo Colon and Brad Penny.

By Game Five, Matsui's inability to hit home runs had so upset the Yomiuri sponsors that they hastily arranged a home run contest between Matsui and MLB slugger supreme Barry Bonds. But even then Matsui could only muster four out of the park blasts to Bonds's nine, batting against an easy-throwing batting practice pitcher. After-ward, Bonds snootily declared that Matsui would be lucky to hit 10 to 15 homers in his first season in America (an assessment that would prove to be accurate, if unkind).

Hay Group executive and baseball fan Minato Asakawa, who spent years watching baseball in both Tokyo and New York, pre-dicted, "I think Matsui will have a hard time, at least in his first year, because he's *too Japanese*. Ichiro and Nomo are not like other Japan-ese. They are independent. Too independent, perhaps. But to suc-ceed in the U.S., you've got to debug your own Japaneseness. Matsui is too humble, too reserved, too accommodating. He'll have a hard time . . . at least in his first year, until he becomes less Japanese."

Former Giant captain Kiyoshi Nakahata told *New York Times* cor-respondent Ken Belson, "He is so kind that his kindness doesn't mesh well in the game. In games he is not so bold. His strong point is that he's nice. But also his weak point is that he's too nice."

Japan's oft-lurid tabloids found other potential difficulties for Matsui to fret about. One series in an evening daily warned that in addition to problems arising from language, food and travel, there were potential dangers from the rising use of steroids, amphet-amines and marijuana in MLB.

One newspaper article breathlessly noted recent revelations about gays in major league baseball and stressed the need for Matsui to be vigilant in the Yankee Stadium shower room when he bent over to pick up the soap. That same article mentioned the reportedly keen interest of the San Francisco gay community in Tsuyoshi Shinjo's "tight little butt" and Ichiro's boyish charm. The writer quoted ex-Expos and Mets hurler Masato Yoshī as saying he had been propositioned by a San Francisco taxi driver, and reported the interesting fact one player always carried around a condom just in case he was raped in the U.S.; he wanted to be able to provide protection.

In January, after being sent off to the U.S. by a small gathering of 800 of his closest friends at a downtown hotel, Matsui finally crossed the Pacific and signed his contract ($21 million over three years) at a ceremony presided over by New York mayor Michael Bloomberg. Then he headed for the Yankees training facility in sunny Tampa, Florida, trailed by more than 150 reporters, photographers and other media personnel from Japan, who gave new meaning to the term blanket coverage.

Matsui's first *batting practice* in Tampa was televised live back to Japan at one o'clock in the morning. His first exhibition game home run earned several pages of analytical articles in each of the leading sports dailies. And when he missed practice one morning because of a root canal, a photo of his open mouth adorned the front page of the *Sports Nippon* daily newspaper. All in all, there were more Yankees preseason games televised live nationwide in Japan than were shown in New York City.

The presence of so many Japanese reporters—the Yankees fielded 90 separate requests for interviews with Matsui on Opening Day alone—quickly became an irritant to the Yankee front office, which had to deal with their constant demands. George Steinbrenner growled at his media relations personnel to exercise more control, and they in turn began to vent their frustrations at the unending requests for entry. (Said a representative of *Time* Asia, repeatedly rebuffed while pressing for a photo shoot of Godzilla, "It was the first time in my career anyone yelled at me just for requesting access.")

The Yankees would eventually restrict admission to the Yankee Stadium home locker room, limiting entry for the reporters from Japan to groups of three at a time, moving them in and out in shifts of five to ten minutes each, like tourists in the Sistine Chapel, while putting no such limits on the 25 or so New York–area-based reporters who regularly covered the team. Since space in the Yankee Stadium press box was limited, most of the Japanese contingent was consigned to a dank workspace in the bowels of the stadium where the field was visible only on TV monitors. The dismal state of affairs prompted more than one Japanese media man to label the individuals ultimately responsible for the restrictions "racist."

The only person who seemed unfazed by all the media hoopla was Matsui himself, who, after all, had spent years enduring such scrutiny in Japan. He patiently sat for interviews, wearing a smile of seraphic sweetness on his face, answering the same banal questions in session after session in a marathon display of courtesy. One memorable evening, he even took a dozen New York baseball writers to dinner at an expensive restaurant, playing host through his interpreter and the smattering of English he was picking up from the textbooks he studied daily, charming his guests with his polite attentiveness. It was a first in Yankees history.

"Talking to the press and signing autographs as often as I can is my way of fulfilling my obligations as a player," he told startled and bemused MLB reporters. It was a view decidedly out of sync with the vast majority of current big leaguers.

After charming New Yorkers with appearances on *Regis and Kelly* and the *Late Show with David Letterman*, Matsui started off the official season with a bang, smashing a dramatic grand slam home run in his first game at Yankee Stadium, a feat which understandably caused paroxysms of joy back in Japan. The historic ball was immediately flown back to Neagari, where it was enshrined in the Matsui museum. Said one aged farmer, staring at the ball in wonder as a TV crew filmed him, "You can see Hideki's character in it."

Then, however, came a difficult period of adjustment. After one month, Matsui was hitting .255, with only two home runs, and was in the midst of a 9-for-47 slump. The only bright spots were his fielding and his 22 RBIs.

"It's quite different here," he confessed to the everpresent writers.

"The MLB is much harder than I thought. It took me a while to realize it, but American pitchers will throw a strike on 2–2. In Japan, they try to get you to hit something off the plate." He kept trying to pull those two-seam fastballs, resulting, unfortunately, in a succession of infield grounders.

Particularly embarrassing was the greatly anticipated first matchup between Seattle's Ichiro and New York's Matsui, a three-game set scheduled for April 29 through May 1 at Yankee Stadium. The series did not live up to its fanfare. That included, for the first time, simultaneous big spreads on the back page of the tabloids in both New York and Tokyo. The headline in the *New York Daily News* was "Ichiro vs. Godzilla" and featured cartoon caricatures of the two icons with the caption, "Japan's big shots battle in the Bronx."

The confrontation was viewed by tens of millions of people and analyzed by an NHK guest commentator, Matsui's ex-mentor and manager Shigeo Nagashima (who took the opportunity of his visit to Yankee Stadium to inform New Yorkers about the "great nationalistic pride as a Japanese that Matsui had inside"). It also featured one of the briefest pregame handshakes in MLB history—so fast that most in the mob of photographers on the scene were unable to record it—as a distinctly uninterested Ichiro appeared out of the dugout, offered a limp wrist without even removing his batting glove and then quickly escaped to the outfield. Adding injury to insult, the Yankees were swept and Matsui managed only three miserable, insignificant singles.

Going into the last week of May, Matsui was on the verge of oblivion. His average stood at .249, with but five home runs (one less than Ichiro, to add to his shame), contributing to a serious Yankees swoon. He had also taken a commanding MLB lead in infield groundouts, earning the uncomplimentary nickname "4–3'" for his one-bounders to second base, and was becoming an embarrassment to executives at NHK, who had filled their sports programming schedule with wall-to-wall Matsui coverage.

The typical telecast of Yankees games featured numerous reruns of Matsui at bat—in slow motion, wide screen, split screen comparison with other at bats, and all from as many different angles as the on-the-spot producers could think up. Being thrown out at first time after time and vying for the league lead in double play balls (he would finish second with 25) was not an automatic crowd pleaser in Japan. Nor was the title of "Groundball King," as he was also known.

The absolute low point for Matsui came during that period when George Steinbrenner, tired of watching Matsui flail away helplessly, declared, "This isn't the man we signed on for." That public insult was featured prominently in the tabloids back in Japan.

The normally unflappable Matsui fell into what was for him a depression, albeit one that was indiscernible to anyone else. In reply to a question from a *Tokyo Supōtsu* reporter as to how "enjoyable" his experience had been thus far, he said, "My heart's in a slump. . . . I thought I was going to have a good time playing. But I would not call this fun. It's *hisshi* [desperation] every day. I'm just trying to keep up."

"It's not just one or two pitchers here who have great velocity," he told another inquirer ruefully. "*Everyone* does."

Matsui lived alone in a Manhattan high rise. He did his own laundry and socialized mostly with his assistant Isao Hirōka, a few Japanese writers, visitors from Japan, and occasionally his teammates, if the services of an interpreter were available (Matsui's English having not yet arrived at a conversational level). Like most ballplayers, he eschewed the museums and art galleries and other such NYC attractions, preferring to spend his free time eating at Japanese restaurants and going for long reflective drives along the Hudson River in his new Chevy. At night, he patronized the sedate, refined Manhattan hostess clubs for Japanese ex-pats—such establishments a noted feature of the exclusive Japanese community in New York. One Tokyo tabloid, worried about Matsui's sex life, interviewed a top porno actress in Japan who volunteered to fly to the States and service Matsui whenever required, just in case blonde, Western women were not to his liking.

Despite Matsui's struggles at the plate, Yankees manager Joe Torre defended his new left-fielder from the Far East, praising his defense and his ability to drive in runs even while having to adjust to a new league. Torre and Matsui, in fact, exchanged numerous missives during the season, translated by Matsui's assistant Hirōka, about how to cope with MLB pitching, and the Yankees pilot was certain that it was just a matter of time before Hideki would show what he was really made of. "Stand closer to the plate" was Torre's advice.

Team batting coach Rich Down (destined to be ex–batting coach by the end of the year) added his analysis. "In Japan Hideki only had to face two major-league-level pitchers per team. Here, it's a different story, but sooner or later he'll catch fire and I predict he'll single-handedly carry this team for long stretches at a time."

Both predictions proved to be accurate. At the end of May, Matsui suddenly righted himself. The reversal in his fortunes was triggered by a discussion with Yankees catcher Jorge Posada about Matsui's stance, which had grown increasingly timid and defensive. "You're not swinging aggressively enough," he said. "And you're not hitting the ball where it's pitched. Cock the bat and get your body into the swing." The advice worked.

On May 29, Matsui hit a huge home run to help Roger Clemens win his 300th career game and delivered several more key hits after that, including a three-run homer in Cincinnati and a dramatic grand slam versus the Mets in the widely watched crosstown matchup on June 30. The blast was his 10th homer of the year. He had also raised his average to .300 and moved into the top 10 in the American League in RBIs.

Back home, a greatly relieved Japanese public participated vigorously in the All-Star balloting, overwhelmingly voting for Hideki and putting him into the starting lineup for the 2003 midsummer classic, to the dissatisfaction of some in the American media who thought there were more qualified players.

As ESPN.com's Sean McAdam pointed out, for example, Matsui's 64 RBIs at the midway point tied him for sixth place in the A.L., but he was not among the league leaders in batting average, total bases, run scores, slugging percentage, OBP or extra-base hits. Nor was he even close to the top 10 in batting average with runners in scoring position.

Said McAdam, criticizing the ballot box stuffing by fans back in Japan, "Matsui's RBI total shows him the beneficiary of the many base runners in front of him in the powerful Yankees batting order."

He added "There are more regulars in the Yankees lineup who have more homers than Matsui than those who have fewer. . . . This is an All-Star?"

Nonetheless, it was a historic game for Japan because there were an unprecedented three native sons selected to play: Matsui, Ichiro Suzuki and Shigetoshi Hasegawa. In fact, ratings for the telecast of that game in Japan were higher than they were in the United States. (Shown on NHK General, the network's terrestrial channel beamed to nearly every household in Japan, the game drew a viewer rating of 11.6 percent, meaning nearly 12 million people watched the morning telecast. The rating was higher than for the Fox telecast of the contest in the United States, and higher even than certain Tokyo Giants games that year.) Fans missed the last two innings of that game, one of the most exciting All-Star games in years, with the A.L. rallying in the bottom of the eighth inning for three runs to take a come-from-behind victory, because of a previously scheduled half-hour news break. It hardly mattered to most of them, though, because the last Japanese player had already been removed from the game. Indeed, a subsequent survey conducted by the *Mainichi Shimbun* asked the question, "After you see the day's news on Matsui, do you remember who won the day's game?" Seventy-eight percent of respondents said no.

Matsui continued to impress as play resumed in the second half of the season, with a number of crowd-pleasing hits, foremost among them a towering walk-off home run to right field to beat the Cleveland Indians on July 18; it was the first *sayonara* home run ever hit by a Japanese in MLB history. On September 17, he became only the third Yankees rookie in history—after Joe DiMaggio and Tony Lazerri—to drive in 100 runs in a season.

Although Matsui did not ultimately prove to be the franchise player (or even the home run threat) that many Japanese had anticipated, he did finish with a set of statistics you could send home to Mama. They included a batting average of .287, 16 home runs and his 106 RBIs, which was second on the team and was the highest total for a Yankees rookie since DiMaggio in 1936. Showing "gap power," he also led New York in doubles, batted .335 with runners in scoring position and earned kudos from fans and sportswriters alike for his other talents—the fielding skills, the quickness with which he got the ball back to the infield ("He's like a second baseman in that regard" said YES broadcaster Michael Kay), his heads-up baserunning ability and mastery of the other fundamentals. Thomas Boswell called him "a left-handed version of the elegant Hall of Famer Al Kaline."

New Yorkers especially took to his unfailingly polite demeanor, which fit in nicely with the clean-cut, almost bland Yankee persona. Had Matsui been less of a nice guy during his down periods, the New York press would most certainly have been harder on him, but, as it was, there were no howling back-page headlines of the "Iraboo" sort about his performance.

No one was more satisfied than Yankee manager Joe Torre, who said, summing up, "He does everything well. Sure, he's a different player than I thought we were getting, but I think he's better. It's tough for a slugger to switch leagues and switch countries because most of them take advantage of pitchers' mistakes, pitchers they've faced over and over again. But Hideki is much more than a home run hitter. He's a line drive hitter who covers the whole plate. He hits to all fields. He has good at bats. And he knows how to play the game. I can't think of anyone else I'd rather have at bat with men on base than Hideki." High praise indeed.

And there was more to come as shares in Matsui's stock enjoyed a major postseason rally. He whacked a powerful home run in Minnesota to give the Yankees a 3–1 lead in the American League Division Series. He slammed a scalding double down the right-field line off Pedro Martinez in Game 7 of the American League Championship Series, while his alert baserunning allowed him to score the tying run in the eighth inning of Game 7, which New York won in extra innings. He was so excited after touching home plate on that play that he jumped three feet into the air, pumping his fists in jubilation. Said one Japanese writer watching wide-eyed back in Japan, "That's more emotion than he ever showed in his life."

In Game 2 of the 99th World Series (which the Yankees would lose in six games), he hit a 3–0 fastball off Florida starter Mark Redman

over the center-field fence, 408 feet away. That blast made him the first
Japanese ever to hit a World Series home run and earned him gushing
headlines the next morning—"A Classic Yankee!" blared the *New York
Post*. "Matsui Earns Stripes!" went another—and a public prediction
by Steinbrenner that Matsui would hit "35 homers" for sure the following year.

In the end, Matsui's most important contribution may have been financial, as he single-handedly created new ways for tourists to blow
their money in New York. Sales of Yankees tickets to Japanese tour
groups went through the roof, as did sales of Matsui goods. In midseason, an autographed Hideki Matsui baseball sold for $379, com-
pared to $269 for teammate Derek Jeter (and a Barry Bonds ball for
$279), prompting one baffled Yankees official to remark, "The peo-
ple from Japan don't seem to give a damn about Yankee baseball. All
they want is to see Matsui get a hit, to buy a Matsui souvenir and go
home feeling good about their country. Watching the other Yankees
play is incidental."

Be that as it may, according to one estimate, the intense Japanese
interest in Matsui brought in roughly 500 million much-needed dollars for the city's economy, about five times what Ichiro had done for
Seattle in his debut campaign.

Godzilla himself didn't do so badly either with lucrative endorsement contracts for Upper Deck sports cards, Lotte ice cream, a
Mizuno sports drink and Japan Airlines, among others. In midsummer of 2003, JAL launched a new fleet of Boeing 747 jets, two of
which flew to Matsui's hometown airport in the city of Komatsu (of
which Neagari is a suburb) bearing a 20-foot image of the star's
puss on the fuselage. One of the many advantages for Matsui of
being a Yankee was that unlike the Yomiuri Giants, the Yankees did
not demand control over his endorsements or a 20 percent cut off
the top.

The city fathers of Neagari certainly welcomed the publicity gener-
ated by their native son's emigration to New York. Plans were laid to
ignite a tourist boom by merging their town with two nearby commu-
nities and bestowing upon the new mini-metropolis the name "Matsui

City." A train station near the local ballpark was to be renamed "Godzilla Station."

Not everybody in Japan was eager to share in the joy. One, of course, was Watanabe, who saw his TV ratings slip to under 15 percent, the team's lowest since the Japanese Nielsen system began in 1965. Another malcontent was a fan named Kiyoko Morishita who wrote a letter of complaint to a newspaper in which she decried the fuss over American games. "Many players seem to think that success in the major leagues means more than success in Japan," she sniffed. "The attitude is similar to some Japanese people's adoration of Western culture. I want Japanese players to respect Japanese fans. The media and TV shows actually give more attention to the achievements of Japanese major leaguers. I'm bored with that. They should focus on Japanese baseball. . . . If the Professional Baseball Association doesn't consider ways to change the situation, it will become unable to attract spectators. My hope is that more young talented players will come out and show us more exciting games."

One who wasn't about to fly back to the rescue of the NPB was Hideki Matsui, who, by season's end, was standing as erect and as proud as anyone else in the park during the playing of the "Star Spangled Banner" and "God Bless America"—shoulders back, cap respectfully over his heart—as if he truly were an American citizen. Said Yankees vice president Jean Afterman, "Hideki absolutely reveled in being a New York Yankee."

"I'm a American major leaguer, now," Matsui said emphatically, after a year of enjoying American-style freedom. "And I'm here to stay. . . . This is only the beginning."

EPILOGUE

The funny thing is not how different Japanese and American baseball is, but how, in some ways, each country longs to be a little more like the other.

JOE POSANASKI, *KANSAS CITY STAR*

Ichiro Again

For Ichiro Suzuki, 2001 proved hard to match. The shades-wearing teen idol followed his gilt-edged first season with successively declining marks of .321 and .312, starting off like an F-1 racer in both years but then developing engine trouble and running out of gas by September. It was a pattern that accompanied the Mariners' frustrating dissipation of huge division leads in both of those campaigns, which ended with their failure to make the playoffs two years running. In 2002 Ichiro hit .357 in the first half of the season, but only .280 after. In 2003 his collapse was even more striking, as he nose-dived from .352 at the All-Star break all the way down to .243 over the final two months.

This prompted some observers, like sports columnist Jack Gallagher, to suggest that perhaps Ichiro's famed work ethic was inappropriate to the long MLB grind, with its grueling travel schedule. Others believed that the problem was caused by opposing pitchers who had been pounding the Seattle Flash more than ever with inside fastballs, which Ichiro had taken to pulling for fly outs. This caused a significant drop-off in the number of hits he slashed to the opposite side of the field—such infield singles being a hallmark of his unforgettable first year.

Ichiro himself, who had once aspired to hitting .400 in MLB, was said to be so upset by his inability to perform well for the Mariners down the stretch that he lost his famous composure. He told his old friend Leon Lee, who had spent 2003 managing Ichiro's former team, the Orix BlueWave, "It was killing me that I was letting my teammates down. I felt so much anger and anxiety at times that I threw up."

"Don't worry so much," Leon counseled him. "Your problem is that you're getting stronger. You're only 29 and you're still developing as a player. Add to that the fact that you know the pitchers in the majors better, so you're being more aggressive. This all goes to why you're hitting more flyballs. What you should be doing is easing up and trying to hit more to left field. Hit inside out and you'll be fine."

It was a theory that remained untested as this book went to press.

Certain other distractions may have affected Ichiro's mental state as well. Among them was his irrepressible father, Nobuyuki, who was now spending all his time running the Ichiro museum in Nagoya, an amazing operation that housed, among other delectations, every conceivable bit of Ichiro childhood memorabilia, from his preschool baseball glove to his dental retainer. It was all maintained "as lovingly as the Shroud of Turin," to use the words of one writer. Nobuyuki had been funneling Ichiro's ancillary income from endorsements and other sources through the museum's accounting books, a practice that unfortunately came under the inquiring gaze of the National Tax Office. Tax officials subsequently required Ichiro to pay back taxes to the tune of $168,000. Then there was the report that his father had attempted to charge ESPN $800 for an interview. According to Orix beat reporters, Nobuyuki had been making up to $100,000 a year from such endeavors in Japan, where paying for press interviews was a custom. Most Japanese sports figures understood that such practices were not generally welcome in the West and declined to invoice American reporters for their time. Nobuyuki, however, had apparently not gotten the word. ESPN predictably declined to pay and the interview never took place. (Hideki Matsui, chosen in the postseason by *People* magazine as one of the 23 Most Lovable Men on the Globe, suffered a similar embarrassment when his father, a noted karaoke buff, took advantage of his son's exploding popularity to record a CD in a duet with a popular *enka* songstress named Kaori Kozai. Matsui's exasperated response to the album, entitled *Yukizuri Monogatari,* or "A Tale of Passing Strangers," might be loosely translated as "Dad, you really ought to know better.")

By 2003, Ichiro's media star had begun to fade somewhat in Japan, if only fractionally, as his comings and goings were partially eclipsed by the surge of interest in the new Yankee samurai Matsui. Coincidentally or otherwise, it was about this time that Ichiro began to lower his guard and make himself more accessible to U.S. media. The highlight of this new availability was an interview he did with Bob Costas in which he revealed his favorite English expression: Kansas City in August was "as hot as two rats fucking inside a sock."

If his own late-season pace had been less torrid than that, it was still impossible to ignore the raw fact of his three-year average of .328 and aggregate total of 662 hits, stats that few players in MLB history had ever approached. He had opened a door that was swinging ever wider, and more and more of his confreres were willing to walk through it. And stay.

They were led by Hideki Matsui, despite the fact that he found adjustment to MLB extremely difficult. Although he had complained about the two-seam fastball—"Even when you know how the ball is going to break, there is no guarantee you can hit it solidly," he told a gathering at the National Press Club in Tokyo in November—and had adjudged the NPB and MLB to be so different that it took a special kind of individual, one with mental strength as well as physical adaptability, to make it, he could not wait to get back. He pronounced 2003 the most satisfying season of his career and vowed he could do even better in seasons to come.

Little Matsui

The prize catch of the 2004 season was a New Age paragon named Kazuo Matsui, who played for the Seibu Lions and had been voted the best shortstop in the history of the NPB when he was only 24 years old. Favorably compared by the high priests of *yakyū* to Derek Jeter, Nomar Garciaperra and even Alex Rodriquez, the 5'10"

183-pound Matsui, who could hit from either side of the plate, was pursued by no less than nine different MLB teams. All were dazzled by his industrial-strength numbers: seven straight seasons of .300, with a high of .332 in 2002; four straight seasons with more than 20 home runs; five years of stealing more than 30 bases, with a high of 62 in 1997, a season in which he was voted MVP of the Pacific League. He also had four gold gloves. In his best year, 2002, he became the first switch hitter in the history of Japan to hit .300 with 30 home runs and 30 stolen bases in the same season. His career-high 36 homers that campaign, playing in the drafty, semi-domed Seibu Stadium, was the most ever for a switch hitter, while his 88 extra-base hits broke a 52-year-old Japan record. Equally notable, perhaps, was his sturdiness: He played in 1,143 games straight, the 5th longest streak in NPB history and the longest ever in the Pacific League.

On the basepaths he was a blur, half a step faster than Ichiro, and he possessed a rocket-propelled throwing arm from short that was every bit as intimidating. He was also more versatile and more dynamic than steadfast Hideki Matsui. Said one scouting report, "If he wanted to bunt, he could hit .350 every year. If he wanted to concentrate on stealing, he could swipe 100 in a year."

Matsui was born in teeming Osaka in 1975 and started playing baseball in the third grade. He became a star in junior high school and at P. L. Gakuen, Japan's premier baseball factory, where, aping players in MLB, he started lifting weights to build upper-body strength and a stronger arm. Despite a subsequent spate of injuries—to back, shoulder and elbow, the last requiring surgery—he continued to build his body, converting himself from a short, frail pitcher into a muscled moundsman with a V-shaped physique. His goals as a youth were twofold: One was to turn professional, and the other was to buy a Benz. By 1994 he had accomplished the first, when the Seibu Lions drafted him at age 18 and turned him into an infielder; and by 1998 he had achieved the second.

A self-described "baseball brat," he called his mother, Sachiko, the most influential person in his life. A strong, determined woman, she had raised him alone from the age of 12 after Kazuo's father had deserted the family and had given him three rules of life to follow: (1)

Don't boast. (2) Don't be arrogant. (3) Don't forget to express gratitude to others who have helped you. She was not averse to slapping
her son if he neglected to follow these rules.

Matsui, a natural right-handed hitter who unfortunately could not
hit right-handed pitchers very well, undertook took the highly unusual
step of converting himself to a switch hitter in 1996, his second year
in the pros. He had seen the advantages fellow Pacific Leage player
Ichiro Suzuki enjoyed by hitting from the left side of the plate, and
had made it his habit to come out on the field in pregame practice to
study Suzuki's form. It was as a switch hitter, in 1996, that Matsui batted above .300 for the first time. He also sparkled in the postseason
exhibition series that fall between All-Stars from the NPB and MLB,
manufacturing 10 hits and 5 stolen bases. It was then that the manager of the MLB team, Dusty Baker, whose mastery of Japanese had
not yet attained to the finer points of pronouncing "Kazuo" and
"Hideki," dubbed him "Little Matsui" to distinguish him from "Big
Matsui," Hideki standing four inches taller than Kazuo and outweigh-
ing him by 30 pounds. Kazuo did not much care for the nickname,
given the pride he took in his chiseled tree-trunk torso, which to some
invited comparisons with Bruce Lee, a kung-fu star whom Kazuo idolized so much he had the team play the theme song from Lee's signature film, *Enter the Dragon,* whenever he came to bat. It was around
this time that he also began to display the leadership qualities that
made him the rock of the Seibu infield. Said one observer, "You could
watch him play without knowing who he was and you automatically
knew that this guy was the team leader."

In the first game of the 2002 seven-game series with the MLB All
Stars, while "Big Matsui" was flailing helplessly away, "Little Matsui"
hit screeching home runs from both sides of the plate and went on
to finish with a batting average of .423, capturing the "Fighting
Spirit" award.

In person, he was an engaging, energetic, self-effacing young man
with a resplendent mane of hair streaked with colors like metallic silver, electric mustard, sea-urchin blue and reddish-orange, as well as
a taste for modish dress (black velvet vests, shiny silk shirts, and six-
button suits), who still believed in the old-school work ethic that in-

cluded six hours of workouts a day during the off-season. Matsui was also known for being superstitious. He always put his socks on starting with his left foot, and if his team lost, then he would take a different route to the ballpark the next day. In 2000, before embarking on road trips, he initiated a purification ritual, *kiribi*, introduced to him at a Japanese restaurant, in which he would strike iron and stone pieces together to create sparks as a way of praying for a safe and successful trip. The formula seemed to work. In 2004, coming off a season in which he hit .305, with 33 homers and 85 RBIs, he stood as the finest all-around player in Japan.

Subjects Matsui did not like to discuss were his ancestry and his estranged relationship with his father, a former *yakiniku* restaurant proprietor, who had remarried a woman 20 years his junior and who had been borrowing money recklessly, according to the *Shukan Shincho,* using his son's income as collateral.

Matsui's decision to declare free agency and play in the States came in November 2003, after much agonizing over whether to remain in Japan in 2004 in order to play for the Japanese entry in the Athens Olympics. He eventually made up his mind after listening to former Seibu star outfielder Koji Akiyama, one of the finest all-time NPB players, confess that he had deeply regretted not challenging the majors and that Kazuo should not make the same mistake. Matsui turned down reported three-year offers from both Seibu and the Yomiuri Giants in the $27 million range, and signed with the New York Mets, accepting a three-year pact for slightly more than $20 million. In regard to the lower salary figure, he told *Sports Illustrated*'s Franz Lidz, in a nod to the pressure that NPB stars now felt to prove themselves in America, "It's more important for me to see how much I can improve as a player."

In the wake of the "Metsui" signing, there was the predictable level of excitement among fans and the press in Japan, for now the nation had stars playing in what, one could argue, were the two most famous baseball teams in the United States, located, of course, in the most famous city in the world, hailed in song by the great *Furanku Shinatora.* If that wasn't cachet, what was?

The story dominated the sports dailies for a while and fans basked in the glow of all the coverage of Matsui #2 by the New York media, which bordered on worshipful. It included major pieces in all the important sports publications, as well as the cover of *ESPN Magazine,* which gushed that Matsui was one of the "top five short-stops on the planet," that he might be "the best pure athlete the Japanese game has produced" and that, as the first infielder from Japan, he had the "talent and the temperament to assume a big league leadership role," despite linguistic and cultural barriers that might stop ordinary shortstops. Sound bites of New York's mayor welcoming Matsui to the Big Apple in slightly fractured Japanese were rerun on every major news show.

However, after the all-out media assault on Japanese senses that had accompanied the migrations of Ichiro and Matsui, one sensed a slight trace of "been there, done that" in the popular reaction. How long could you keep up the euphoria before it started to get old? The Americans had even wearied of moon landings after a while. And be-sides, no one really expected the Osaka Flash to surpass Ichiro in bat-ting average or hits, or even belt more home runs than Godzilla. In fact, Matsui's former Seibu manager Haruki Ihara, who had moved to Orix at the end of the 2003 season, publicly criticized Matsui for los-ing his hunger and letting minor injuries get the better of him, noting that, after all, Kazuo had let his batting average drop to .305, and that 84 RBIs *was* a comedown from previous years.

The NPB had now lost another one of its jewels. This meant that, along with Hideki Matsui and Ichiro Suzuki, three active players from the NPB All Millennium team were now in major league uni-forms. And there were others lining up behind them to board the love train to MLB. Former Chunichi Dragon Akinori Otsuka, a late-inning sinker-ball specialist of some note (17 saves in 2003), signed a modest two-year deal with the San Diego Padres for the 2004 sea-son, while closer Shingo Takatsu, who racked up 34 saves for the 2003 Yakult Swallows, was eyeing Los Angeles. Ex-Hanshin Tigers starter Tsuyoshi Shimoyanagi (10–5, 3.73 in 2003), became super agent Scott Boras's first Japanese client.

Also eager to go was an insouciant 28-year-old Yomiuri Giants right-hander named Koji Uehara, who struck out Barry Bonds three times in a 2002 postseason exhibition game between the NPB and MLB All-Stars in Tokyo with an assortment of *shōto* balls, sliders, forkballs and fastballs, and also nailed Jason Giambi twice. Another potential candidate was phenom Daisuke Matsuzaka, a 23-year-old workhorse for the Seibu Lions who could throw the ball at 96 mph. Matsuzaka once threw 250 pitches in a nationally televised high-school game that went 17 innings. Also waiting in the wings was left-handed pitching artist Kei Igawa, who led the Central League in wins (20) and ERA (2.80) in 2003; and outfielder Kosuke Fuku-dome, a line-drive hitter who denied Hideki Matsui his triple crown in 2002 by hitting .343 to cop the Central League batting title. As of this writing, however, all of them were four or more years away from free agency.

In the face of the latest Matsui defection and the public avowals of other stars like Uehara and Matsuzaka to follow suit, NPB fans remained remarkably nonplussed. The Rubicon had, after all, already been crossed when Hideki Matsui defied the shoguns of Yomiuri and purchased his one-way ticket to the big leagues. That was the Last Taboo, and it symbolically ended any remaining pretensions Japanese owners had of claiming parity with the U.S. Kazuo Matsui had not played for Yomiuri and had therefore not been a nightly fixture on nationwide TV. It was less painful to let him go.

Ardent baseball fan Machiko Kawamura, a grandmotherly resident of Hodogaya (outside Yokohama), who watched Yankee games religiously (she had memorized the entire Yankee roster) and tuned in the Mariners as well, was thrilled at the prospect of adding the Mets to her viewing schedule. "Kazuo should go," she said. "It's exciting for us to think that he will be a valuable player in the U.S. Of course, some people are worried about the future of Japanese base-ball, but after we see the quality of the games of the MLB, which are faster, stronger and more dynamic, we want to see more and more Japanese succeed over there. It's the fault of the NPB for not keeping pace. Besides, it's not the end of the world. Americans watch the NFL on Sunday, but they also watch high-school football on Friday and college football on Saturday. Japanese watch professional European and Latin American football and their own J.League. There's room for all."

Unlike the NPB stars cited above, among those not eager to depart were Alex Cabrera, Tuffy Rhodes and Roberto Petagine, all of whom won home run titles in Japan. Advancing in years as they were, none, it was said, was certain to hit the 96 mph fastballs so common in the U.S. but so rare in Japan. And no one in MLB was willing to pay them the millions they were making in Japan—Rhodes had a two-year deal worth $10 million with Yomiuri for the 2003 season—to find out.

Living in America

There were a variety of reasons why the seepage of players to the U.S. seemed certain to continue. In addition to the challenge, there was the looseness of the MLB system: For the first time in their lives, Japanese players who went to the States had a real say in dictating their own salaries and their own practice routines. Said Hideo Nomo, who played for eight different comparatively laid-back Amerian managers, "It's a great feeling to be responsible for yourself and to be free to be yourself. In Japan, you're treated like a child."

But there were other factors as well, if somewhat less significant. Money, of course was one. Although many players did accept less money to play in the U.S., they stood to pocket more lucre in the long run given the higher MLB salary structure and the potential for increased commercial endorsements back home. Another was the preference for natural grass in American parks, which allows outfielders to dive for balls they might not go after as enthusiastically in Japan, where artificial grass is so prevalent and is such a potential cause of injury to players sliding or diving to make a catch. Japanese imports even professed to like the unequivocal expressiveness of American fans, even those in New York. As Hideki Matsui put it, "In the U.S., they are easy to understand. When you play well, they give you a big round of applause. When you do bad, they boo you. In

Tokyo, it's always the same. Trumpets, whistles and chanting in the *ōendan*. Silence in the rest of the stands." Ichiro Suzuki agreed: "They're fun to watch. They're every bit as individualistic as the players. In Japan, without the cheering section, it's deathly quiet."

Of course, not everything about the American experience has been pure unalloyed joy for the Japanese *yakyū* migrant (something that has also been said in reverse for Americans playing in Japan). While, on the one hand, most Japanese players appreciate the unconstrained nature of the U.S. system, they also think that it helps create "unfinished" athletes, baseballers who are less skilled in the fundamentals and the finer points of the game—like the bunt, the hit and run, hitting to the opposite field, base running, defensive relays and such—because they do not practice them endlessly from Little League on up the way young ballplayers in Japan did. The Japanese have a term that they use to describe the American ballplayer in general. It is *sabitteru,* and it means "rusty." The constant American emphasis on power, they believe, is a detriment to equally important parts of the game, like advancing the runner.

Japanese also look askance at certain long-standing American baseball customs like the quaint practice of chewing tobacco and spitting it on the dugout floor—"disgusting" is the word cleanliness-conscious Japanese players commonly use to describe it as they weave their way through the pools of tobacco juice. They find confusing the myriad unwritten rules of behavior that major leaguers have concocted to protect their all-important "Major League Pride." No bunting or stealing with a big lead is one. No crowd-pleasing fist in the air (or *gattsu pozu,* as folks back home put it). The Japanese cannot understand why opposing players took offense at Tsuyoshi Shinjo's gaudy show of touching home plate with his hand, or why American players in the Hawaiian Winter League took exception to Kazuo Matsui's celebratory gestures when he played there some years earlier. To fans in Japan, such behavior is reminiscent of former Seibu star Koji Akiyama, who would do a cartwheel and a somersault whenever he hit a game-ending blast. It is a mystery to the visiting *nihon-jin* why that kind of conduct is viewed as "showing up the opposition" in MLB and regarded as an invitation to reprisal in the form of a fastball to the ribs, while similar behavior is seen and tolerated all the time in the NFL and the NBA. Then there is the puerile tendency of their American teammates to play practical jokes on each other—like, say, putting itching powder in a teammate's talcum powder container. This is simply not done back home, where group *wa* is so important.

Other puzzlements include the presence of loud and abusive fans willing to fight to the death over possession of a foul ball in the stands—a marked contrast to Japan, where batting-practice balls are politely returned to the ushers—as well as umpires who cannot be intimidated, a phenomenon unknown in Japan, where they rank at the very bottom of the totem pole. What would be considered a normal interrogation in Japan would get you thrown out of a contest in America and possibly suspended.

Outside the ballpark, adjustments are even more difficult. Few Japanese speak English well enough to carry on a conversation with their teammates, and it is such a wearying experience to spend an evening over dinner communicating through an interpreter that the development of meaningful cross-cultural relationships is impeded. Thus most Japanese players spend their off-duty hours consorting with other Japanese expatriates or visitors from Mother Nippon, catching up on the news from back home and trying to figure out what makes Americans tick. The 300,000 or so Japanese residents of the United States and the constant flow of baseball tourists across the Pacific ensure that they do not totally lack for company. (Hideki Matsui, for one, complained that hardly an evening went by in New York City that there wasn't some group or another in from Tokyo that he was required by social custom and good manners to favor with his presence.)

But their sense of isolation is heightened by the constant travel, the long airline rides and countless nights in strange cities where most people have never even met a Japanese. (Kansas City is one of the least desirable destinations because it is so difficult to find a decent Japanese restaurant there.) Tsuyoshi Shinjo described his three years on the MLB road as a constant battle against loneliness and boredom. "You fly into a city," he said, "you play a game that ends at ten and then you're ready to go out, but all the restaurants—Japanese or otherwise—are closing up. You go back to your hotel room, order a cheeseburger from room service and turn on the TV, but you can't understand what the people are saying. It can really get to you after a while. I had to start carrying DVDs from Japan with me to keep my sanity." Unlike many MLB players, most Japanese athletes on the road leave their wives at home, in conformance with Japanese custom. In many cases, they leave them all the way back in Japan, where the school system is considered more suitable for their children.

Life in America is a smorgasbord of new and strange experiences. In contrast to Japan, where public transportation is spotless, state-of-the-art and run with the smooth efficiency of a Swiss watch (excuse me, Seiko), the American system is a disaster. American subways, trains and buses often appear filthy and inefficient, and U.S. airplanes always seem delayed. Compared to Tokyo taxis, which are models of comfort and hygiene (often featuring internal air fresheners and even backseat television sets, among other accoutrements), riding in a New York cab could be, as Hideki Matsui put it, "scary."

Then there is the American custom of tipping for such services which, many Japanese will tell you, is unfathomable and uncivilized. On top of that are the subtle and not-so-subtle discriminations that people of Asian origin sometimes face. While Ichiro, for one, claimed that he had never experienced any kind of anti-Japanese bias in America at all, others complained of hearing racially derogatory insults from the stands, if not from other ballplayers, and not infrequent rudeness from salespeople, who would then turn around and treat whites with the height of politeness.

In 2003, in fact, a young Japanese woman was moved to file a multi-million-dollar lawsuit against MLB, her former employer, for "unreasonable, offensive and demeaning anti-Japanese and anti-Asian hostility," charging an executive with repeatedly referring to people of Japanese ancestry by the term "Jap" or "Japs." Later that same year, a scout for the New York Mets was fired for mocking the ancestry of an Asian Los Angeles Dodger executive.

If you asked Japanese what they like most about the U.S., they would probably mention the vast spaciousness of it all—the large houses and the accessibility of golf courses (ideal for golf fanatics like Ishī and Hasegawa). It compares most favorably to the cramped conditions on Japan's four crowded islands. Added Seattle-based sportswriter Masayoshi Niwa, who has covered the Mariners for years, "These guys absolutely love the freedom of being able to walk downtown in the cities without wearing any sunglasses. It's something they can't do back in Japan—especially Ichiro. It's why he finally decided to stay in Seattle to train after the 2003 season ended. If he goes back to Japan, the media follows him everywhere."

Ballplayers' wives, if they come, might mention the enhanced social status of women in the United States, which stands in marked contrast to Japan, where men often treat their spouses like servants. Shinjo's wife experienced considerable shock when she visited her husband in New York in 2001 and he peeled some fruit for her. "He never did anything like that for me back in Japan," she said.

If you asked Japanese, coming as they do from a relatively peaceful country with a comparatively low crime rate, what they dislike the most about the U.S., they would probably mention the confrontational side of American society and its pervasive crime—symbolized, to their minds, by America's fixation with guns (ownership of which in Japan is severely limited). Said sportswriter Niwa, "The players I know really worry about security, especially those with children. Dirty taxis and late-arriving planes are one thing. That's just part of life in the United States. But they really do worry about crime and guns and safety. It's one reason why Hasegawa, who has a son, likes Seattle so much. It's safe."

Shōrai, "The Future"

In the fall of 2002, Ichiro Suzuki predicted that the day would come when there would be "four, five and more Japanese players on every MLB team." As if to make his prediction come true, scouts from North America, impressed by the all-around ability, the work ethic, the obedient manner and the comparative lack of greed at the salary table that the Mariners' Nipponese Whiz and his compatriots have demonstrated, have flocked to Japan in search of more new talent. The National High School Baseball Spring and Summer tournaments at Koshien Stadium in Osaka, showcase for some of the best high-school talent in the land and long a gathering spot for NPB scouts, has begun attracting MLB scouts as well—hoping to sign amateur stars right out of high school and train them in the States. So have big-time college games.

Evidence of an intriguing future supply of talent could be seen at the 2003 Little League World Series, in Williamsport, Pennsylvania, captured by a contingent from Fuchu, Japan, the third Japanese squad in four years to win the title. They were so dominating that they outscored their opponents in the 18 tourney games they played 222–21, easily winning the final against Boynton Beach Florida, 10–1. Their star player was 5′5″ pitcher Yūtaro Tanaka, who weighs 181 pounds and resembles a small truck.

The Fuchu club is but one of 679 such teams in Japan, the second largest number in the world, after the U.S. But, unlike their American counterparts, these Japanese play a season that lasts nearly the entire calendar year. They grow up superbly coached, highly skilled in all the fundamentals, and with a better appreciation of the word "preparation" than their counterparts in the U.S.

No doubt the MLB scouts were encouraged by the widely reported remarks of the Fuchu nine who visited Yankee Stadium in the afterglow of their victorious world championship game and professed to dream of stardom in the States, *not* their native land. Young Tanaka flatly declared the only place he wanted to play when he grew up was in the majors. He said he rarely missed a telecast of Hideki Matsui's games with the New York Yankees, even if it meant he had to arise at two in the morning to watch the first pitch of an afternoon Yankee Stadium contest.

The increasing foreign attention, and the steady hemorrhaging of baseball talent from Japan, raises the question of what will happen to the NPB—a proud organization that had once thought of challenging the U.S. in a "Real World Series" but is now seemingly reduced to feeder status for MLB, helpless to stop the flow of the game's best players out of the country. Sports columnist Masayuki Tamaki, ruefully comparing the kidnapping of NPB players by MLB to the infamous abductions of Japanese citizens by North Korean agents, said, "It makes me want to become a sports terrorist. . . . But then again, maybe you've got to destroy the game in order to save it."

However, others argue that the loss of the NPB's biggest stars, however painful, is not exactly the end of the world, because realistically speaking, the NPB does not have that much talent to lose. Experts estimate that there are anywhere from two dozen to three dozen MLB-level players in Japan—Valentine's claim of "a hundred" notwithstanding. Few of them approach the Ichiro or Matsui level, while the liberty to move abroad via free posting and free agency takes years to attain. Then too, not every professional in Japan is that eager to take on MLB. Many borderline players of, say, Shinjo's level, are afraid to risk their well-paying jobs and their stature in Japan for a spot on the bench with some MLB team. After Kazuo Matsui, in fact, legitimately available stars are few and far between.

Said Shigetoshi Hasegawa of the game he had left behind, "While players from the Dominican Republic or Venezuela must leave their homeland to make a good living at baseball, Japanese players can still make a good salary at home. That's why I don't think everybody wants to come to the States. With the different culture and the different language, it's pretty tough. So Japan will continue to have good baseball. The game is still strong."

Moreover, many young amateur players are reluctant to start their careers in the U.S. minor leagues, where teams do not provide interpreters, where pay is barely above subsistence level and where their games are not televised back in Japan for family and friends to see. Better, they believe, to start in the comfort of the NPB minors, where at least they are paid a living wage and have a dormitory room in which to hang their baseball cap and *fundoshi*, or perhaps try a season or two on one of the industrial league teams, where one can play ball as a company employee. *Shakai-jin yakyū*, as it is called, provides a steady number of players to the NPB each year (17 in 2003, as opposed to 67 from high school and universities). For most players, it makes sense to build up a name, make some money and enjoy some recognition at home before thinking about a move abroad.

A merger between the NPB and MLB is one idea that has been mentioned occasionally. In such a scenario, a handful of teams, utilizing both local and imported talent, would form a Japan division, joining either the American or the National League (or perhaps both, if two Japan divisions were created). Japanese stars who want to test themselves against big-league competition would not have to pack up and move all the way to North America to do so; they would simply join one of Japan's entries in MLB. At the same time, according to MLBPA attorney Gene Orza, there are any number of skilled major leaguers who, having participated in exhibition tours of Japan, would jump at the chance to play in a city like Tokyo, as long as it was *major league* baseball and not the practice-until-you-die variety.

Speculations about an NPB–MLB merger are highly speculative. Among the many obstacles it would face are ten-hour flights (unless Lockheed-Martin's new super-fast passenger jet program, which would cut flight time in half between Japan and the West Coast, is resurrected), debilitating jet lag, higher costs, and other logistical headaches, such as the need for work visas and processing through customs. The Chicago Cubs played their first two official games of the 2000 season in Tokyo (versus the New York Mets), but then returned home and, exhausted, lost their next 10 in a row; no one on the team was eager to repeat the experience. A season opener between the Seattle Mariners and the Oakland A's was canceled in 2003 due to terrorist worries. But the New York Yankees are slated to open their 2004 season in Tokyo, and with all the fans they have acquired there, it may well seem like just another home opener.

Any serious attempt at a merger of such great pith and marrow, however, would require a wholesale restructuring, from a system of corporate sponsorship to one of business orientation, the building of a better minor league system and overcoming what seems sure to be virulent owner opposition to any American invasion of their markets. The Yomiuri mandarins, in particular, seem unlikely to smile.

Of an NOB–MLB merger, sniffed *Kyojin honcho* Tsuneo Watanabe, "It's totally impossible. The idea is nonsense and has no merit;

[people like] Whiting who favor such an idea show they don't understand anything about Japanese baseball."

The sense of national pride that many Japanese players feel further confuses the issue. Ichiro Suzuki, a man who three years earlier had said that "the only thing I will miss about Japanese baseball is my dog," seemed to contradict himself in a joint interview with Nagashima for the *Yomiuri Shimbun* New Year's Day issue in January 2003. "My wish in the long run," he said, "is for Japanese baseball to be recognized as the best in the world, even though that distinction belongs to the major leagues at the moment. I feel that way because I am Japanese. Sure, I want fans to see regular-season games (like Seattle vs. Oakland) to feel the seriousness, the aggressiveness of them all. But take Koji Uehara's performance at the 2002 Japan-MLB All-Star Series. He fanned Barry Bonds and Jason Giambi three, four times each, and that made me happy. I was on the other [MLB] bench, but rooting for Uehara. I want Japanese baseball to be the best in the world."

When asked about Hideki Matsui's then-impending defection to the States, Ichiro further replied, "It's impossible to control your growing desire to play in the major leagues because we all know that it's the best in the world. Many are worried what effect Matsui's move to the majors would have on Japanese pro baseball. But I don't think that shock would last long. . . . As an athlete, you have to compete against the world's best. In that sense, Japanese baseball lags behind a bit. I hope Matsui's move will open the closed doors. In the short run, the popularity of baseball might recede a bit. But in the long term, I believe, it would have more positive effects than negative ones. It has to happen to become the No. 1 baseball. If you remain an outsider, you never know what's going on inside. There're many things that you haven't got a clue about if you have no first-hand experience."

Overlooked in discussions about the death rattle of the NPB is the fact that it is still very much alive. Although MLB has made real inroads—an average of 1.5 million viewers were estimated to have watched the 272 regular games shown in Japan, with 12.5 million viewers watching the early-morning casts of the six games of the 2003 World Series (this compared with an average of 20.1 in the U.S. on

Fox in prime time), and a month later MLB signed a TV deal with Japan estimated to be worth $275 million over six years, which was triple the previous contract—surveys still show that *Nihon Puro-Yakyū* has remained the favorite sport of well over half of all sports fans. Although Yomiuri TV ratings dropped to 14.6 percent on average in 2003, an all-time low for that team, that still works out to approximately 18 million viewers a night. Moreover, overall attendance was up by 3.1 percent, to 23,664,500, an all-time high—a state of affairs some people actually attribute to the success of Japanese in MLB, which, perversely, has lent more credibility to the local game even though its top stars are no longer in the country.

The enhanced interest in the 2003 version of the NPB was also due in part to the Osaka Hanshin Tigers, a team frequently compared to the Chicago Cubs or the Boston Red Sox in terms of passionate local fan support and historical futility. The Hanshin club won their first pennant in 18 years, drawing over 3,000,000 fans for the first time in the team's history (the third franchise in either league to surpass the figure in 2003, after Yomiuri and Daiei), earning prime time "Golden Hour" ratings for many of their games, mostly those versus the Giants. In fact, four national networks interrupted their regular evening programming to telecast the moment that Hanshin clinched the flag. The event caused so much excitement that an estimated 5,300 fans, overcome with elation, leapt exuberantly into the highly toxic Dotonbori River in downtown Osaka to celebrate—an act of lunacy that has become a local ritual in that boisterous metropolis, previously demonstrated after Japan's last victory in 2002 World Cup play. It resulted in the death of one overexcited soul, who made the jump three times but only came up twice.

On the other hand, pessimists were happy to point out that Hanshin had *not* won the Japan Series, falling to the Daiei Hawks in seven games, and that their manager's subsequent retirement, forced by bad health, did not bode well for future repeats of the Miracle of '03. Moreover, the Japan Champion Hawks were so financially unstable that the front office deemed it necessary to unload their popular power hitter/third baseman Hiroki Kokubo to the Yomiuri Giants— for nothing—just to rid themselves of his expensive contract.

The future of the NPB was increasingly being seen in the establishment of an Asian League, or, in lieu of that, a round-robin playoff system involving the champions of the ROK, Taiwan and Japan pro leagues, in which the winner would be awarded a wild card slot in the MLB postseason. Still another was the creation of a World Baseball Cup tournament, like that in soccer, to be held once every four years, an idea the MLB had penciled in for March 2005. (MLB had, incidentally, set up an exploratory office in Tokyo in 2003 captained by one Jim Small. Ironically enough, it was located right above the NPB commissioner's office in the Imperial Towers.)

In the meantime, with the player exodus to North America destined to continue, some speculate that both sides are in line to reap benefits. Said noted playwright Tetsu Yamazaki, a longtime NPB fan, "Let Japanese players go to the States. That is good for Japanese baseball because someday they will come back and raise the level of the sport." This is in fact what happened with Irabu, who helped lead the '03 Tigers to their miracle, not only with his pitching but also through his positive influence on the younger members of the squad and the lessons he had brought back from MLB, such as proper care of the pitching arm. A similar theme was echoed in the words of Kazuo Matsui, an avid observer of the MLB way, who told a magazine interviewer, "The 100 fungo drill makes more sense than the 1000 fungo drill. What's important is your concentration level when you practice. I don't like being tired in vain. I want to take what's best from both places." And, miracle of miracles, the Yomiuri Giants even allowed their pitching ace Uehara to use an agent/attorney in contract negotiations for 2004—although they could not bring themselves to actually refer to the man as an agent, publicly insisting he was only an "advisor."

At the same time, Japanese organizations *appear* to be becoming more flexible about adopting American ways, as indeed evidenced by the hiring of Trey Hillman and the rehiring of Bobby Valentine—although how the sagas of these two men, especially that of the latter, would play out remains a keen point of interest. There is, after all, still resistance to the idea of full and unlimited participation in the Japanese game by foreign players, led by the NPBPA, as evidenced by the 2004 restrictions of no more than four foreign players per varsity team.

The flowback seems to be working the other way as well, as MLB coaches and players, marveling at Hideki Matsui's solid fundamentals and Ichiro's determined grace and style, are beginning to incorporate certain Japanese ideas about extra training—as evidenced by Mariners manager Bob Melvin's 2003 spring camp routine. Many are beginning to wonder if Japan's system—where players start lengthy training from Little League on, stressing basics and such old-fashioned ideas as bunting, advancing the runner and stealing—might not be such a bad idea.

Americans are always grumbling about how nobody plays the game right anymore. Maybe that's about to change.

NOTES

I n researching and writing this book I conducted over 100 interviews, traveled nearly 100,000 miles, read nearly 100 books and
waded through countless newspaper and magazine articles. Specific sources for all the material in *The Meaning of Ichiro* and accompanying notes can be found in the extensive End Note section on
a special *Meaning of Ichiro* Web site set up by Warner Books at
www.twbookmark.com. What follows here is but a brief sampling.

The All-Time All-Star Team

According to a poll conducted to determine Japan's All-Century
baseball team, Ichiro was the fans' favorite selection, leading all
candidates including Shigeo Nagashima and Sadaharu Oh, with
587,426 votes. The lineup consisted of Atsuya Furuta at catcher, Oh
at first base, Hiromitsu Ochiai at second, Nagashima at third, Kazuo
Matsui at shortstop, Hideki Matsui, Isao Harimoto, and Ichiro in the
outfield. Yutaka Enatsu was the pitcher. (*Kyodo News*, October 19,
2000).

About TV Ratings

With a few exceptions, all of the Seattle Mariners games were telecast on the NHK's satellite channel system, which was established in
the '80's and was not as diffuse as the terrestrial TV system used by
most houses in Japan. NHK did not give out ratings, or even the number of households that had the new system installed. Thus, the impact
of the Mariners telecasts was difficult to accurately gauge. However,

the vast outdoor crowds that watched the games on Hi-Vision screens around Tokyo and Osaka and other major cities, and the slippage in the ratings, were clear evidence that a dramatic change had occurred. According to Video Research, which took over the TV ratings from Japan Nielsen, a rating of one percentage point equaled 1.2 million viewers. Thus a 15 percent rating for a Giants game meant that 18 million people watched it. 30 percent meant 36 million viewers. On October 31, 2003, *The Wall Street Journal* reported that there were only 4.41 million houses with satellite TV in Japan, a country with a population of 127 million. *The Wall Street Journal* estimated that there were an average of 1.5 million viewers for a satellite gamecast. In games occasionally shown on NHK General, their terrestrial network, ratings sometimes reached 10 percent, or 12 million viewers, which was quite remarkable for an early morning telecast.

About the Early History of Baseball in Japan

Baseball was a by-product of Japan's all-out effort to learn from the West. In its nascent years, baseball was considered less a "sport" than a kind of competition, like archery or shooting, where the object was to hit a target.

The first game ever played in Japan is believed to have been a contest between the crew of the U.S. battleship *Colorado* and foreign residents in Yokohama in September 1870 (*Mainichi Daily News*, Sunday, May 7, 2000, "Baseball History blasted into past" by Akio Nikaido). The first game played by Japanese was said to have been organized by an American professor named Albert Bates at Kaitaku University in 1873. What was perhaps the first game ever played between Japanese and Americans was a pickup affair involving unequal sides of university students and visitors from the U.S. which took place in 1876. The first organized baseball team, with uniforms, was the Shimbashi Athletic Club Athletics, formed in 1878 by railway engineer Hiroshi Hiraoka, who had recently returned from a stay in Boston where he became an avid Red Sox fan. Hiraoka, according to historical accounts, was the first person in Japan to throw a curve ball (NPBHoF).

The Ichiko practice routine was described in the following manner by Suishu Tobita in *Tobita Suishu Senshu, Yakyū Kisha Jidai, Bēsubōru Magajin sha,* in 1960 (pps 30–31). "For their practice, there was no snow or hail . . . If it snowed, the team would clear the field . . . Then they started practice. And the word 'ouch' was prohibited for the members of Ichiko during practice. For ordinary people, there was no doubt that they would express their pain by screaming, however in their (Ichiko's) case, there was no word uttered. The pain was overcome. In case it wasn't, the word *kayui* (it itches) was used . . . The balls were thrown against the cold chilly wind and occasionally their fingers were colored with blood, and the balls, being thrown left and right, were also covered with blood. This was the way of practice . . . Balls that hit their shins and feet felt like iron."

An Ichiko alumnus would later write this spirited summation of the philosophy of his school's adopted and highly popular pastime. "Sports came from the West. In Ichiko baseball, we were playing sports, but we were also putting the spirit of Japan into it . . . *Yakyū* is a way to express the samurai spirit. To play baseball is to develop this spirit . . . Thus, our members were just like the warriors of old with their samurai spirit." From '*Yakyū Bushi*," an article appearing in a commemorative work published by the Alumni Association of the first Higher School of Tokyo, February 28, 1903, entitled "*Yakyū Bushi Fukisoku Dai Ichi Koto Gakkō Koyukai.*"

The Ichiko triumphs, no less significantly, also represented the first step in making baseball accessible to the masses. Up until that time, baseball had been a game played and watched by a relatively affluent and socially advanced elite. Early in the Meiji Era, social inequities were still so pronounced that some families had to resort to selling off their daughters to the brothels of Yoshiwara just to put food on the table. For the average person, mingling with foreigners was out of the question. There were only a handful of senior high schools in Japan, and they were elite schools like Ichiko—far removed from the sweaty realities of the hoi polloi. But the Ichiko victories served to make baseball the number one sport in the nation's middle schools as well, spreading out to all corners of the archipelago. They helped popularize terms like "*seishin yakyū.*"

Ichiko won their first encounter with the American squad on May 23, 1896, in Yokohama by an astonishing score of 29–4, in what is known as the first formal game between Japan and the U.S. When the recently retired school principal Hiroji Kinoshita was telegraphed the news that day, he exhorted Ichiko to "demonstrate the true spirit of Japanese *Bushido*" by not boasting about their triumph. The victory was reported on page 1 of the *Hochi Shimbun*, May 25, 1896, and page 2 of the *Yomiuri Shimbun*, May 25, 1896. Ichiko went on to win two rematches later that year by scores of 35–9 and 22–6. See the encyclopedic collection of material that is Ichiko's history entitled "*Koryoshi*," pp. 799–810, published by the *Dai-Ichi Koto Gakkō Kishukuryo*, September 10, 1930.

An account of Ichiko's games versus the Americans appears in two installments of a series entitled *Yakyū-bun-nan Shiwa*, by Saburo Saito, the first appearing in the *Yomiuri Supōtsu*, vol. 5, No. 8, July 1952, pp. 71–73, continued in the Vol. 6, no.9 edition of August 1952, pp. 64–66. A good general description of how Ichiko provided a catalyst in turning baseball into a martial art appears in Masaru Ikei's book, *Hakkyu Taiheiyo wo Wataru*, Chuko Shinsho, Tokyo, 1976. See pp. 38–46 for an account of Ichiko victories over Yokohama in 1896 and their impact on the country as a whole. Also see "*Kindai Puro Supōtsu*" *no Rekishi Shakiagaku*, by Koichi Kiku, Tokyo, Fumaido, 1993, pp. 88–122, as well as the chronological chart on pp. 52–53. Also see *Gekan Bēsubōru*, January 10, 2001, for a good summary of the development of Ichiko baseball. Moriyama's practice routine was described in "*Yakyū Nenpo*," published by *Mimatsu Shoten Nai Yakyu Nenpo Henshu-bu*, in 1912. Tokyo, pp. 309–17. The article was written by Suishu Tobita. Also see *Zuihitsu to Tsuiso*, Suishu Tobita, *Bēsubōru Magajin*, 1960, p. 229. For another article dealing with Moriyama's mound exploits, also written by Tobita, see *Undokai*, No. 47, April 1912. Also *Yakyu Hyakunen*, by Kyushi Yamato, Jiji, 1976. A photograph of the brick wall bearing the hole Moriyama put in it appears in *Nihon Supōtsu Reikishi*, by Ki Kimura, *Besuboru Magazine* sha., 1978, p. 103 An excellent description of Moriyama's Ichiko career, as well as the early years of baseball in Japan, appears in Chapter 4 of Joseph Reaves's fine book "*Taking in a Game: A History of*

Baseball in Asia," published by the University of Nebraska Press in 2001. The *Yakyūbuka* appears in *Schooldays in Imperial Japan*, p. 125, by Donald Roden, Berkeley: University of California Press, 1980, which also features a thorough and fascinating history of Ichiko. An interesting, if incomplete, account of games between the Ichiko ball club and the Yokohama Country and Athletic Club nine is on pp. 124–26. Ichiko baseball alumni published accounts of their experiences in a series entitled *Ichiko Yakyū Bushi,* published in the turn-of-the-century magazine *Undokai*. The spread of *Bushido Bēsubōru* to Waseda and Keio was described in *Kindai Puro Supōtsu no Reikishi Shakai Gaku,* by Koichi Kiku, published by *Fumaido Shuppan*, Tokyo, 1993, p. 102.

The Waseda trip to the U.S. is described in Masaru Ikei's book, *Hakkyu Taiheiyo wo Wataru*, Chuko Shinsho, Tokyo, 1976, pp. 46–51. Also see the article in the *San Francisco Chronicle*, October 31, 1996, C-1, entitled "U.S.-Japanese Baseball History—It Happened in 1905." Also see *Kindai Puro Supōtsu no Reikishi Shakai Gaku,* by Koichi Kiku, published by *Fumaido Shuppan*, Tokyo, 1993, p. 102, pp. 100–122. Waseda pitcher Yasushi Kono, who started every game of the tour, earned the nickname "Iron Kono," and was occasionally greeted by cries of "On to St. Petersburg." Iso Abe, the leader of that Waseda contingent to the States, envisioned baseball as a peaceful substitute for war. He recommended modifying Ichiko's *bushido* approach and maintained that the Anglo-American concept of fair play could be applied as well. He added that it wasn't necessary to practice every day all year to play one game. Needless to say, his imprecations were ignored. "superior to that of the U.S." from *Saikin Yakyū Gijutsu,* written by Makoto Hashido and published by *Haku Bunkan*, Tokyo, 1905, pp. 5–7.

In Tokyo the Keio-Waseda rivalry grew so heated that, after opposing groups of supporters confronted each other on the streets of the city in the midst of a three-game series in 1906, authorities suspended matches between them for two decades.

About *Bushido*

The term "Bushido" means "way of the warrior" and refers to the code of the samurai in feudal Japan, which stressed loyalty, duty, obligation and obedience and valued honor above life. It has been dismissed by some historians as an "invented tradition," because it was essentially a warrior code that had been created in the 17th century after the major civil wars had been concluded and the samurai were no longer needed to fight in battle. Although the original idea developed during the Kamakura era, 1192–1333, the name Bushido was not used until the 16th century with the advent of the new peacetime era of the Tokugawa shogunate (1603–1867). The concept of *Bushido* was something that masterless samurai used to market their skills as martial arts instructors, bodyguards and peacekeepers and was refined to incorporate Confucianist, Zen and Buddhist thought. In the mid-19th century, it was made the basis of ethical training for the whole society, with the emperor replacing the feudal lord as an object of loyalty and sacrifice, and as such it played a role in the rise of Japanese nationalism and mustering popular support for wartime efforts to come. Embedded in its value system were piety, frugal living, loyalty, selflessness, kindness, honesty, learning, filial and ceremonial propriety and military skill. It was even said to parallel Anglo American concepts like chivalry and fair play in the 19th century.

The Way of the Samurai received wide exposure in the early part of the 20th century, after the publication of Inazo Nitobe's English-language tome *Bushido*, which was an attempt to introduce "traditional Japanese culture" to the West. Some critics characterized it as an overcooked myth given its overly rosy portrayal of old samurai as men of highest honor while ignoring the brutality and treachery they often practiced. "Professional killers," some historians have called them.

That said, however, the impact of *Bushido* on the Japanese culture and consciousness since the time of *The Book of Five Rings*, written in the 17th century, can hardly be dismissed. Generations of children have heard its core principles—dedication to self-perfection, submergence of ego, martial spirit, development of inner (spiritual) strength, courage—expounded by their fathers, tachers, coaches and, in adulthood, corporate bosses, right to the present day.

About the 1,000 Fungo Drill

The "1,000 Fungo Drill" does not usually mean a player has to field a thousand ground balls. The idea is to make him dash to his left and to his right and then back again, chasing balls hit just out of his reach until he becomes exhausted. It is a spirit-strengthening drill, not a conditioning one. In the Morinji Camp, such drills consisted usually of 200 balls per player, although Shiraishi was said to have been worked much longer. A similar drill—with fly balls—was used for outfielders. According to Kazuo Matsui, "There are a lot of my former teammates I know of who have done up to 700 or 800 . . ." (January 16, 2003. Seibu Stadium)

About Mihara and "Gattsu"

Osamu Mihara's managerial career was distinguished, from others of his era, by the fact that he never raised his hand in anger to his players. Some say this was because he served as a private in Japan's wartime imperial army and had been routinely punched by his superiors. At any rate, he was fond of saying, "I can win without hitting my players" (*Kon-shu no hon*, Saichi Maruyama, *Mainichi Shimbun*, November 24, 2002). He also had a strong dislike for base-by-base style of play, preferring the long ball instead. He recalled with special disgust a game with the Giants when he was their manager in the 1947–1950 era. Slugger Noboru Aota, batting third in the order, took it upon himself to sacrifice bunt with runners on second and third and no out. But Mihara did not mind abusing his pitchers. The Lions' Kazuhisa Inao (who won 42 games in 1961) appeared in six of the seven games of the 1958 Japan Series. In the 1958 pennant stretch, Mihara started Inao in 18 of the team's last 27 games and used him in relief in 7 others. Inao's career, not surprisingly, was over by the time he was 32, thanks to a damaged arm. See *Majitsushi–Mihara Osamu to Nishitetsu Lions*; Yasunori Tateishi, *Shogakkuan,* 2002; and *Puro Yakyū Kiroku no Techo*, Isao Chiba, *Baseball Magazine,* 2001.

Yale anthropologist William Kelly, who has been studying Japanese baseball, argues that "guts"did not become "ideologically central" in pro baseball until the V-9 era of Kawakami and the Yomiuri Giants, 1965–1973. This would come as a surprise to Mr. Inao, as well as to Motoshi Fujita, who pitched 359 innings for Mizuhara and his Giants in 1959, and to Tadashi Sugiura, who pitched all four games of the 1959 series against the Giants for the Nankai Hawks, coming off a season in which he won 38 games while pitching 371 innings. These individuals uncomplainingly pitched their arms out for their managers, relying on "guts" when the inevitable pain from so much wear and tear manifested itself in their elbows and shoulders. Their careers ended early, but as Hiroshi Gondo, a pitcher who threw 429 innings in 1961, put it, "The code of Bushido was strong . . . Many times my fingers and arms hurt, but I could not refuse my manager's request." Inao, for his part, continued to speak of his great affection for Mihara long after his retirement, despite his teammate Yasumitsu Toyoda's bitter complaints that Mihara shortened Inao's career. "Heart is the important thing," he said. "Younger players should pitch more." Toyoda Home page. Toyoda/Inao interview. Sugiura often expressed similar sentiments, despite his own arm-damaged shortened career.

Mr. Kelly's comments on "guts" would, of course, also be news to the men who participated in the Morinji Camp. (See "The Blood and Guts of Japanese Professional Baseball, by William W. Kelly. Department of Antrhopology. Yale University, *William.Kelly@yale.edu* for the professor's "ideologically central" and other such remarks contained therein.)

About Tobita and *Seishin Yakyū*

Shortly before his death in 1967, Tobita did an extensive interview with NHK in which he continued to cite the Ichiko approach as the foundation for all Japanese baseball. However, he also expressed his concern that modern baseball players were overdoing things in practice. "We were thought to have practiced hard in my era," he said, "but watching these guys today at Waseda, it looks a lot tougher. Maybe I'm just getting old, but it seems more regimented."

Concerned over a slump in the fortunes of his alma mater, he instigated the removal from power of yet another in a long line of Waseda managers noted for their Spartan training, Renzo Ishī, a.k.a. "Renzo the Ogre," and had him replaced with a former Waseda star and one of the luminaries of amateur baseball, a witty, warm-hearted individualist, Tokichiro Ishī, who believed that "baseball should be fun." Tokichiro's first words as manager—"It's too cold today. Let's forget about practice"—were revolutionary and went down in Waseda history. His idea of a manager's duties was to encourage his players to make choices (including what position they played) and to bring out the best in their talents through mix of discipline and laughter. He ushered in a new golden era at the university, where the watchword was "take risks, realize the joy of the game, and get out of the meeting as soon as possible and go drink." He is one of the few lifelong amateurs to be enshrined in the Japanese Hall of Fame.

Elsewhere, however, *seishin yakyū* continued to hold sway. At Meiji University, "*konjō, konjō*" was the watchword for three decades under manager Kīchiro Shimaoka. At Keio, there was a sign in the baseball clubhouse—"3000 swings in the morning; 3000 more in the afternoon. If you don't do that, you can't win"—that reminded players what their priorities were. Said Keio player Shozo Eto, who later went on to coach and manage in the pros, "If you screwed up, they made you do *seiza*, sitting on your heels with a bat lodged behind your knees, under your thighs. There's nothing more painful. I'd rather be beaten up any day."

Draconian discipline eventually made its way back to Waseda as well. After his namesake departed and the school went through 15 losing seasons, Renzo Ishī returned to Waseda as manager in 1988 to win the championship of the Big Six, Tokyo's top university league. All in all, Renzo's mainstream approach made the baseball world more comfortable than Tokichiro's iconoclasm: a *konjō* philosophy was easier to apply and did not require a patient affection for one's athletes or an irrepressible sense of humor, traits not shared by everyone in the game. Baseball remained a taxing endeavor, which separated it from its American cousin.

Tobita's NHK radio interview was recorded in August 1962, five years before his death. The adventures of Tokichiro Ishī were related in the book *"Sekihaku san no Home Run,"* by Junji Tominaga, Chukei Shuppan, Tokyo, 2003. See pp. 1–16, 356–66. The latter segment contains a description of Suishu Tobita. David Shapiro, a personal friend of Tokichiro, provided additional details. Izu "Hell Camp" described in *Sports Nippon,* July 25, 2003, p. 3. "Bashing the players this way . . ." from *Nikkan Sports,* November 2, 1996, at start of that year's "Hell Camp" in Miyazaki. Ichiro Suzuki's comments about *seishin yakyū* or *konjō,* as he referred to it, came in an author interview November 7, 2002.

About Kazuhiro and Seishin Yakyū

Still another believer was Kazuhiro Kiyohara, the burly Giants hero who joined the team in 1997 after 11 years with the Seibu Lions. In the mid-'90s, Kiyohara, who was famous for his long line of girlfriends and nighttime escapades, but also for his attitude of respect toward the game—he always bowed upon entering and leaving a park—experienced a series of injuries that affected his batting average and threatened his career. In the Giants 25-day autumn camp in '97, Kiyohara took what was perhaps a record 30,000 swings, which works out to about 1,200 a day. (On hearing of this, New York Yankee manager Joe Torre remarked, "I don't think I've ever heard of a player swinging a bat 1,000 times a day, let alone 30 days in a row." Neither had his 2003 batting coach Rick Down.) Kiyohara's "30,000 swings" from *Nikkan Supōtsu,* October 28, 1997, p. 5. Torre and Down's comments on Kiyohara came in author interviews, March 14, 2003 and April 29, 2003 respectively.

In the winter of 1999, coming off yet another disappointing season in which he was also accused of associating with organized crime figures, Kiyohara shaved his head, donned the robes of a Buddhist monk and spent several wintry days, from 5:30 in the morning until midnight, chanting and meditating at a Buddhist temple in Kagoshima, interrupting his daylong spiritual practice only long enough to swing the bat. It was an effort, he said, to "regain the purity of his high school days."

Kiyohara's schedule:

    5:30 Wake up.
    6:00 Ring Temple Bell. Clean Temple.
    6:00 Radio Calisthenics; Vocal Training.
    7:00 Supplicant Drills—Hands, Knees and Face to the Floor.
    8:00 Breakfast.
    10:00 Incense Burning, Chanting.
    1:00 Reading Scriptures.
    4:00 Lunch.
    5:00 Shadow Swings.
    8:00 Sermon by Chief Temple Priest.
    12:00 Lights Out.

Kiyohara's sojourn to the Kagoshima zen temple was described on the front page of the *Tokyo Supōtsu*, December 22, 1999. Gary Garland, author of the terrific *"japanese insider"* on *baseballguru.com* described the visit of Hanshin Tiger righthander Taiyo Fujita, as "one of those ludicrous attempts at a spiritual toughening up that many Japanese players engage in." Fujita spent on Friday in January 2003 camping under a freezing cold waterfall in Gifu Prefecture for 110 seconds. "I thought it would kill me," said the player, who was shaven bald and wore white garments that made him resemble a Buddhist monk doing *"omisogi,"* a kind of cleansing rite. The account appeared in Garland's portion of the *Baseball Guru.com* web site, January 10, 2003.

Not all of them were addicted to practice—Koji Uehara, the man who easily struck out Barry Bonds three times in that 2003 exhibition game, preferred American style workouts between starts.

The Guttman-Thompson book "Japanese Sports: A History" provides some interesting material about the early development of baseball. But beware a book that gives you page upon page about *kemari*, an ancient "game" in which elegantly robed Heian courtiers stood in a circle and contrived to keep a gaily colored ball in the air by kicking it—an exercise akin to the equally bold practice of strewing beans for expecting royal princesses (exalted above other forms of exertion) to be picked up as a way of maintaining muscle tone—but not even a brief introduction to the wildly popular Koshien High School Baseball tournament, a mecca for the sport even before there ever was a professional game, or a mention of the contributions made by Moriyama and Tobita. Granted, this is an academic work, but given the theories espoused therein—i.e., "the attraction of baseball is as a 'bittersweet comic drama of the dysfunctions of corporate life'"—one wonders if the authors ever put down their research treatises and interviewed real-life ballplayers, fans and other flesh-and-blood, on-the-scene participants. If they had, they would at least have understood that it was Nagashima the public most identified with, not Oh, as they erroneously suggest.

About Fan Behavior

Not everyone agrees with the idea the fans in Japan only let loose when they join the highly organized ōendan or cheerleading groups. The aforementioned Kelly studied fan behavior at Koshien Stadium for a time in the mid-'90s and claimed this view of the fans "conforms too neatly to certain stereotypes about an alleged Japanese character of mindless collectivism (their 'undividualism' we might say)." He quotes a passage in the book *You Gotta Have Wa* that describes the Japanese fan in the ōendan as shedding his usual "restraint" and becoming a "veritable wildman, yelling and screaming nonstop for nine solid innings," implying this author sees the fans as automatons.

He declares that, in Japan, in general, the "more numerous infield audience . . . by and large behaves rather like crowds at American ballparks," and goes on at great length about the "sociality" of the Hanshin bleacher fans, in a labored article layered in social science terminology. ("*Sense and Sensibility at the Ballpark: What Fans Make of Professional Baseball in Modern Japan,*" available on the professor's website, *william.kelly@yale.edu.* It also appeared as "An Anthropologist in the Bleachers," *Japan Quarterly,* 1997.)

While Kelly's article appears well-researched, to suggest that there may be more going on in the grandstand than mindless groupthink or cathartic transformations from salaryman to screaming savage is hardly an epiphanous leap toward the understanding of the subject. And to argue that fan behavior away from the influence of organized *ōendan* or cheering group sessions is no different than that of the fan in America is to dismiss the perception of individuals who have watched far more games in both Japan and the United States than Professor Kelly and who see something else entirely.

Ask Ichiro Suzuki, a baseball player who spent nine years in Japan and three in the U.S. as of this writing. Said Suzuki, "I think Japanese fans, like the Japanese players, suppress their emotions too. They are very *otonashī* (quiet). You have the cheerleaders blowing trumpets and all. But when they're not doing anything, the stadium is really quiet. American fans, by contrast, do their own thing—people stand up and dance. The fans get up and express themselves, they show their own individuality, just like the players. You get the feeling they are really enjoying themselves." Asked why the Japanese fan is so quiet—was it courtesy or shyness?—he responded, "I think it's shyness. When I'm sitting in the stands in Japan as a fan, I can really understand that feeling" (author interview November 7, 2002). Said Jim Colborn, another who had spent years in ballparks on both sides of the Pacific, some as a coach, some as a scout, "Compared to the American fans, the Japanese in the infield stands are polite, orderly and reserved. They save their screaming for the *ōendan.* In the U.S., they have got to be participants" (interview August 29, 2003).

Wayne Grazcyk, baseball writer for the *Japan Times* for three decades and one of the world's foremost experts on the game: "The Japanese are not as exhibitionistic as the Americans. A baseball crowd is a more formal situation in Japan. They're not as boisterous or as innovative as the Americans. Even the vendors are monotonous. U.S. vendors are more showy. They'll deliver the peanuts behind their back, or they'll say, "You want some peanuts or what?"

Everybody's got a shtick. All in all, aside from the *ōendan*, stadiums are a lot quieter in Japan" (interview, November 8, 2002).

Marty Kuehnert, another longtime Japan-based writer: "In America, when you're quiet, you're quiet. When you cheer, you cheer. You make noise. You really cut loose. Most Japanese fans are quiet in general. They keep things at arm's length. I took a U.S. TV producer to Game 1 of the 2002 Japan Series. He couldn't believe the people in the stands were so quiet. 'Why don't they get excited?' he asked me." In the spring of 2000, Kuehnert wrote, "In this writer's opinion, the 2000 MLB opener in Japan was a resounding success in so many ways. I have one gripe, however. I would like to ask Japanese fans to wake up and learn how to cheer properly. It seems that without trumpets, drums, flags and cheerleaders, Japanese fans do not know when and how to cheer. One of my frequent complaints about Japanese baseball is that it is too noisy, with the din of brash instruments and organized cheering sections being constantly loud throughout the game, regardless of the score or the drama, or lack of it, on the field. . . . One sportswriter from New York described his impression of the *ōendan*-less Tokyo Dome during the Mets and Cubs exhibition games with Kyojin on March 27 and 28 and the official MLB opening games on the 29th and 30th, like being in a cemetery." (MSN Japan, April 5, 2000). Kuehnert also interviewed an *ōendan* leader who confessed that he did know what was happening on the field during the game because he was too busy leading cheers. It was only when he got home and watched a videotaped replay that he saw the game for the first time (interview, November 15, 2003). MLB second baseman Jeff Kent, after an exhibition tour in Japan in November 2002 in which *ōendan* were not in attendance, said, "I was surprised at the atmosphere in the ballparks. My wife even noticed it. She said that everyone was just glued to their seats. There wasn't anybody dancing or anything" (press interview, November 16, 2002).

Masa Oshima, interpreter and longtime fan of the game in both countries: "Fans in Japan who sit in the infield seats are more reserved than the *ōendan* fans, especially at Tokyo Dome for a Giants game, where you have more corporate or yuppie types, whereas the cheering section fans are less inhibited and more willing to make fools out of themselves . . . there is a 'strength in numbers' mentality" (interview, October 20, 2002).

Seiyu Hosono, Ph.D. in Molecular Biology, Senior Research Scientist at Biotech, New Jersey, and longtime fan of Japanese and American baseball: "Americans are more participatory for sure. This is not only in baseball, but also true at a music concert, etc. For example, I live in NY and I can never become like some American fans when I go to Yankee Stadium or Shea. Even though I was educated in the American School and have lived in the United States for almost 29 years, I can never act like an American" *(Japanese baseball.com, posted October 15, 2002)*.

Ken Belson, *New York Times* reporter and longtime Japan resident: "There is a big difference between the IF [infield] stands fans in the U.S. and Japan. Watch video highlights of people in the stands in the U.S., there are guys with beer bellies, doing dances, pumping fists. In Japan, they just sit there. In the OF [outfield], they just follow the leader. They don't cheer defense. They only yell on offense. U.S. fans are much more participatory. So it really is different. Osaka, however, is one exception. Fans are a lot more earthy there. Noisier. More vulgar _____" (author interview, October 10, 2002).

Gareth "Torakichi" Swain, a New-Zealand-born, Osaka-based translator and Hanshin Tiger fan: "I speak from the point of view of a semi-permanent resident of the right-field terraces of Koshien. While there are always exceptions, in general, the *gaiya* (OF) crowds are deafening, hyperactive, and often oblivious to the fact that our team is being thrashed, and the *naiya* (IF) are not as raucous (note I refrain from calling them 'quiet' or 'subdued' or whatever). I too have pondered this, and while I think it'd probably take a sociologist or shrink to give authoritative answers, I draw some parallels with baseball crowd behavior and that in other situations. The one that leaps to mind first is the 'traffic light' mentality, *aka-shingo, minna-ga watareba daijobu* (It'll be OK to cross the road on a red signal if everyone crosses at the same time). While I'm sure that people in all areas of the ground want to sing the cheer songs and whack their little skittles, perhaps the fact that the *ōendan,* armed with their trumpets and drums, are concentrated in the outfield stands means that only those in the cheap seats have the courage to do so" (*Japanese baseball.com, posted October 15, 2002*).

Said soccer expert and *Asian Wall Street Journal* reporter Sebastian Moffet, "Football crowds in most countries have a hard core of fans, usually behind the goal, and the tension gradually tapers off towards the edges and in the side stands. In Japan, there was no gradual tapering. The hard core could make as much noise as any crowd in the world, and generally had a fantastic time. But a few rows away, the other side of an invisible line, shouting and singing became as embarrassing as it would be in a shopping center. These fans were purely spectators and remained silent apart from clapping along with the drumbeat or gingerly slapping their thighs with a plastic megaphone" (see *Japanese Rules*, Yellow Jersey Press, London, 2002, pp. 78–79). Jim Allen, *Yomiuri* baseball columnist, has this take: "The Tigers fans at Koshien definitely do not fit the mold, with more spontaneous—albeit alcohol-fueled—razzing everywhere around the park. People all around the stadium get into the action—including applauding their team's good defensive plays far more than what is typical in most parts . . . Chiba Lotte Marines fans remind me of the European soccer model described above. People want to get close to the ōendan because it's so entertaining and the amount of cheering activity tapers off as you approach home plate (author interview, December 20, 2003)." Kazuhiro Sasaki, Seattle Mariners baseball pitcher, on Safeco Field: "Here, the fans are really knowledgeable. They know when to cheer and when to shut up. It's not mindless, frantic cheering the entire game" (*Japan Times*, December 17, 2003).

About *Wa*

Some scholars question the use of concepts like *wa* to describe the Japanese. They argue that modern society in Japan is too varied and too dynamic, especially after exposure to the West, to be described as a "homogenous society that marches in lockstep," to quote one historian. As Yale's Gary D. Allinson puts it, the "static and superficial stereotypes of Japan, so common in the United States today, stigmatize the Japanese people and jeopardize our understanding of Japan's history." Kyoto-based writer Roger Pulvers speaks of the intersecting of cultures, not only from overseas to home but to the interaction and intertwining of differing cultures emanating from within Japan—from the unique traditions of Okinawa and the Korean-influenced arts of Northern Kyushu to the pristine spirituality of northeast Honshu (http://homepage2.nifty.com/uesugihayato).

Others believe that there are trends in Japan that are distinct from other societies. Tama University president Gregory Clark talks of a continual emphasis on "tribal" values—gut feelings, direct human relations, instinctive groupism, familial styles of management, taboos, rules rather than principles, traditions and animistic legends rather than firm ideologies, and so on. Said highly regarded Tokyo-based business leader Glen Fukushima, of Harvard Law and Business schools, and *Todai*, among a long list of other institutions of higher learning, "While I believe it's harder now to define the Japanese national character as it applies to the Japanese, concepts like *shūdan-shugi* (groupism) and *wa* and deference to authority are still relevant to Japan and set Japan apart from most other advanced industrial societies (i.e., North American and Europe) and even from many other Asian societies. However, I believe the concepts have relevance as *tendencies* in the society. That is, there may be a larger proportion of individuals in Japanese society than in, say, American society who are affected by thinking or behavior related to these concepts, but that is not to deny that some Japanese people may be more 'individualistic' and 'rebellious' than some Americans." Added Keio University professor Masaru Ikei, a specialist in international law and a noted baseball expert, "In Japan, standing up and insisting on your rights is not very popular. Japan is still a society of 'wa' or harmony."

Some of these tendencies are documented in studies like "*Nihonjin no Kokuminsei no Kenkyu*" ("A Study of the Japanese National Character") and the public opinion polls conducted every five years by the *Tokei Suri Kenkyujo* (Institute for Statistical Mathematics), which regularly show that filial piety and social obligation outweigh respect for individual rights. See "*Kokuminsei no Kenkyu Dai 10 Ji Zenkoku Kensa,*" published by the *Tokei Suri Kenkyu Jo,* March 1999, p. 89.

Fukushima remarks made in author interview, October 13, 2003. In 2003, the *Asahi Shimbun* conducted its annual survey, in which pollees were asked to describe the character of the Japanese. 54 percent of the respondents chose the word "warmhearted," 50 percent "diligent" "45 percent" "cooperative" and 41 percent "honest." Lowest on the list came "original" (28 percent) and "independent" (31 percent) (*Asahi Shimbun*, Friday, February 14, 2003).

According to a survey conducted in the *Kokuminsei no Kenkyu*, published in March 1999 by the *Tokei Suri Kenkyujo* (The Institute of Statistical Mathematics), 33 percent of Japanese believed Japanese superior to Westerners in 1998. This compared with 53 percent in 1983 and 20 percent in 1953 (see p. 140). Twenty-nine percent in 1988 would permit their children to marry foreigners, while 36 percent would not. In 1998, 40 percent supported the idea, while 29 percent did not (see p. 146).

About Japanese-American Athletes in the U.S.

There were numerous teams of Japanese-American players on the West Coast in the early part of the century, ranging from Los Angeles to Vancouver, with names like the Stockton Yamatos and the San Jose Asahi's. Because of racial discrimination at the time, these *issei* or first-generation Japanese in America had no place to play, so they built their own baseball grounds and formed their own leagues. The first such club was founded in San Francisco in 1902 and was called the Fuji club. For more on this subject (100 years' worth more), read the fascinating book *Through a Diamond* by Kerry Yo Nakagawa, Rudi Publishing, 2001. A Japanese Waseda graduate and student at Knox College in Gettysburgh, Illinois, named Goro Mikami and nicknamed "Jap Mikado," is said to have been the first Japanese to play professional baseball in the U.S. He played for a club known as the All-Nations, a barnstorming team that included Cubans, American blacks, American Indians, a Hawaiian and a Filipino—decades before Jackie Robinson broke the color barrier. He played exhibition games in 1914 and 1915 against teams in the short-lived Federal

League (then recognized as a third major league). He was the subject of a 1997 book in Japanese by author Kazuo Seyama entitled *Jap Mikado no nazo,* published by Bungei Shunju in 1996.

About Abitration

The advent, in 1989, of a system of arbitration was equally instructive. Whereas arbitration committees in the United States, as negotiated by the union, included a neutral, independent, third party (a system that many big league owners complained was most responsible for the rise in MLB salaries), the newly established Japanese arbitration committee, by contrast, was composed of the baseball commissioner and the presidents of the two professional leagues. In addition, the player requesting salary arbitration could not, under the NPB arbitration rules, which forbade agents, employ an attorney during arguments. It was an arrangement about which the NPBPA remained conspicuously, but not surprisingly, acquiescent. The first player in NPB history to file for arbitration, at the end of the 1990 season, was the iconoclastic superstar Hiromitsu Ochiai, whose request for a 25 percent in increase in salary for leading the league in home runs was, not unexpectedly, turned down. The subsequent arbitration report warned that potential imitators of Ochiai should take due caution, stressing that arbitration was not something to enter into lightly. "I don't expect to have many more arbitration cases," said then-commissioner Ichiro Yoshikuni. "It's not the Japanese way of doing things." Subsequent applicants for arbitration could be counted on two hands. In the next dozen years, there were six applicants, two of whom actually won.

"Unimaginable" Okada quotation in IHT, January 1993. A form of free agency had been allowed, in which players had the option of changing teams at the 10th and 14th year plateau, in their careers. It was arbitrarily removed in December 1964 with the inauguration of a draft system, instituted to curtail wild bidding on young amateur talent. "Watanabe didn't give a damn about the other teams," author interview with Shigeyoshi "Steve" in March 2001. "The behavior of people who belong to a welfare state," quotation by baseball critic, author interview with Masayuki Tamaki, December 15, 1996. "Publicly scolded his field manager Shigeo Nagashima for being seen at a dinner party talking to one," from *Nikkan Supōtsu*, November 30, 1999. "If one of my players brings an agent into contract negotiations . . . then we'll cut his salary," Tsuneo Watanabe quotation from *Asahi Shimbun*, November 4, 2000, and *Tokyo Supōtsu*, November 9, 2000. Another major NPB figure against agents was 400-game-winner Masaichi Kaneda, who wrote in his *Shukan Posuto* column of November 11, 2000, p. 190, "I strongly oppose the use of an agent in salary contract negotations. A player who can't negotiate and speak for himself is not a pro!"

About Free Agency

One of the five players who filed for free agency in 1993 was ace pitcher Hiromi Makihara, who was looking for a three-year deal. However, he obligingly withdrew his free agency application along with his request for a multiyear contract, after a personal appeal by Giants manager Nagashima—who showed up at Makihara's front door with a bouquet of freshly cut roses and his "personal promise" not to trade him for the next three seasons. Makihara, who was quoted as saying he was "deeply moved" by the "gesture of sincerity" from his famous manager, signed a one-year contract (*Nikkan Supōtsu*, November 22, 1993). Masayuki Tamaki interview, November 22, 1993. "Bad influence" quotation by Kimiyasu Kudo from Interview in *Shukan Bunshun*, December 1, 1994, pp. 218–19. Manabu Kitabeppu, a Carp ace eligible to file for free agency, declined to do so, declaring simply, "I have an obligation to Hiroshima" (quoted in *Asahi Shimbun*, September 28, 1993, p. 23).

In 2002, Kintetsu Buffaloes slugger Norihiro Nakamura declared free agency and experimented with the idea of going elsewhere, holding serious talks with the Hanshin Tigers as well as the New York Mets, but found himself uncomfortable with the strangeness of the new process. Nakamura and the Mets had nearly come to an agreement for a two-year deal worth seven million dollars, but he backed out at the last minute, upset over a premature leak about his contract in the U.S. media, before he had had a chance to convey his decision to Kintetsu and Hanshin.

"It may be the difference between the Japanese and American styles. But I first wanted to decline the offers (from Kintetsu and Hanshin) by following the Japanese way of *giri* and *ninjō* and then accept an offer from the Mets. . . . This factor accounts for turning 180 degrees at the last minute."

His wife was reportedly relieved at his decision to stay in Japan and remain with the Buffaloes, worried as she was about how she was going to raise three little girls in a big intimidating city like New York.

Nakamura summed his experience up by saying, "Japan is a world of *giri-ninjō*. America is a severe country where you can often say what you want to whomever you want. But I chose the way of *giri-ninjō*. That's why things got so messed up. I don't think I've hurt my image at all. I kept to my policy and things eventually worked out. But the free agency system is really bothersome" (*Nikkan Supōtsu*, February 14, 2002, p. 4).

About Attendance Figures and the Tokyo Dome

All teams in Japan inflate their attendance reports, somewhat, but none as blatantly as the Tokyo Yomiuri Giants. The Tokyo Dome became the home of the Tokyo Giants when it was completed in 1987. The capacity of the Dome, according to stadium officials and Yomiuri executives, was 56,000, which was the attendance the Giants reported for every game they played there until the late '90s when the figure was reduced to 55,000. This change reflected an actual reduction in the number of seats. However, an unauthorized count of the seats in the Dome in 1990, conducted by this author and published in the weekly magazine *Shukan Asahi*, revealed a total of only 42,761 seats, while a subsequent count of maximum standing room totaled some 3,000. The publication of this news had absolutely zero effect on subsequent attendance reports.

About the Irabu Affidavit

An important document of reference was a declaration that Hideki Irabu dictated in February 1997 and had translated into English. In 17 pages, it described in detail his dealings with Lotte in his efforts to reach the major leagues as outlined in chapter 6. It includes his description of the infamous secret letter he was required to sign, Shigemitsu's adventures with George Steinbrenner, and the trade to San Diego against his will. Irabu signed the document on February 13, 1997, and submitted it as evidence to the MLB Executive Council held shortly thereafter in San Diego. As a sworn affidavit, it subjected him to perjury charges if false. Since Lotte did not formally respond to it at the hearing, it was regarded as a truthful account of what actually happened.

The secret letter proffered to Irabu was the type of solution one often saw in harmony-conscious Japan, with distinct facets in two different dimensions—surface and reality. The Japanese even had terms to describe them: *tatemae* and *honne*.

"I subject myself to your will," Irabu had said rather dramatically, as he signed the secret letter. He revealed later that he and Nomura had been particularly persuaded by the team officials' use of the word "sincerity" to describe his attitude toward the accord. Sincerity was a word that in Japanese meant everything, and in this case, Irabu believed, imposed on the Marines a "very high duty and obligation." (Later, when push came to shove, Lotte would refuse to confirm that such a deal had ever been made, but again, failed to refute Irabu's account at the San Diego Executive Council hearing.)

To Shigemitsu, the Yankees refusal to accept his proposal was clear evidence that the Yankees were not demonstrating the all-important "sincerity" on their part. According to the Irabu affidavit, he added that of all the major league owners that he knew George Steinbrenner was the worst. He said that if Mr. Steinbrenner were sitting next to him he would turn his back on him.

"If Irabu had the name John Smith," from Gene Orza author interview, January 25, 1998. Also see transcript of Orza's argument before the Executive Council in San Diego, February 27, 1997.

Orza's "blond hair and blue eyes" remarks were prompted by an off-the-cuff statement he'd overheard by an MLB team executive, to the effect that the flow of Asian players into the United States had to be "controlled." Nomura also charged discrimination, noting that there were high school stars in America who were offered more money to sign than what San Diego had offered Hideki Irabu, a proven professional.

About Restrictions on Foreign Membership on Japanese and U.S. Teams

It should be noted that American professional baseball has its own restrictions. According to Jeff Pfeifer of MLB, while there are no U.S. government restrictions for P-1 type visas, meaning those for major league players with valid big league contracts, there are restrictions for the second type of visa used, H-2B, which is for minor league players. Each year MLB requests a certain number of H-2B visas from the U.S. Labor Department, submitting a lengthy report regarding usage and requests. Each year, the number varies but is close to 1,300. In 2003, the total stood at 1,350. Each club annually receives a different amount depending on past usage and current requests. Numbers vary from club to club, from 35 to 45. Again, however, there is no limit on P-1 visas (Jeff Pfeifer, MLB NY, via Jim Small MLB Tokyo, December 8, 2003).

Also, according to the officials at the *nyukoku-ka* (immigration office) of the *homusho* (Ministry of Justice), there are no limits on foreign baseball player visas. If the Tokyo Giants decided they wanted to employ 70 *gaijin senshu* on their farm team and the NPB said okay, there is no law in Japan prohibiting it. Visas would be granted to all. The limit imposed of four players on each "varsity" is a policy of the NPB (author interview December 8, 2003).

"Back in the Meiji Era . . . according to the *Asahi Shimbun* . . ." to end of paragraph. See "Pointing a nondiscriminatory finger . . ." Jane Singer, *Asahi Shimbun*, October 30, 2002. Also see "*Nikkan Supōtsu*, July 15, 1991. A survey conducted by *Japan Today*, October 5, 2003, found that 48.9 percent of respondents thought the Japanese words *"gaijin"* was racist or derogatory; 37.5 percent said "no"; 13.6 percent said I don't know. "kinugasa wasn't really Japanese." *Chrysanthemum and the Bat*, p. 203.

About Minorities

Some observers like to paint the NPB as an equal opportunity employer that accepts people regardless of race, creed or color and criticize those who emphasize the "Japaneseness" of the game. They point out that there have been hundreds of North and South Americans that have played the game, as have ethnic Koreans, Chinese and men of mixed ancestry. "Let's stop calling it the Japanese game," you will hear, "and instead refer to it as the Game in Japan." It would be easier to agree with that those sentiments if the NPB removed its restrictions on the number of foreign players allowed per team and at the same time removed the restrictions limiting the participation by foreigners in the All-Star games to three position players and one pitcher. Such restrictions have kept many a league leader in batting or other categories at home watching on TV.

It would also be easier to accept the theory that the NPB is one big melting pot if Korean players did not feel compelled to hide their identities for fear of social ostracism.

This writer personally knows of several players and coaches in Japan with Korean backgrounds who will talk about their ancestry privately but refuse to discuss it in public. I know of one lawsuit that resulted when a player was identified by a teammate in a Japanese magazine as having Korean grandparents on one side of his family. The fact of the ancestry was not disputed. But the propriety of its publication was. The magazine offered to run an apology that stated, "We're sorry so-and-so identified you as being part Korean." The subject was so sensitive that the player's lawyer demanded the reference to Korean be taken out of the apology. Thus, the apology read simply, "We're sorry we identified you as we did."

About the NPB Schedule

The NPB schedule has varied over the years. The most common schedule has been 130 games, and experiments were occasionally made with 135- and 140-game seasons. The Pacific League tried a 150-game schedule briefly in the early 1960s; both leagues went to a 140-game schedule in 2001. Voluntary training traditionally begins the first week of January, and "joint voluntary training" (there is nothing "voluntary" about it), in the presence of coaches, begins January 15.

BIBLIOGRAPHY

Abrams, Roger I. *Legal Bases*. Philadelphia. Temple University. 1998.

Allen, Jim. *Ichiro Magic*. New York. Kodansha International. 2001.

———. *Guide to Japanese Baseball*. Tokyo. Slug Books. (Versions published in 1994, 1995, 1996, 1997, 1998.)

Baseball Magazine. *Nihon Puro Yakyū Kiroku Nenkan*. 1990–2004.

Buruma, Ian. *A Japanese Mirror*. London. Johnathan Cape. 1984.

Chiba, Isao. *Puro Yakyū Kiroku no Techno*. Tokyo. Baseball Magazine. 2001.

Chimu 51, Ichiro no Nazo. Tokyo. Libero, KK. 2001.

Chuman, Kanae. *Yakyū*, Tokyo. *Maekawa Buneido Shuppan*. 1897.

Cromartie, Warren, with Whiting, Robert. *Slugging It Out In Japan*. Tokyo. Kodansha International. 1991

Dai-Ichi Koto Gakkō Koyukai. Yakyū Bushi Fukisoku Dai Ichi Koto Gakkō Koyukai. Tokyo. *Dai-Ichi Koto Gakkō Koyukai*. 1903.

Dai-Ichi Koto Gakkō Kishukuryo. Koryoshi. Published by the *Dai-Ichi Koto Gakkō Kishukuryo*, September 10, 1930.

Draeger, Donn F. *Modern Bujustu and Budo*. Weatherhill. New York and Tokyo. 1974.

Graczyk, Wayne. *Japan Pro Baseball Fan Handbook and Media Guide*. Tokyo, Wayne Graczyk. 1977–2003.

Guttman Allen, and Thompson, Lee. *Japanese Sports. A History*. Honolulu. University of Hawaii Press. 2001.

Hasegawa, Shigetoshi. *Fukano wo Kano ni Suru Koto (Boku no meja rigu nikki)*. Tokyo. Gentosha. 2003.

———. *Tekisha Seizon Meja e no Chosen*. Tokyo. Gentosha. 2003.

———. *Chansu ni Katsu Pinchi de Makenai Jibun Kanrijyutsu*. Tokyo. Gentosha. 2002.

———, with Ninomiya, Seishun. *Meja Rigu Pureyas Fairu 2001*. Tokyo. Za Masada. 2001.

Hashido, Makoto. *Saikin Yakyū Gijutsu*. Tokyo. Haku Bunkan. 1905, 5–7.

Helyar, John. *Lords of the Realm*. New York. Ballantine Books. 1995.

Ichiro-ban Kisha Gurupu. Ichiro. Tensai no Shinjitsu to Himitsu. Tokyo. Zenisu Planning. 2001.

Ikei, Masaru. *Hakkyu Taiheiyo wo Wataru.* Tokyo. Chuko Shinsho. 1976.

———. *Meja Rigu Chosensuru Otokotachi.* Tokyo. NHK Shuppan Kyokai. 1998.

———. *Yakyū to Nihonjin.* Tokyo. Marzuen Raiburari. 1991.

Ishida, Yuta. *Ichiroizumu boku ga kangaeta koto kanjita kotō to shinjiru koto.* Tokyo. Shueisha 2002.

Ishī, Kazuyoshi. *Meija no Ryugi.* Tokyo. Shodensha. March 2003.

Kawasaki, Noboru. *Kyojin no Hoshii* (11 parts).

Kawamoto, Tak. *Shinjo ga '4-ban' Utta Riyu.* Tokyo. Asahi Shimbun-sha. 2002.

Kī, Mutsuo. *Chuman Nakae Den.* Tokyo. Baseball Magazine. 1988.

Kiku, Koichi. *"Kindai Puro Suptōsu" no Rekishi Shakai Gakku.* Tokyo. Fumaido. 1993.

Kimura, Ki. *Nihon Suptōsu Bunka-shi.* Tokyo. Besuboru Magajin. 1978.

Kingston, Jeff. *Japan in Transformation.* Pearson, Longman. 2001.

Kodama, Mitsuo. *Ichiro "Tensai" to Iwareru Ningen no Kyotsu Ten.* Tokyo. Kawade Shobo Shinsha. 2001.

Komatsu, Narumi. *Ichiro Intabyu. Attack the Pinnacle!* Tokyo. Shinchosha. 2001.

———. *Ichiro on Ichiro; Interview Special Edition.* Tokyo. Shinchosha. 2002.

———. Trans. Gabriel, Philip. *Ichiro on Ichiro.* Tokyo. Shinchosha Publishing Co. 2002.

Kuehnert, Marty, *Suta Senshu wa Naze Bomei Suru ka.* Tokyo. KK Besuto Seruazu. 1998.

Kure, Mitsuo. *Samurai: An Illustrated History.* Tuttle Publishing. 2002.

Matsui Hideki. *Tanto Kisha Gurupu (Hen), Matsui Hideki Chosen.* Tokyo. Line Books. 2002.

Matsui, Kazuo. *Meja Saishuu Heiki.* Tokyo. Futabasha. 2003.

McClain, James L. *Japan. A Modern History.* New York. W.W. Norton & Company. 2001.

Mihara, Osamu. *Kyojin Gun to Tomo ni.* Tokyo. Sakuhinsha. 1949.

Mimatsu Shoten nai Yakyu Nenpo Henshu-bu. Yakyu Nenpo. Tokyo. Tobita, Suishu. Tokyo *Mimatsu Shoten.* 1912.

Miyamoto, Musashi (Trans. Wilson, William Scott). *The Book of Five Rings.* Kodansha International. 2002.

Moffett, Sebastian. *Japanese Rules.* London. Yellow Jersey Press, Random House. 2002.

Muguruma, Mamoru. *Mei Sukauto wa Naze Shinda Ka*. Tokyo. Kodansha. 2002.

Murakami, Masanori. *"Tatta Hitori no Dai Reega."* Tokyo. Kobunsha. 1985.

Nagatani, Osamu. *Amerika ga Ichiro wo hyoka suru honto no no riyu* Tokyo. *Kirutaimu kommunikashion*. 2002.

Nakagawa, Kerry Yo. *Through A Diamond*. Rudi Publishing. 2001.

Nihon Puro Yakyū Senshu Kai. Puro Yakyu no Ashita No Tame Ni. Tokyo. Heibon-sha. 2001.

Nitobe, Inazo. *Bushido*. Tokyo. ICG Muse. 2001.

Ogawa, Masaru. *Ichiro wa Tensai de wa nai*. Tokyo. Kadokawa shoten. 2002.

Raines, Rob. *Baseball Samurais*. New York. St. Martin's Paperbacks. 2001.

Reaves, Joseph. *Taking in a Game*. Lincoln. University of Nebraska Press. 2002.

Rhoden, Donald T. *Schooldays in Imperial Japan*. Berkeley. University of California Press, 1980.

Sasaki, Kazuhiro. *Rokka Rumu Boku to Meja Riga Tachi no Eiko to Kutsujoku*. Tokyo. Shodensha. March 2003.

Seyama, Kazuo. *Jap Mikado No Nazo*. Bungei Shunju. 1996.

Shinjo Tsuyoshi Kenkyukai Shinjo Goroku. Tokyo. Kindaieiga. 2002.

———. *"Dreaming Baby."* Tokyo. Kobunsha. 2001.

Starfin, Natasha. *Roshiya kara kita esu*. Tokyo. PHP. 1993

———. *Hakkyu ni eiko to yumei wo nosete*. Tokyo. Baseball Magazine-sha. 1993.

Strange, F. W. *Outdoor Games*. Tokyo. Tokyo University. 1883.

Suzuki, Nobuyuki. *Oya to Musuko (Ichiro to Watashi no Ni-ju Ichi Nen)*. Niken Shobo. 1995. (Reprinted below under different title.)

———, *Musuko Ichiro* (My Son Ichiro). Tokyo. Niken Shobo. 2001.

Tachibana, Ryuji. *Poshitibu Kochinggu*. Tokyo. Kodansha. 2002.

Takaoka, Eiyo. *Musashi to Ichiro*. Tokyo Shogakkan. 2003.

Takarajima Henshu-bu. Kishingeki Nihonjin Dairiga, Tokyo. Takarajima. 2001.

Tamaki, Masayuki. *Puro Yakyū Dai Dai Dai Jiten*. Toto Shobo. 1998.

Tamaki, Masayuki, and Whiting, Robert. *Yakyū-do to Besuboru-do (400 Chigai)*. Tokyo. Kodansha. 1991.

Tateishi, Yasunori. *Majitsushi–Mihara Osamu to Nishitetsu Lions*. Tokyo. Shogakkuan. 2002.

Tobita Suishu. *Tobita Suishu Senshu (1) Yakyū Seikatsu no Omoide*. Tokyo. Bēsubōru Magajin-sha. 1960.

———. *Tobita. Suishu Senshu (2) Nekkyu San-Ju Nen*. Tokyo. Bēsubōru Magajin-sha. 1960.

———. *Tobita Suishu Senshu (3) Yakyu Kisha Jidai.* Tokyo. Bēsubōru Magajin-sha. 1960.

———. *Tobita Suishu Senshu (4) Kogeki Hen, Renshu Hen.* Tokyo. Bēsubōru Magajin-sha. 1960.

———. *Tobita Suishu Senshu (5) Shubi Hen.*

Tokei Suri Kenkyujo. "*Nihonjin no Kokuminsei no Kenkyu*" (A Study of the Japanese National Character). Tokyo. *Tokei Suri Kenkyujo* (Institute for Statistical Mathematics). 1999.

Tokyo, Bēsubōru Magazine-sha. 1960.

———. *Tobita Suishu Senshu (6) Zuihitsu to Tsuiso* (Essays and Recollections). Tokyo. Bēsubōru Magajin-sha. 1960.

Tominaga, Junji. *Sekihaku san no Home Run.* Tokyo. Chukei Shuppan. 2003.

Watson, Brian, *The Father of Judo, A Biography of Jigoro Kano.* Tokyo. Watson, Kodansha International. p. 55.

Whiting, Robert. *Bēsubōru Junki.* Tokyo. Asahi Shimbun. 1990.

———. *Bēsubōru Junki.* Tokyo. Asahi Shimbun. 1991.

———. *Nīzuru Kuni no "Dorei Yakyu."* Tokyo. Bungei Shunju. 1999.

———. *The Chrysanthemum and the Bat*, Avon Books, 1983.

———. *You Gotta Have Wa*, Vintage Departures. 1990.

Yamamori, Keiko. *Yakyū Sunya-de Dai Riga Ohka Tomokazu no Chosen. Besuto Serazu.* October 2002.

Yamato, Kyushi. "*Nihon-yakyū shi—Meiji hen*," Tokyo. Bēsubōru Magajin. 1977.

———. "*Nihon yakyū shi—Taisho hen*," Tokyo. Bēsubōru Magajin. 1977.

———. *Nihon Yakyū shi. Showa-hen Sono* 1. Tokyo. Bēsubōru Magajin-sha. 1977.

———. *Nihon Yakyū shi. Showa-hen Sono* 2. Tokyo. Bēsubōru Magajin-sha. 1977.

———. *Yakyū Hyakunen.* Tokyo. Jiji Press. 1976.

———. *Yomiuri Gurupu, Tokyo Yomiuri Kyojin Gun 50-nen*, Tokyo. Yomiuri Group in 1985.

There is a treasure trove of material on the NPB in Japanese. Unfortunately, there are limited numbers of English sources for neophytes interested in learning more about Japanese baseball—although they have been growing in recent years. Readers might try online versions of *Japan Times, Yomiuri Daily News, Mainichi Daily News* and the *Asahi Shimbun*, as well as the highly informative websites *baseballguru.com* and *japanesebaseball.com*.

INDEX